THE LETTERS
of
John Baptist de La Salle

John Baptist de La Salle, portrait by Pierre Léger, 1734

THE LETTERS
of
John Baptist de La Salle

Translation, Introduction, and Commentary by
Brother Colman Molloy, FSC

Edited with Additional Commentary by
Brother Augustine Loes, FSC

1988
Lasallian Publications
Romeoville, Illinois 60441

This first volume of the Lasallian Publications is dedicated to Brother Maurice-Auguste Hermans, FSC (1911–1987), Doctor of Canon Law, former Assistant Superior General and procurator general of the Institute of the Brothers of the Christian Schools, in appreciation for his scholarship and his commitment to Saint John Baptist de La Salle and to the Institute.

Lasallian Publications

Sponsored by the Regional Conference of Christian Brothers
of the United States and Toronto

———— ◆ ————

The Letters of John Baptist de La Salle is volume 1 of Lasallian Sources: The Complete Works of Saint John Baptist de La Salle.

Copyright © 1988 by Christian Brothers Conference.
All rights reserved

Printed in the United States of America

Library of Congress catalog card number 87-83220
ISBN 0-944808-01-8

Cover: John Baptist de La Salle, engraving by Manigaud (before 1888), reproducing quite faithfully the portrait by Léger from which it was copied.

A Note about Lasallian Publications

This volume is the first in a series of publications intended to make available to the English reader the life and writings of John Baptist de La Salle together with the rich heritage bequeathed by this seventeenth-century French saint, educator, spiritual writer, and Founder of the Institute of the Brothers of the Christian Schools.

Lasallian Publications will include 13 volumes of the writings of De La Salle, the 3 early biographies, 4 volumes of thematic studies of various aspects of the life of De La Salle and the origins of the Institute, 3 volumes of current research, and several volumes devoted to Lasallian studies.

These publications will be drawn mainly from the documents published and analyzed in the monumental collection known as the *Cahiers lasalliens*. Presently numbering some 46 volumes, that series is the result of a decision by the 38th General Chapter of the Institute (held in Rome in 1956) to sponsor Lasallian research.

The inspiration for this decision came from Father André Rayez, SJ, whose essays on Lasallian studies and Lasallian spirituality appeared in 1952 and 1955 in the *Revue d'Ascétique et de Mystique*. In the course of his research for these essays, Father Rayez took the occasion to alert the superiors of the Institute to what had already been done and what needed to be done for a more sophisticated and scholarly study of the Lasallian texts. Fortunately at that moment, perhaps for the first time in its three-hundred-year history, the Institute had the qualified men and the resources for such an undertaking.

Since its inception, *Cahiers lasalliens* has been under the general direction and editorship of Brother Maurice-Auguste Hermans, who spent over 50 years of service to the Institute in the Generalate in Rome. Brother Maurice died in 1987.

The first volume of the *Cahiers* is a study by Brother Michel Sauvage of the New Testament sources for De La Salle's *Méditations pour le temps de la retraite*. Volumes 2, 3, and 11, authored by Brother Maurice, treat the various aspects of the foundation of the Institute prior to the papal Bull of Approbation granted in 1725. Volumes 45 and 46 contain the doctoral dissertation of Brother Miguel Campos, an extensive and profound study of De La Salle's spiritual odyssey as manifested in specific moments of his life and expressed in the *Méditations pour le temps de la retraite*.

The biographies of De La Salle written by his contemporaries are presented in their original published form, with appropriate introductory material, in volumes 4 through 9 of the *Cahiers*. All of De La Salle's extant writings, with introduction and commentary, are to be found in volumes 10 through 25.

Volumes 26 through 42 of the *Cahiers lasalliens* contain the published results of the lifelong research of Brother Léon de Marie Aroz. These volumes present documents pertaining to all aspects of the life and work of De La Salle: familial, civil, ecclesiastical, theological, educational, and financial. Not content with the documents that were known to exist, Brother Léon conducted an intensive search of municipal, departmental, and national archives all over France. This material is published, much of it for the first time, in the *Cahiers,* with photographs of the original documents, extensive introductions and scholarly commentary.

The *Cahiers* series is by no means complete and Lasallian scholarship continues to develop. Volume 5 of the *Cahiers,* dealing with the Founder's *Mémoire sur l'habit,* has yet to appear. Volumes 43 and 44 presumably await further results from the research of Brother Léon de Marie Aroz. Meanwhile a new Lasallian scholar is emerging in the person of Brother Jean-Guy Rodrigue, a Canadian, whose research on the sources of the Founder's *Méditations pour les Dimanches et les principales Fêtes de l'année* is soon to be published in the *Cahiers.*

Not all the recent research and publication relative to De La Salle and the origins of the Institute is confined to the volumes of the *Cahiers.* A notable exception is the doctoral dissertation of Brother Michel Sauvage published in 1962 in Paris under the title, *Catéchèse et Laïcat.* This seminal work treats of the role of the laity in the ministry of the Church, with special attention to the originality of the role De La Salle established for the teaching Brother in this context.

Another independently published doctoral dissertation that has contributed significantly to our understanding of De La Salle and his times is the work of Brother Yves Poutet. Comprising two enormous volumes and published in Rennes, France, in 1970, the study is entitled *Le XVIIᵉ Siècle et les Origines lasalliennes.*

De La Salle's educational and catechetical writings have been the special object of the research of Brother Jean Pungier. To date he has published commentaries on De La Salle's *Conduite des Ecoles chrétiennes,* and a source study with commentary on the catechetical sections of the Founder's *Les Devoirs d'un Chrétien envers Dieu.* Brother Jean continues his research in the Generalate of the Brothers in Rome.

In addition to these studies by seasoned scholars, many other monographs and essays have appeared over the last 20 years dealing with the educational or spiritual vision of De La Salle. Most of these were originally research papers or dissertations written to fulfill the requirements for advanced degrees in European universities and catechetical centers such as the Lateran University and the now defunct Jesus Magister Institute in Rome, the Institut Catholique in Paris, Lumen Vitae in Brussels, the Catholic University at Louvain, and the Pius X Pontifical Institute conducted by the Brothers in Salamanca.

This brief survey of recent Lasallian scholarship provides a context in which to understand the timeliness of Lasallian Publications.

Contents

*Entries placed in brackets are conjectural based on internal evidence.

Illustrations

Abbreviations

AE   Archives, District of England

AM   Autograph Manuscript

AMG   Archives, Generalate of the Brothers of the Christian Schools, Rome, Italy

BL   *De La Salle: Letters and Documents,* edited by W. J. Battersby, FSC

BR   *Conduite admirable de la divine Providence en la personne du vénérable serviteur de Dieu Jean-Baptiste de La Salle,* by Brother Bernard, FSC

CL   *Cahiers lasalliens*

EC   *Les Lettres de Saint J.-B. De La Salle: Edition Critique,* by Brother Félix-Paul, FSC

Ms. 22   Manuscript 22, a notebook containing extracts from letters written by De La Salle, preserved in the archives of the Generalate of the Brothers of the Christian Schools, Rome, Italy

Acknowledgments

Translator's Acknowledgments

It is a great pleasure to have the opportunity to acknowledge the assistance given by so many in the preparation and compilation of this volume. In the first place my thanks go to Brother José Pablo Basterrechea, FSC, Superior General (1976–1986) of the Brothers of the Christian Schools, for his authorization to publish in English the letters of Saint John Baptist de La Salle, as well as pertinent material taken from the *Cahiers lasalliens* and other documents belonging to the Institute of the Brothers of the Christian Schools. My thanks are due, too, to Brother John Johnston, FSC, Superior General, who first suggested that I undertake this work and who kept it alive by his continued interest and encouragement.

My thanks and appreciation are due also to the following people:

✦ Brother Léon de Marie Aroz, FSC, for allowing me to make use of the results of his research published in the *Cahiers lasalliens* and to include in English in this volume the letter of De La Salle to Canon Jean-Louis, his brother, which was recently discovered in the Thiénot chambers in Reims (CL 39: 25–32); Jean-Louis de La Salle's letter to De La Salle (CL 26, D. 20; CL 41 I, D. 31); as well as evidence of De La Salle's presence at Epernay in 1711 (CL 41 I: 258, n. 5)

✦ Brother Emile Rousset, FSC, for permission to reproduce from his pictorial production, *J. B. De La Salle, Iconographie,* no. 5, Portrait of De La Salle (Léger); no. 41, Signature of De La Salle

✦ Brother Saturnino Gallego, FSC, for permission to quote his estimate of the number of letters written by De La Salle to the Brothers, taken from his article in the *Lasalliana*, N. 02–A–08

✦ Brother Leander Lenihan, FSC, Visitor of the District of England, for allowing the inclusion of the autograph letter of De La Salle, both in translation and as an illustration

✦ John Down, staff member of Oakhill College, Castle Hill, Brother Thomas Normoyle, FSC, and Brother John Brady, FSC for their work in preparing material for illustrations

✦ Brother John Hazell, FSC, archivist at the Generalate, for his guidance

✦ Brother Raphael Bassett, FSC, and Brother Quentin O'Halloran, FSC, Visitor and former Visitor, respectively, of the Australian Province, for the time and financial help generously made available

✦ The many Brothers of Australia, New Zealand, and Papua New Guinea, for the encouragement they have given by their interest

✦ Brother Peter Gilfedder, FSC, in a particular way, for the care he brought to the reading of the early drafts and for his constructive criticism

✦ Brother Laurence Woods, FSC, and Brother Baptist Will, FSC, for the readiness with which they researched seventeenth- and eighteenth-century French legal and administrative terminology
✦ The Benedictine Monks of the Arcadia Monastery, for the use of their library, and Brother Terry Kavenagh, OSB, for his willing and expert guidance in research into Benedictine monastic life
✦ Sister Kym Harris, OSB, of the Benedictine Priory, Croydon, Victoria, for explaining the essence of Benedictine prayer and for her encouragement to persevere in the preparation of the publication
✦ Val Peters and Barbara Oakes, for all the time and skill they generously devoted to typing the manuscript

Brother Colman Molloy, FSC
1984

Editor's Acknowledgments

Special thanks are due to the following people:
✦ Brothers Edwin Bannon, FSC; Luke Salm, FSC; Erminus Joseph, FSC; Joseph Murphy, FSC; and Leonard Marsh, FSC, who served on the editorial committee for this work
✦ Brother Miguel Campos, FSC, for many helpful suggestions during the final editing
✦ Brothers Francis Huether, FSC; Hilary Gilmartin, FSC; Lawrence Oelschlegel, FSC; and Richard Rush, FSC, for research assistance, proofreading, and editorial suggestions
✦ Mrs. Carol Hamm for typing the manuscript
✦ Brother Edwin Bannon, FSC, present archivist at the Generalate, also for providing photographs of eight letters
✦ Brother Conrad Kearney, FSC, for preparing the index.

Three communities of Brothers have also been very supportive of this project:
✦ De La Salle Hall, Lincroft, New Jersey
✦ Queen of Peace, North Arlington, New Jersey
✦ The participants in the Buttimer Institute at Manhattan College, New York, and Saint Mary's College, Moraga, California, during the summers of 1986 and 1987

Acknowledgment is also due to Brother Joseph Schmidt, FSC, who, as executive director of Lasallian Publications, supervised the preparation of the final draft of the manuscript through several revisions. His corrections and suggestions have enhanced the final work considerably.

Brother Augustine Loes, FSC
1987

Introduction

I

When Adrien Nyel arrived from Rouen to establish the first tuition-free school for boys in Reims in 1679, Canon John Baptist de La Salle of the Reims Cathedral gave him valuable assistance. De La Salle did not, however, have any thought of taking more than a passing interest in this good work. But as time went on and Nyel moved from Reims to promote schools elsewhere, De La Salle began to feel that if he did not take a closer interest in the venture, it would quickly come to nothing. Step by step, he became more and more involved and eventually became convinced that the direction of the work of schools in which poor boys could be given a thorough Christian education was to be for him the expression of God's will. He soon found himself the guide and superior of a small band of dedicated teachers. Under his direction this little community increased in numbers, developed existing schools, and opened new ones as their services were requested elsewhere.

By 1688 De La Salle decided that the Community of the Brothers of the Christian Schools, as the teachers now called themselves, should move beyond the boundaries of the Archdiocese of Reims. That year he went to Paris with two of the Brothers at the invitation of Father De La Barmondière, the parish priest of Saint Sulpice. In this parish De La Salle and the two Brothers took charge of the charity school for boys.

This move to Paris brought to De La Salle and the Brothers a host of problems, some of which beset De La Salle for most of the remaining years of his life. The Writing Masters and the Masters of the Little Schools of Paris had established associations to protect the interests of their members. They believed that De La Salle's schools robbed them of some of their students and thereby deprived them of a means of livelihood. These associations brought lawsuits against De La Salle and the Brothers, and these court battles plagued them for many years. In the meantime, the situation of the Brothers in Reims deteriorated. They were not ready to function without their Founder.

De La Salle had left behind him in Reims a flourishing community of Brothers engaged in conducting a school for boys, a training school for teachers who were destined for schools in small rural centers, and a training house for young men who wished to join the new community — in all, a community of some fifty persons. By 1690 he had taken with him to Paris the boys, *les petits Frères,* who were preparing to enter the novitiate, but in the capital city they lost interest in the life of the Brothers and withdrew.

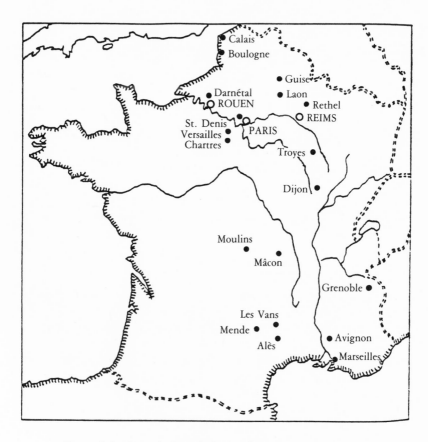

Sites of the French foundations of the Institute in 1719

Meanwhile, deprived of De La Salle's guiding hand, the training college for rural teachers soon closed. Eight of the 16 Brothers in the Reims community and two of the four now in Paris left the struggling congregation. There were no replacements. Brother Henri L'Heureux, who was studying for the priesthood in view of succeeding De La Salle as superior, suddenly died. At this critical juncture, De La Salle himself was confined to bed for six weeks. Several of the Brothers became physically ill, suffering from exhaustion because of their work in the overcrowded classrooms. Others, their initial enthusiasm waning, began to falter in their commitment.

Still, De La Salle did not waver in his conviction that it was God's will that Christian schools were to be maintained for poor boys. As usual he spent considerable time in prayer. He consulted the more experienced and dependable Brothers and then with characteristic vigor set about taking measures to restore the situation, for he feared that otherwise the Brothers' work in the schools would completely fail. One of the steps he took to stabilize the situation was the introduction of monthly correspondence with the Brothers. The Brothers were to write to him regularly each month, telling him of their community relationships, their efforts in the classroom, their progress in prayer, and their fidelity to their community practices. He hoped in this way that the Brothers would reflect on their progress as teaching Brothers and that he would be able to keep in touch with those Brothers whom he could not see and talk to personally, giving them encouragement, guidance, and advice. He continued this practice of monthly correspondence until he relinquished his position as superior in May 1717. By that time there were just over 100 Brothers in the community, so that during the years of De La Salle's superiorship, there must have been thousands of letters written by the Brothers and thousands sent back in reply by De La Salle. The letters from the Brothers were received in confidence, and De La Salle would have destroyed them. Very few of De La Salle's replies have come down to us. We do not know with certainty what became of the great majority of these replies.

De La Salle's early biographers—Brother Bernard, Canon Blain, and Dom Maillefer—certainly had a number of De La Salle's letters at their disposal, for many letters are quoted either in full or in part during the course of their biographies. Blain also refers to a number of letters De La Salle wrote to Sister Louise, the hermitess of Parménie, whom De La Salle consulted when he visited her retreat near Grenoble. Brother Barthélemy tells of a number of letters written "in defense of the Constitution of Our Holy Father Pope Clement XIII, which had considerable effect." Yet, only one copy of one of these letters is known to exist. Furthermore, De La Salle himself remarks that several of his letters to Gabriel Drolin in Rome either went astray or were intercepted. But these missing letters would add only a small number to those we already possess. After his death, a concerted effort was made to gather together De La Salle's correspondence, with a view to the publication of his biography. The recovery of some letters (for example, those addressed to Brother Mathias that were found in the attic of a house in a village near Avignon around 1850) possibly gives us a clue that the loss of many others occurred during the period of the French Revolution, when the Institute of the Brothers was all but destroyed.

In his *De La Salle: Letters and Documents,* Brother Battersby estimates the number of letters written by De La Salle to the Brothers at about 18,000. In *Lasalliana,* N. 02–4–08, "An X-Ray Photograph of Saint John Baptist de La Salle," Brother Saturnino Gallego, FSC, gives the more conservative estimate of 7,000. In his essay in *Circulaires Instructives et Administratives,* No. 335, Brother Félix-Paul concludes that perhaps as many as 2,000 or 3,000 letters have been lost.

II

Soon after he became interested in Adrien Nyel's work in 1679, De La Salle also became convinced that if the schools were to be of any significant value to the poor boys of the city by giving them a solid foundation for Christian living, something would have to be done to give his teachers a good religious and pedagogic formation. De La Salle took advantage of the frequent absences of Nyel to try to supply this need. Despite his first tentative measures—bringing the teachers into his house after class hours, instructing them in the methods of prayer, and giving them some form of simple education, both secular and religious—the venture seemed doomed to failure. The first group of teachers simply wanted some form of employment that would provide them with a modest living. They had not bargained for what De La Salle was asking of them. Soon, they departed. New volunteers, who knew what De La Salle was trying to do, arrived, and before long the little band of teachers evolved into a kind of religious community.

De La Salle was aware of previous efforts in France to establish and to ensure tuition-free Christian schools for children. In the early seventeenth century, numerous congregations of women were founded for the education of poor girls, but the situation was different for poor boys. The aristocratic and rich provided amply for the quality education of their sons and daughters, and those who had a more modest degree of wealth could send their children to elementary tuition schools. But the really poor had no choice but to allow their children to roam the streets. Saint Peter Fourier had tried to interest the Augustinian Canons Regular in the Diocese of Toul in providing schools for poor boys. He had succeeded in the reform of the canons at the request of the bishop, but he failed to win their support for tuition-free schools.

Charles Démia, another educational reformer, had founded the Society of Saint Charles in Lyons in 1672 for the Christian instruction of poor children. The members of the society were either priests or young men training for the priesthood. Démia died in 1689 and shortly thereafter the Society of Saint Charles ceased to exist. De La Salle's own friend and guide, Father Barré, a religious of the Order of Minims, established two congregations in Rouen, the Sisters of Providence to teach in schools for girls and the Brothers of the Holy Child Jesus to conduct similar schools for boys. The Sisters of Providence flourished and came to Reims where, under the direction of Canon Roland, they developed into the Congregation of the Sisters of the Child Jesus. Barré, like Démia, however, had little success with his congregation of Brothers.

De La Salle was convinced that the work of Christian education of poor children was an expression of God's plan of salvation. However, the first teachers, whom he had tried to prepare for the work, quickly abandoned him. He realized, therefore, the urgent need to gather men who would be dedicated and who would undertake this educational work for religious motives, since there was no prospect of earning a rewarding livelihood through it. He addressed himself totally to the task of building up such a group of men. Initially, he drew up a simple rule of life for the new group of teachers. They adopted a distinctive form of attire and took the name, "Brothers of the Christian Schools," to underscore their relationship with one another and with their students not only as teachers but also as Brothers.

The rule of life was adapted throughout De La Salle's lifetime and was finally completed after the General Chapter of the Brothers in 1717, when he handed over the superiorship of the community to his successor, Brother Barthélemy.

In the development of the Brothers' Rule, De La Salle used the Rules of other religious orders, but he adapted them to the needs of his Brothers. According to the Lateran Decree of 1215, the establishment of new religious orders within the Church was forbidden. Only four Rules were recognized — Saint Basil's, Saint Augustine's, Saint Benedict's and Saint Francis'. Such disciplinary regulation did not allow for new forms of religious life in the Church to meet new needs arising in society. But approval was requested and given during the sixteenth century for numerous new congregations of women and for at least nine groups of Clerks Regular. The most notable of the new Clerks Regular was the Society of Jesus. De La Salle had to demonstrate that a new congregation such as the Brothers of the Christian Schools responded to a contemporary need as yet unprovided for within the Church in France and also that its Rule and Constitutions were based on the traditional principles of the religious life.

Thus, we find prominent in the Rule of 1718 in chapter 16, the following statement:

> It is necessary for the Brothers to apply to themselves and to take as the basis and support of their fidelity to the Rule what Saint Augustine says at the beginning of his Rule, that those who live in a Community ought before all else love God and after him their neighbor, because these two commandments are the most important that God has given us and because any form of fidelity which is not based on the observance of these commandments is useless for salvation. . . .

The members of religious life follow certain basic principles that are common to all orders and congregations at all times. The application of these principles and the means taken to put them into effect vary according to the needs which give rise to the foundation of the religious bodies. We find, then, that De La Salle studied the Rule of Saint Benedict, the prime model of all Rules of the religious and monastic life in the Western Church, and was aware of the reforms and writings of Abbé Armand-Jean Le Bouthiller de Rancé, the Abbot of La Trappe, which were being widely discussed in France at that time. Paragraph 1 of Letter 106 refers to one of De Rancé's books. Also during the seventeenth century, the Benedictine Congregation of Saint Maur became established and spread throughout France. De La Salle was a close friend of Dom Claude de Bretagne, Prior of the Maurist monastery of Saint Remy in Reims. Moreover, François-Elie Maillefer and Simon-Louis Maillefer, two of De La Salle's nephews, sons of his sister Marie, were Maurist Benedictines, so De La Salle had ample opportunity to study the life and Rule of a Benedictine monastery at close hand.

Dom P. Salmon, OSB, in an article published in 1959, "Ascèse Monastique et Exercices Spirituels dans les Constitutions (Saint Maur) de 1646," wrote that the basic principles of the monastic life have always been separation from the world, silence, stability, poverty, celebration of the Divine Office, obedience, and the formation of young religious. The Divine Office, the *Opus Dei*, or Work of God, is the particular community duty of the Benedictine monastery, and except for the recitation of the Office, the remaining principles as enunciated by Dom Salmon formed the bases of the Rule and Constitutions that were adopted by the Brothers of the Christian Schools at their General Chapter of 1717, after having been written by De La Salle himself at the request of that Chapter.

In his letters De La Salle never tired of reminding his Brothers of these principles of Benedictine spirituality. For the Brothers, however, their *Opus Dei* was the Christian education of the children in their classes. Not being priests, they were under no obligation to say the Divine Office. Their daily schedule, moreover, made it impossible for them to recite the office together in choir. De La Salle himself came to the decision that he would have to choose between devoting his time either to the responsibilities of being a canon or to those of being a superior of the new body of religious teachers. He chose to resign from the canonry. He frequently stated that the Brothers were to make no distinction between the work of their own salvation and the work of the Christian education of the children in their classes.

Separation from secular affairs, strict silence within the community, the austerity of the life of poverty, insistence on the importance of un-questioning obedience — these practices De La Salle mentioned again and again in his letters to his Brothers.

Noteworthy, too, is that when the Brothers made their first perpetual vows in 1694, they included the vow of stability in the formula. Under the original Benedictine Rule, stability was promised to the monastery into which the monk was received. In the Maurist Congregation, this vow was made to the congregation, not to the individual monastery. In like manner the Brothers vowed stability to their Society.

There were other influences on De La Salle which also affected the lives of the Brothers. In *Explication de la Méthode d'Oraison* which he wrote for the Brothers' instruction, De La Salle followed closely the method of prayer he practiced during his days at the Seminary of Saint Sulpice. The school schedule of the Brothers required that formal community prayer be restricted to fixed times each day, but prayerfulness was to be cultivated throughout the day both in and out of class by frequently recalling the presence of God. The Brothers' practice of saying the rosary when walking through the streets, also, no doubt, came from the Sulpician custom.

De La Salle, additionally, showed a marked appreciation for the Society of Jesus, whose Rule and Constitutions he knew well and whose loyalty to the pope was much in line with his own. He was indebted to the Jesuits for the rule on modesty and the regulations for community recreation.

De La Salle makes frequent reference in his Letters to the various spiritual and community exercises practiced throughout the day by the Brothers. The following is a summary of these practices:

◆ **4:30** A.M. Rising and a quarter of an hour spent in preparation for prayer.
◆ **5:00** A.M. Vocal prayer for about 15 minutes. Personal prayer until Mass at 6:00 A.M.
◆ **After Mass until 7:15** A.M. Either secular or religious studies, followed by breakfast, during which an instructive book was read publicly.
◆ **After morning classes.** Religious studies until 11:30 A.M., when the community assembled in the oratory for examination of conscience regarding a particular fault (called Particular Examen, employing the method developed by Saint Ignatius), followed by the midday meal.
◆ **After the meal.** Community recreation together for an hour.

✦ **Afternoon classes from 1:30 P.M. to 4:30 P.M.** Religious studies until 5:30 P.M., followed by spiritual reading and prayer until 6:30 P.M.; then the evening meal and community recreation for one hour.

✦ **8:30 P.M.** Religious study for one-half hour, followed by community night prayer and retiring.

The monastic chapter of faults was divided into two parts. Every day before the evening meal, each Brother confessed to the Brother Director, in the presence of the community, any exterior faults he had committed during the day. On Fridays the Brothers assembled at the end of the evening recreation and, in the presence of the Director, pointed out to each other defects that had been apparent in the conduct of one another during the week. For many years these two practices were known among the English-speaking Brothers as the *accusation of faults* and the *advertisement of defects.* Both practices have been officially abandoned in recent years.

III

De La Salle's letters addressed to the Brothers have quite a different tone from those addressed to persons not belonging to the Institute. In the latter group there is generally a great deal of formality. This more formal tone is illustrated in De La Salle's letter to his own brother, Canon Jean-Louis. On the other hand, all correspondence with the Brothers begins without any formality at all, but in a familiar manner, with the words *My very dear Brother* occurring usually within the opening sentence. Similarly, these letters invariably close with *tout à vous,* which is rendered *devotedly yours.* The body of each of these letters reads like a conversation, while letters to people outside the Institute are often in a style almost impossible to translate into the more familiar style of contemporary times. De La Salle identifies himself completely with the Brothers, abandoning all claims to the social status he possessed in a century and a society where such claims were rigorously maintained.

From the letters we learn scarcely anything about the difficulties that De La Salle personally experienced or the opposition that dogged him throughout his life. His correspondence with Gabriel Drolin is the only exception to this pattern, for De La Salle liked to keep his disciple in Rome aware of what was happening to the Institute in France. But even in these letters, references to himself and his problems are few. The violence of the Writing Masters and the Masters of the Little Schools, their physical attacks on the schools, the court cases they brought against De La Salle, the fines imposed, and the prohibition against teaching in Paris are but obliquely mentioned. Brother Nicolas Vuyart's betrayal of his responsibility and of the confidence placed in him as Director of the training school for rural teachers is only indirectly mentioned in a reply to Drolin's complaint about what Drolin considers to be De La Salle's lack of confidence in him.

De La Salle's replies to the Brothers are direct and precise. They give the impression that De La Salle had his correspondent's letter in front of him as he wrote his reply point by point with here a word of encouragement, there a reprimand, now a little irony, but mostly with advice for living in community and the management of classes. He makes no attempt to use the polished phrase. The replies seem to be those of a man with more work to do than he really has time for, a man in a hurry.

To many readers it might appear that De La Salle spends too much time dealing with trivialities, insisting on minor points of the Rule, like sounding the bell the correct number of times for the various spiritual exercises. But we have to take into consideration that the Brothers of those days were all beginners in the religious life. None of them had experience in this kind of lifestyle; there were no established traditions for them to follow. They were often living in houses in groups of two or three without the support of a community of experienced men. The original local superiors were men who had been members of the Society for only a few years.

De La Salle was not only the superior of the Society of Brothers, he was also at their own insistence their spiritual director and confessor. Thus, in several of his letters we find him readily giving encouragement and help to Brothers with troubled consciences. He won a reputation outside his new community, too, as a spiritual director, and people were recommended to his guidance. Often he found himself asked to direct men and women in their search for a greater spiritual progress in their lives. It is interesting to note that the letters he wrote to these persons outside the Institute of the Brothers are much more detailed and more filled with spiritual guidance than the majority of those written to the Brothers themselves. At least, this is certainly the case of those letters that have come down to us from Canon Blain, one of De La Salle's first biographers.

In addition to the letters to the Brothers and to others who sought his guidance, this volume contains one letter De La Salle wrote to refute the claim that he was one of those who had appealed against the Papal Bull *Unigenitus,* a document which condemned as unorthodox certain dogmatic statements drawn from the *Augustinus* of Bishop Jansenius. There is also a strongly-worded letter, written very probably to his nephew, Canon Jean-François Maillefer, who had appealed to the civil courts against a decision handed down by the bishop in a matter of ecclesiastical discipline. Jean-François was the brother of François-Elie, another early biographer of De La Salle. In these two letters De La Salle clearly manifested his position of adherence to the magisterium of the Church — the Church universal in the person of the pope and the local Church as represented by the bishop.

IV

The first English edition of the letters of John Baptist de La Salle was prepared and published in 1952 by Brother W. J. Battersby to commemorate the 300th anniversary of the birth of De La Salle. In the same year and as part of the same commemoration, No. 335 of the *Circulaires Instructives et Administratives* for private distribution among the Brothers of the Christian Schools appeared under the title of *Les Lettres de Saint Jean-Baptiste de La Salle.* Like all such circulars until recent times, it was published in French. In the preparatory notice to this French edition, written by Brother Athanase Emile, Superior General from 1946 to 1952, no mention is made of the man who prepared the letters for publication. The Superior did, however, thank the archivists of the Generalate for their meticulous work over a period of two years. A second edition in French, the *Edition Critique* (1954), reveals that both Circular No. 335 and the *Edition Critique* are the work of one man, Brother Félix-Paul.

Although Battersby's English edition of the letters and Félix-Paul's Circular No. 335 both appeared in 1952, and although both were introduced by Brother Athanase Emile, there is no mention in either publication of the other. Brother Battersby would have used the same source material of the original autograph letters of De La Salle, the same authenticated copies, and the same letters contained in the so-called Manuscript 22, all kept in the archives of the Generalate in Rome. There is nothing to suggest that Battersby made use of Brother Félix-Paul's modernized French version of the originals. This fact makes Battersby's contribution to the study of the spirit and work of De La Salle all the more remarkable. He most surely read the autograph letters in the original or their facsimile reproductions (which were made in view of the damage done to the originals over the course of two and one-half centuries) and brought his expertise to bear on the French of the seventeenth and early eighteenth centuries with its own orthography, style, and idiom as well as its numerous historical allusions.

Because of his accomplishment, we cannot speak highly enough of Battersby's pioneer work in making De La Salle's correspondence available to English-speaking readers. However, there has been much research done on the life, the work, and the writings of De La Salle since the General Chapter of 1956. That Chapter decided to promote research into the publication of texts and documents capable of serving as a basis for a scientific study of the life and work of John Baptist de La Salle. As a result of this decision, more light has been shed on his writings, some earlier dubious renderings of the texts of these writings have been clarified, and letters and documents hitherto unknown have been discovered.

The results of all this study and research are published in the *Cahiers lasalliens,* a series of over 45 volumes. This scholarly and extensive work is the result in a special way of the competence of Brothers Michel Sauvage, Maurice-Auguste Hermans, Léon de Marie Aroz, and Miguel Campos.

The present volume is based mainly on the *Edition Critique* of Brother Félix-Paul, which had been prepared for publication by Georges Rigault, author of *Histoire générale de l'Institut des Frères des Ecoles chrétiennes (1936)* (hereafter, *Histoire générale*). It is Georges Rigault who notes that at the time Circular No. 335 was published, Félix-Paul was already well advanced with his preparations for the *Edition Critique.* He had just completed his work for that edition when, in the first week of July 1952, he took ill. He died on July 17 of that year. Brother Athanase Emile died shortly after. His place as Superior of the Institute was taken by Brother Denis, Vicar General, who requested Georges Rigault to prepare Félix-Paul's work for publication.

It is difficult to give an adequate appreciation for the work of Brother Félix-Paul. His *Edition Critique* is an excellent example of a scholarly study, providing the results of careful historical and sociological research into the background and details of all the letters. It is especially valuable for the extensive documentation of information about the Brothers to whom the letters were addressed and about Brothers and other persons mentioned in the letters, as well as about the events alluded to by De La Salle. Most of the commentary in this present English edition of the letters is based on the work of Brother Félix-Paul. Brother Battersby's observations have also provided useful information.

In Battersby's English translation, the letters of De La Salle are arranged in two principal groups: (1) autograph letters and (2) those letters preserved only as copies. These latter are in two categories according to their arrangement in the archives of the Generalate in Rome. Within each of the groups, the letters are arranged chronologically as far as possible. Battersby's edition has a special value in presenting, along with the English translation and commentary, the original French text with only minor accommodations to modern typesetting.

In Brother Félix-Paul's *Edition Critique*, the letters are arranged in the alphabetical order of the names of the recipients, from Brother Anastase to Brother Thomas. There then follow letters to unidentified recipients, arranged according to their office (e.g., Directors, other Brothers) and persons outside the Institute, even though some of these latter recipients are known. The *Edition Critique* also includes excerpts of letters that are quoted in Blain's biography of De La Salle and that do not appear in Battersby's translation. Some of Blain's quotations from the letters are also known from other sources, including the other early biographies by Bernard and Maillefer. The most important of these other sources is Manuscript 22, a collection of copies of 36 letters of De La Salle, all written in the same hand, probably before the French Revolution. The *Edition Critique* made use of these other sources to reconstitute the texts of Blain when it seemed appropriate. A comparison of Blain's version with these other sources is made in volume 10 of the *Cahiers lasalliens*, pages 137–150. In the present volume this comparison is illustrated in the commentary following Letter 80.

In the present volume also an attempt is made to arrange the letters in chronological order regardless of whether they are autographs or copies, or whether the names of the recipients are known. At the same time, the letters addressed to the same correspondent are grouped together. It is hoped that this arrangement will give an appreciation for the gradual development of the Institute as well as insight into the various stages in the life of De La Salle himself. The exact dates of some letters, of course, are not known, but letters whose dates can be estimated by their contents have been inserted into approximate chronological order. Letters whose dates cannot be determined follow those De La Salle wrote during the period when he was carrying on an active correspondence with the Brothers and with persons outside the Institute.

Throughout the text, John Baptist de La Salle is most often referred to as *De La Salle*, which is how he himself signed his letters, or simply as the Founder of the Brothers of the Christian Schools. On the left side of the appropriate pages, at the beginning of each letter, the documentary sources are given. When the date of the letter or the place from which it was sent is not part of the letter itself, but this information must be inferred, the information is placed in brackets at the head of the letter. Finally, each letter is separated into numbered paragraphs, following the arrangement of the *Edition Critique*.

THE LETTERS

of

John Baptist de La Salle

LETTER 1
To the Mayor and Councillors of Château-Porcien

This is the earliest letter of John Baptist de La Salle that we possess. It was written at a critical moment in the history of the Institute. De La Salle was 31 years old and living in his family home in Reims. He had just made the decision to leave his home on the Rue Sainte-Marguerite to live with the teachers he was training in a house he had rented on the Rue Neuve. This is the house that Maillefer, in one of the earliest biographies of De La Salle, called the "cradle of the Institute" (CL 6: 45). The Saturday mentioned in paragraph 3 of the letter, when the two teachers were sent to Château-Porcien, was the very day when the new community moved into the house of its own.

This letter was discovered by Archbishop Gousset of Reims in the episcopal library in 1843 during the investigation leading to the process of beatification of De La Salle. The original was lost during the beatification process but has been preserved in a lithograph facsimile. Battersby thought this facsimile was actually the original and placed it first among his presentation of the autograph letters.

Letter 1: To the Mayor and Councillors of Château-Porcien
lithographic facsimile; AMG; EC 111; BL I.1

Reims
June 20, 1682

Gentlemen,

1   Even were I to take but little interest in what concerns the glory of God, I would indeed be quite insensitive not to be moved by the urgent pleas of your Reverend Dean and by the courteous tone of the letter with which you have honored me today.

2   It would be wrong of me, Gentlemen, not to send you school teachers from our community, in view of the enthusiasm and zeal you show for the Christian education and instruction of your children.

3   So please be assured that nothing is dearer to my heart than to support your good intentions in this matter. By this Saturday I will send you two school teachers, with whom I trust you will be satisfied, to open classes the day following the feast of Saint Peter. I assure you that I am very much obliged to you for your courteous remarks.

I beg you, Gentlemen, to believe that, with respect
and in Our Lord,
I am, your very humble and obedient servant,
DE LA SALLE, Priest, Canon of Reims

———— ✦ ————

Château-Porcien was the capital of a territory acquired in 1666 by the Duke
of Mazarin. It is located about ten miles from Rethel, where in March 1682
Adrien Nyel had opened a school. The school in Rethel may have prompted
the request from Château-Porcien. Also, in Reims not far from De La Salle's
house lived a very pious priest, Jean Faubert, a native of Château-Porcien
according to biographer Brother Bernard, to whom De La Salle would resign
his canonry on August 16, 1683 (CL 4: 54). This priest may have spoken
approvingly to the people of Château-Porcien about De La Salle's work
with teachers.

Adrien Nyel, who had been so instrumental in involving De La Salle
in the work of Christian education for the poor, may have been one of
the two teachers mentioned in paragraph 3, or he may only have helped
the other two get started, since he opened two other schools the same year,
at Guise and Laon.

It is noteworthy that De La Salle uses the expression "teachers," not
"Brothers." This latter title was probably not adopted until the first
assembly of the teachers in 1686. Nevertheless, even at this date in 1682,
he does speak of "our community."

The school in Château-Porcien probably lasted for only a short time.
In his biography of De La Salle, Blain mentions that De La Salle's confessor opposed his move to Paris in 1683 because the new society had only
15 members in Reims, Laon, Rethel, and Guise. Blain does not mention
Château-Porcien. In the *Mémoire sur l'habit,* written by De La Salle about
1690, mention is made of Château-Porcien as one of the places where the
Brothers neglected their school to take part in ecclesiastical functions.

It is possible that whatever information Blain knew about Château-
Porcien was obtained from Brother Jean Jacot, Assistant Superior General,
who was living at Saint Yon when Blain was writing his biography of
De La Salle. Brother Jean was born in Château-Porcien in 1672 and entered
the Institute as a junior novice in October 1686. He may well have been
a student of the Brothers in his native town and therefore one of the first
members of the Institute to have been a student of a Brothers' school.

Even at this early date De La Salle reveals his ideals, namely, his zeal
for "the glory of God" and his interest in "the Christian instruction and
education" of children. In fact, he says, "Nothing is dearer to my heart."
This letter gives evidence that De La Salle's zeal was often in response to

Letter 1, to the Mayor and Councillors of Château-Porcien, the earliest known letter of De La Salle

the initiative of others. Responding to needs identified by others was
De La Salle's characteristic way of allowing Providence to guide his actions,
and this mode of acting became characteristic of the development of the
Institute during the whole life of De La Salle. He says explicitly to Brother
Gabriel Drolin in paragraphs 17 and 18 of Letter 18 that this is his usual
way of proceeding.

LETTER 2
To a Brother

This is the earliest letter known to have been written by De La Salle to
a Brother of the Christian Schools. The name of the Brother to whom it
was addressed is not known.

The original manuscript of this letter was used in the process of beatification of De La Salle in 1835. It was subsequently lost and was known
only through copies that had been made on that occasion. These copies
were used both in the *Edition Critique* by Brother Félix-Paul and by Battersby in his *De La Salle: Letters and Documents*.

In 1955, however, the original manuscript of Letter 2 was rediscovered
in England. In November of that year, Father Bernard Payne, librarian
of Ushaw College in Durham County, found the manuscript in a packet
of autograph letters of various notable persons. There is no record of how
the packet came into the possession of the college. Father Payne contacted
the Brothers of Hopwood Hall, who verified that the manuscript was indeed an original letter written by De La Salle. The happy outcome of this
discovery was that the president of Ushaw College obtained the permission of the Bishop of Hexham and Newcastle to present the manuscript
to the Brothers of the District of England with the understanding that
it would not be taken from the country.

Letter 2: To a Brother
AE; EC 102; BL II.4

May 15, 1701

1   Be careful, my very dear Brother, not to be led by your
    self-will. That is not right, and God will not bless you if
    you act in this manner.
2   You should not have been annoyed because the dear
    Brother Director tore up what you had written, obviously
    because you had written it without permission. This is
    something that should never be done and it is quite right
    to destroy the work that springs from self-will.

The original of Letter 2 was discovered in 1955 in the library of Ushaw College, Durham, England, and is preserved at Saint John's College, Kintbury, the provincialate of the District of England. This letter is the earliest extant letter written by De La Salle to a Brother.

3   You were quite right to tell your Director of your annoyance. Always be completely frank and God will bless you.

4   Take care not to let yourself fall into thoughtless behavior,
for this is very harmful for you and dries up the heart.

5   Be faithful both in carrying out your penances to the letter
and in doing nothing without permission, for God will
bless you only insofar as you act through obedience.

6   Be quite happy when your defects are pointed out to you,
for this is one of the greatest services others can do for
you. Look upon it in this light.

7   The remembrance of God's presence will be a great advantage in helping you and in inspiring you to do all your actions well.

8   I am delighted that you devote yourself readily to prayer.
This is the spiritual exercise that draws down God's graces
on the others.

9   Be also especially attentive to your spiritual reading, which
will be a great help in preparing you to make your prayer
well.

10 You know that Holy Mass is the most important exercise
of religion. That is why you should bring to it all possible
attention.

11 Don't worry yourself about what your Brothers do. It is for
God to judge them, not you.

12 Be watchful that you do not give way to impatience in
class, for far from bringing order to the class, it prevents
you from achieving it.

13 I pray God to give you his Spirit and
    I am, my very dear Brother,
    Devotedly yours in Our Lord,
    DE LA SALLE

———— ✦ ————

This letter is a good example of the type of guidance that De La Salle provided in response to the monthly letters of the Brothers. This practice of
the Brothers' writing monthly letters to the Founder was called *reddition*
and had been established as an Institute practice ten years earlier (CL 7:
315). De La Salle responded point by point to the letter this Brother had
written: a comment on the failure of self-will, then observations on the
other points of conduct that had been reported by the Brother. Most of
the topics in this letter refer to the religious practices of the community,
but there is also a characteristic observation in paragraph 11 about personal relationships among the Brothers and another in paragraph 12 that
deals with school matters.

As time went on, a directory (see Appendix A) was developed as a guide to the topics about which a Brother should write to the Superior in the monthly redditional letters. This directory is not mentioned in the 1705 Rule, but is in the 1718 Rule (CL 25: 90; 15: 16–22). The first printed evidence of this list appeared sometime before 1725 as an appendix of 20 pages in De La Salle's *Recueil de différents petits traités à l'usage des Frères des Ecoles chrétiennes* of 1711 (hereafter, *Recueil*) (CL 15: 122–130).

In paragraph 8 of this letter, De La Salle expresses his delight that the Brother is devoting himself readily to prayer. The French word here is *oraison*, which has traditionally been translated *mental prayer*. However, that translation could give a false emphasis, since the term *mental prayer* seems to imply that the only, or the most active, faculty of the person in prayer is the mind. De La Salle certainly encouraged the Brothers to engage their minds in prayer in the sense of using their powers to think, reason, and draw conclusions. But he also intended that they engage their entire selves in prayer with their intellect, will, memory, imagination, and feelings, and with their reflective, affective, and contemplative capacities as well. In a systematic and thorough way, and through numerous examples and options, De La Salle, in his primer on prayer, *Explication de la Méthode d'Oraison,* taught each Brother to develop his own style of prayer by bringing his whole person into the presence of God and by engaging in his own way all of his capacities in prayer. In view of this understanding of De La Salle's teachings on prayer, *oraison* is translated here and throughout this volume not as *mental prayer,* but simply as *prayer.*

Letters 3 to 5
To Brother Denis

Very little is known about Brother Denis. The name does not appear in the first register of the Brothers, called the *Catalogue* (CL 3: 24 ff.), which was probably drawn up in 1714. However, a Brother Denis is recorded as having made perpetual vows of obedience and stability at Vaugirard on December 9, 1697. In Letter 3 we find him in community with Brother Claude and two young Brothers at Rethel; in Letter 4 he appears to be at Darnétal. Letter 5 seems to place him at Darnétal in 1708, for De La Salle reproaches him in paragraph 4 of that letter for his unnecessary visits to nearby Saint Yon. No reference has been found concerning Brother Denis after 1708.

The instructions given to Brother Denis in paragraph 7 of Letter 3 may indicate that he was in charge of the community as well as the school at Rethel at that time. The previous Director had died on January 2, 1701.

LETTER 3
To Brother Denis

AM; AMG; EC 10; BL I.2

[Rethel]
May 30, 1701

1   It seems to me, my very dear Brother, that you ought not to spend so much time on thoughts that come into your head about your vocation, for the more time you spend on them, the more trouble they will cause you.

2   Become as interiorly recollected as you can, for only with this recollection can you sanctify your actions.

3   Take care that you often recall the presence of God, for this is the principal fruit of prayer; it will be of little benefit to you if you do not take pains to practice mortification but rather seek your own comfort.

4   It is not enough to think about going to God as perfectly as possible. You must actually do so and this you can only do to the extent that you are hard on yourself.

5   I am not surprised that you find great difficulty in the observance of the rules. Your habit of negligent observance causes you to find them so difficult. If you follow them exactly, you will find a facility in doing so, even a pleasure.

Letter 3, to Brother Denis, has a piece of black cloth sewn into the paper at the lower left and the words "morceau de la couverture de son nouveau testament" have been added. Possibly the fragment of cloth had been given as a relic to Brother Denis after the Founder's death, and Brother Denis thought that the best way to preserve it was to attach it to the letter.

6 It is for this same reason that you feel distaste for Holy Communion.

7 Please, never be absent from the recreations. It is without any doubt a serious matter that you spend the time of recreation with Brother Claude while you leave the two young Brothers to make theirs together by themselves. This is very bad.

8 I am very glad that you abandon yourself to God's will and are unconcerned where you may be sent. This spirit is also needed in your community.

> I am, my very dear Brother,
> Devotedly yours in Our Lord,
> DE LA SALLE, Priest

———— ✦ ————

The "two young Brothers" mentioned in paragraph 7 were probably novices sent to community before they had completed more than a few months of religious formation. It was the practice at that time to put the young Brothers into class shortly after they had commenced their period of formation. After some teaching experience they returned, if necessary, to the novitiate for further religious training.

The Brother Claude mentioned here was the Director of Rethel from 1704 to 1708, but no mention is made of him after that date in any of the extant letters.

This letter and Letter 132, addressed to the Director of Calais, are the only letters we possess addressed to Brothers that De La Salle signs with the title *priest*.

LETTER 4
To Brother Denis

Seven years have elapsed between this letter [1708] and the previous one (1701) to Brother Denis. Much has happened that clarifies references in this letter. In 1705 De La Salle opened a community at Darnétal where Denis was now stationed. (See Letters 33 and 34 about this foundation.) A few months after the establishment at Darnétal, the Brothers took over schools in the nearby town of Rouen.

De La Salle was able to staff several schools in and around Rouen in 1705 as a result of the problems he was experiencing in Paris from the Writing Masters and the Masters of the Little Schools. Because De La Salle's

Christian Schools had been giving the schools of the Masters serious competition, the Masters sued De La Salle on the grounds that he was not limiting his students to the poor. The Masters won their case, and the court forbade the Brothers to continue conducting schools in Paris. In May 1705 De La Salle transferred the Brothers from Paris to staff schools in Rouen.

When this letter was written, the Brothers were teaching in four schools of Rouen: Saint Godard, Saint Eloi, Saint Maclou, and Saint Vivien. Brothers also taught at the General Hospice. All of the Brothers lived in a house in the parish of Saint Nicolas. The community at Darnétal was loosely connected with this community in Rouen, which was only about a mile distant.

Letter 4: To Brother Denis
AM; AMG; EC 11; BL I.43

July 8 [1708]

1   Nothing is farther from my mind than to abandon you, my very dear Brother. If I did not answer your last letter at the same time as I did those of the Brothers at Rouen, it was because I didn't have the time. Indeed there are two Brothers besides yourself whose letters I could not answer.

2   There is no need to buy material for a robe. There is one here made for you. You will not have to go without.

3   I am very glad that you have eased your father's anxieties.

4   I am annoyed with Brother Thomas for treating you as you say. I will see to it that he changes his manner of acting in this matter. It is not true that I wrote to Brother Thomas what you told me about your needs, since I complained to him that he was not supplying what the Brothers require.

5   You must be particularly careful not to be lax with regard to your spiritual exercises. That is not the way to draw down God's blessing. You will have no virtue unless you are hard on yourself, and it is not a question of merely appearing so; your virtue must be solid. It is not by taking your ease and seeking your comfort that you acquire virtue.

6   I am glad that you sometimes practice mortification of the mind and of the senses, but it is also important to practice them when occasions present themselves.

7   Be exact in observing silence out of love for God; this is one of the principal points of Rule.

8   It is a very useful practice to apply yourself to the remembrance of God's presence. Be faithful to it.

9   Nothing will draw down on you the blessings of God so much as fidelity in carrying out small matters.

10   Be especially careful to recite the vocal prayers thoughtfully and to see that they are said in the same manner in class, for what makes vocal prayers pleasing to God is the attention with which they are said.

11   Take care not to become impatient with your Brother, but always speak politely to him.

12   Prayer is the mainstay of piety; so you must bring great attention to it.

13   Be careful to leave everything and everybody as soon as the bell rings.

14   Conclude conversations briefly with persons who come to the school door in order not to let the pupils waste time.

15   Be careful to correct the children, the ignorant even more than the others.

16   It is disgraceful to call them hurtful names. Be careful not to let human respect prevent you from doing good. It is really disgraceful to call your pupils by insulting names, and it also gives them bad example.

17   As you are aware, we make progress in virtue only insofar as we do ourselves violence. For this reason you must be careful to do so.

18   Make a point of practicing mortification of the mind and the senses, which for you is an obligation of your state.

19   At the advertisement of defects you must not look for the motives of others, but rather the good that comes to you from this exercise.

20   There is no doubt that the rules can be carried out, even when there are only two of you. I am very happy that you try to be faithful to the Rule. Praise be to God for the good sentiments that he gives you in this matter.

21   The attitude that you bring to your spiritual exercises is good; keep on with it.

22   It is quite wrong to make your spiritual reading out of curiosity; that is not the way to benefit from it.

23   When you find yourself without good feelings during prayer, humble yourself.

24   You are right that particular friendships among the Brothers cause serious difficulty in a community.

25   I am delighted that you have a good number of students at present. Make sure that you keep them.

26 Keep an eye on that Brother who slaps the students and see to it that he stops doing it. This is most important.

27 I pray that God may keep you in your good dispositions and

> I am, my very dear Brother,
> Devotedly yours in Our Lord,
> DE LA SALLE

———— ✦ ————

This letter is a good example of the range of De La Salle's guidance of his Brothers, especially those like Brother Denis who were responsible for a school or a community. At the very opening of the letter, De La Salle affirms his loyalty to the Brother personally. Apparently Brother Denis had concluded that the Founder had been neglecting him. Then there is mention of a matter of clothing, of the Brother's anxiety about his father, and about a complaint against Brother Thomas, who was responsible for supplying the Brothers' needs. Next follow several exhortations about the spiritual life of the Brother significantly intermingled with matters of school regulations. Notable is De La Salle's concern about the proper correction of students, a topic to which he gave a large section of his *Conduite des Ecoles chrétiennes* (CL 24: 140–179) as well as two entire meditations for the time of retreat (CL 13: 53–63). The detailed instructions of *Conduite des Ecoles chrétiennes* are especially significant, imbued as they are with such moderation and wisdom, and they remain meaningful for teachers even today.

When the Brothers wrote their monthly letters to De La Salle, the letters were all enclosed with the Director's at a community gathering and sealed in the presence of everyone. This was intended, among other possible reasons, to save postage. The letters were likewise returned in one packet and distributed publicly. Hence Brother Denis knew others received answers when he did not.

In paragraph 2 De La Salle reminds Brother Denis of the custom at that time that all robes were supplied from a central source, under the direction of Brother Thomas. The Rule of 1718 states, "He [the Brother] will address to the Brother Superior of the Institute all the letters that he writes to the Brother who provides for the robes and he will never write to him directly" (Article 28).

The community of only two Brothers mentioned in paragraph 20 is the community at Darnétal, composed of Brothers Denis and Robert. Generally De La Salle opposed a community of two. Evidently exceptions were made, especially when such a community could share some of the activities of a community nearby. For example, there is also mention in paragraph 19 of the exercise of the advertisement of defects, which probably was not practiced between Brothers Denis and Robert, but in the central community of nearby Rouen, which numbered ten Brothers under the direction of Brother Joseph.

LETTER 5
To Brother Denis

AM; AMG; EC 12; BL I.44

August 1, [1708]

1   I am quite distressed to hear of the illness that you are suffering, my very dear Brother. We must try to find some way of remedying this.

2   You should apply yourself to prayer as best you can, for this is the exercise that ordinarily draws down graces on the others.

3   You know that it is a shame to speak in anger, so refrain from doing this. Did not the guards have the right to see what you were carrying?

4   You should go to Saint Yon only with the others on the weekly holidays. You have no business there with Brother Hilaire or with the other Brothers.

5   Don't get angry with anybody; it is neither polite nor Christian.

6   Take care that you are not frivolous when you join in recreation with the Brothers in Rouen. It does them no good.

7   As you can see quite well, it is to your advantage to aim at dying to yourself and to your inclinations.

8   Be watchful that you accept the humiliations that come to you with the thought that it is God who sends them.

9   My very dear Brother, to practice real obedience you must be ready to obey all superiors. The difficulty you find in this arises from the fact that you do not see God in them.

10   It is good that you apply yourself to your spiritual reading. It will be very profitable for you and particularly it will help you to pray well.

11   See that you do not let yourself give way to distractions during prayer. They come through your being too occupied with external things. Be careful regarding this.

12 I am told that some clerics who met you alone in Rouen said that you were not a Brother but a layman, walking alone like that through the town. If such was the case, you certainly did wrong.

13 Please, do not go to Rouen any more except on the weekly holidays and with another Brother. Then go straight to Saint Nicolas', for beyond that you have no reason to be there.

14 I have come across your letter of April 21 again.

15 It was wrong of you to leave class to go out for such a thing as you mention to me, and I ask you not to let it happen again.

16 Even if the Brother says or does something to you that is out of order, for your part do not allow any displeasure to show; try to restrain yourself and then you can write and tell me about it.

17 One thing that you must especially aim at is to be faithful to the inspirations that come to you when they lead you to overcome yourself; that is a sign that they come from God.

18 Since you have occasions on which you suffer humiliations when you are in town with Brother Robert, let it appear at such times that you like them, and do not follow the promptings of nature to avoid them.

19 Always be faithful to make your spiritual reading and to go to bed on time. Please, never fail in this, for nothing can dispense you in these matters. Make sure that the rule of silence is observed.

20 You need to recollect yourself often. This will prevent you from falling into faults.

21 It would be good for you to carry out your ideas of living, as it were, a sort of novitiate in order to give yourself up to the interior life. It would be very profitable for you.

22 I am delighted that you ardently desire that God's will may be done in all things regarding you.

23 Make sure that you join in the recreations. Don't allow the children to interrupt this time. In order to keep silence faithfully, you must take recreations at the prescribed time.

24 The students must not say anything disrespectful to a Brother.

25 Make sure that your students come to school punctually and that they attend on Sundays and feast days.

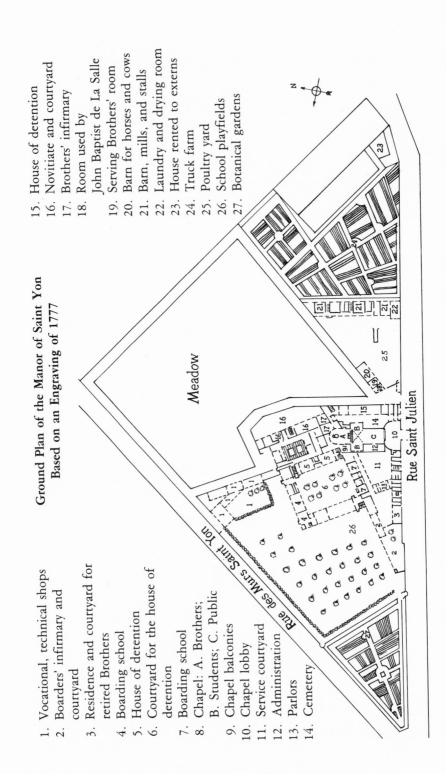

Ground Plan of the Manor of Saint Yon
Based on an Engraving of 1777

1. Vocational, technical shops
2. Boarders' infirmary and courtyard
3. Residence and courtyard for retired Brothers
4. Boarding school
5. House of detention
6. Courtyard for the house of detention
7. Boarding school
8. Chapel: A. Brothers; B. Students; C. Public
9. Chapel balconies
10. Chapel lobby
11. Service courtyard
12. Administration
13. Parlors
14. Cemetery
15. House of detention
16. Novitiate and courtyard
17. Brothers' infirmary
18. Room used by John Baptist de La Salle
19. Serving Brothers' room
20. Barn for horses and cows
21. Barn, mills, and stalls
22. Laundry and drying room
23. House rented to externs
24. Truck farm
25. Poultry yard
26. School playfields
27. Botanical gardens

Meadow

Rue des Murs Saint Yon

Rue Saint Julien

26 Do not fail to carry out my urgent recommendations.
I am, my very dear Brother,
Devotedly yours in Our Lord,
DE LA SALLE

————— ✦ —————

In paragraph 4 De La Salle refers to Saint Yon. This property, near Rouen in the suburb of Saint Sever, was leased by De La Salle to serve, among other functions, as a novitiate. It was finally purchased by the Brothers during the superiorship of Brother Barthélemy.

Saint Yon was also used by the Brothers as a place of rest during their weekly holiday from classes and for retreats during the summer school vacations. Brothers Denis and Robert, who formed the little community at Darnétal, spent their weekly free day either with the Brothers in Rouen or at Saint Yon.

It seems that Denis was going to Saint Yon more often than he should, rather than to his central community of Saint Nicolas in Rouen. Saint Yon was an attractive estate. The property had a spacious building surrounded by 14 acres of gardens and playgrounds for the resident communities of the novitiate and the boarding school. The boarders came from families in Rouen wishing to have special training for their sons. Saint Yon probably also included, by this time, a house of correction for youth. Later this was discontinued, but probably in 1715 a house of detention was opened for young men and adult males who were placed there by special order of the royal court.

Brother Hilaire with whom Denis visited at Saint Yon was at that time a serving Brother.

Brother Robert was Denis' community companion at Darnétal, the same Brother to whom De La Salle wrote Letters 38 to 48. He succeeded Denis as Director of the school at Darnétal in December 1708.

LETTER 6
To a Brother

This letter is one of 36 letters of De La Salle that have been preserved in Ms. 22 and that he wrote to Brothers whose names we do not know. Ms. 22 was transcribed from an earlier collection some time before the French Revolution. It was intended to give the Brothers a kind of anthology of the Founder's letters, arranged under the headings of various virtues. This letter, for example, was under the heading "Il ne faut pas avoir d'humeurs" ("It is necessary not to follow whims"). More than likely some of the letters of Ms. 22 are only excerpts, but their authenticity has never been seriously challenged.

Letter 6: To a Brother
Ms. 22, 9; AMG; EC 93; BL III.9

[1702]

1   You are well aware, my very dear Brother, that we Brothers should not follow our inclinations or our whims. Please give serious thought to this and make every effort to succeed in doing this.

2   As you know, acting through whims is acting as an animal rather than as a human being.

3   Among us mortification is held in highest honor, so you must look upon it as an inseparable companion.

4   We ought to be ready to welcome humiliations in a spirit of simplicity. We often have opportunities to do this, so we must not look on them as strangers. We must become accustomed to them, for they are always good for us.

5   Penances are of little value unless they are carried out with good interior dispositions. That is why you must put your will into doing them. In this way God will bless you.

6   Be faithful to the daily accusation of your faults in the refectory. God will bless this practice with many graces.

   I pray that God will shower his graces on you during this holy season.

   I am, my very dear Brother,
   Devotedly yours in Our Lord,
   DE LA SALLE

———— ◆ ————

When De La Salle speaks of mortification and penances, as he does in paragraphs 3 and 5, he does not advocate severe corporal mortification among the Brothers. He himself practiced such bodily penance and some of his earliest disciples followed his example. But De La Salle soon realized that corporal penances, even when self-inflicted, prevented the Brothers from carrying out their school duties satisfactorily. So we find De La Salle recommending that the Brothers accept those opportunities for mortification of the mind and of the senses that present themselves naturally. The earliest Rule stated, "There will be no corporal mortification required by Rule in this Institute" (CL 25: 25).

   The allusion to the refectory in paragraph 6 refers to a detail included in the Rules of 1705 and 1718: "The Brothers will accuse themselves at least once a day of their faults just before the meal." The daily regulation in the manuscript of the Rule of 1718 is more precise: "Grace before meals is offered, after which the Brothers on their knees in the middle of the refectory accuse themselves to the superior of their faults. This is done by all the Brothers before dinner and before supper."

Letters 7 to 12
To Brother Hubert

Brother Hubert, Gilles Gérard, was born in Romagne in the Archdiocese of Reims, on December 7, 1683. He entered the Institute to make his novitiate in Paris, on April 20, 1700. He became the Director of the community and school at Laon in 1706 and later at Guise in 1708. In October of 1708, he took charge of the community of Brothers at Chartres. In December 1716 he signed the record of Brother Barthélemy's visit to that community to obtain the Brothers' agreement for the forthcoming Assembly of the Brothers, and he participated in the election of Barthélemy as the first Superior General in 1717. He later took part in the election of the second Superior General, Brother Timothée, in 1720.

At the Chapter of 1725, convoked to receive the Bull of Approbation granted by Pope Benedict XIII, Brother Hubert as Director of Paris pronounced his vows according to the terms of the Bull. The year 1734 found him the Director of Meaux in community with Brother Clément, the companion of his novitiate days (Letter 50). In 1745 he was stationed at Noyon and was a member of the Chapter of that year. He took part in the Chapter of 1751 at which Brother Timothée resigned and was succeeded by Brother Claude as Superior General. It is recorded in the minutes of the Chapter that "Brother Hubert, former Director of Angers, was unable to sign as he had lost his sight."

Letters 7, 8, and 9 are addressed to Brother Hubert by name. Letters 10, 11, and 12, though his name does not appear on them, are almost certainly addressed to him. Letters 66 and 67 could also have been sent to him, but conclusive proof is lacking.

As with most of his letters to Directors of communities, De La Salle writes to Brother Hubert in more detail than usual. While many of these details concern the spiritual life of the Brothers, the apostolic character of the spirituality which De La Salle fostered among the Brothers is evident in these letters just as it is in the meditations that De La Salle wrote for the time of retreat and for Sundays and feasts. In all his letters to the Brothers, De La Salle characteristically deals with the issues at hand: school matters, school-parish relationships, relationships of the Brothers with their students, the personal, apostolic, and spiritual development of the Brothers, and relationships among the Brothers in community.

The Sequence of Letters to Brother Hubert

✦ Letter 7, 1702: Brother Hubert, 19 years old, is at his first assignment.
✦ Letter 8, 1706: At age 23 he is already the Director of the school and community at Laon.

✦ Letter 9, 1708: At age 25 he is Director of the school and community at Guise.
✦ Letter 10, 1708: This letter was written three or four months later.
✦ Letter 11, 1709: Brother Hubert is still a Director, probably at Chartres.
✦ Letter 12, 1710: It seems clear he is at Chartres.

LETTER 7
To Brother Hubert

AM; AMG; EC 33; BL I.3

May 5, 1702

1   One of your main preoccupations, my very dear Brother, should be to apply yourself to prayer and to your class work, for these are your two principal occupations and the ones for which you will have to give an account to God.

2   My very dear Brother, you must allow yourself to be led as a child of obedience who has no other aim than to obey and in doing so carry out God's will.

3   Take great care never to use such terms as "I want" or "I won't" or "I must." These are expressions and ways of speaking that are to be held in abhorrence. They cannot but keep back the graces that God offers to those who have no other will but his, for as Saint Bernard says, it is self-will alone that leads to hell.

4   When you have worries make them known to your Director and you will find that God will bless you and either give you the grace to bear them for his love or relieve you of them.

5   Be on your guard against allowing yourself to act according to your whims, for God detests such actions.

6   The principal virtue you must strive for is obedience.

7   In prayer often give yourself up to God's guidance and tell him frequently that all you want is the accomplishment of his will.

8   It is in his love that
> I am, my very dear Brother,
> Devotedly yours in Our Lord,
> DE LA SALLE

LETTER 8
To Brother Hubert

When he received this letter, Brother Hubert, 23 years of age, was already Director of the community and school at Laon, about 40 kilometers northwest of Reims. The school at Laon was one of those established by Adrien Nyel in 1682, when De La Salle was taking his first tentative steps toward total commitment to the Christian education of the children of the poor. The community there consisted of six Brothers who conducted two schools. Brother Clément, about a year younger than Hubert, was in charge of the second school. The position of Director must have been quite a heavy responsibility for so young a man as Hubert. This would account for the detailed advice which De La Salle gives, advice of a personal nature as well as general recommendations for the guidance of the community and the management of the school.

Letter 8: To Brother Hubert
AM; AMG; EC 34; BL I.16

Paris
June 1, 1706

1   It gives me great consolation to learn from your last letter that you are in dispositions of complete abandonment, my very dear Brother.

2   I don't know why you have doubts about your vocation.

3   With regard to the vows, it is not I but you who must decide on that; the decision to make them must be your own. But, since you ask my opinion, I must say that I see nothing in your conduct that could be considered an obstacle.

4   On Thursdays, the day free from class, the Rule is to be observed in the mornings.

5   You are not to read at Holy Mass when you assist at it with your students.

6   Don't be upset by temptations to impurity or by natural movements. Try to think of something else.

7   When you feel yourself giving way to impatience in class, remain still and silent for a short time until the feeling has passed.

8   Take care to be always serious in class; the good order of the school depends a great deal on that.

9   Be careful that the topics of conversation during recreation time are suitable and that useless matters are not introduced.

10 Always have God in view in what you do; this is important if your actions are to be done in a Christian manner.

11 Be faithful to follow the method of prayer.

12 Make sure that Brother Clément keeps well.

13 I urge you not to let anything be done for payment nor for anything else without permission.

14 You did well not to carry out those errands that Brother Cassien gave you. Visits of that sort are not appropriate for us.

15 When there are only a few days before the monthly letter is due, there is no need to write unless the matter is extremely urgent.

16 Brother Robert is not to come back to Paris.

17 There is to be no gardening during recreation time, unless a day is set aside for watering. Even so, a serving Brother could do it. It would be better to have a gardener do it.

18 Nothing must be left undone to ensure that the classes make progress, especially your own.

19 Take care that the Brothers do not talk together.

20 Rest assured that your soul is very dear to me and that I will watch over it; but, as regards a general confession, the reasons you advance are not serious enough to make it necessary for you. Indeed you can do no better than entrust yourself entirely to your superiors.

21 Apparently you have been talking to the Brothers about Brother Charles, since those who do not know him are speaking about him. That is very wrong.

22 You must not let the temptations against purity that you experience upset you. They should not keep you away from Communion.

23 Tell me everything you feel you want to about your conduct and I will try to help you.

24 You must not carry candles at Saint Martin's or anywhere else. If it was done last year, no one has spoken or written to me about it. Tell me who the Director was then.

25 It is not true that the serving Brothers do not make novenas. If Brother Isidore didn't make one, see that he does so.

26 Follow the advice of the parish priest of Saint Peter's and insist that the students be punctual even should you be reduced to having only four. The same for the other classes as for your own.

27 Please take care that the times of recreation are spent properly. You know that giddy laughter is out of place

among us. Recreation is one of the things that you must watch over most carefully. You do well to see that the rules are strictly observed.

28   There is nothing I hope for more in offering you advice than to put your mind at rest regarding the things you write to me about.

29   I am told that the classes of Brother Etienne and Brother Isidore are falling completely into disorder. Please take steps to remedy this.

30   See that the Brothers give an account of their conduct and their consciences.

31   Brother Clément tells me that at the advertisement of defects it was pointed out to him that he goes to the refectory outside of meal times to eat, and that he drinks absinthe, and so on. These are not matters to be mentioned during advertisements, since they are not things that can happen without the Director's authorization.

32   Brother Isidore's work is not to keep him from his religious studies, for it is more important for him to do these than to work. I think, too, that it is not right that he spend the time of the long recreation on Thursdays working.

33   Try to get your community to live a life of complete fidelity to the Rule.

I am, my very dear Brother,
Devotedly yours in Our Lord,
De La Salle

——— ◆ ———

The six Brothers of the Laon community at the time of this letter were Hubert, Director, age 23; Clément, age 22, to whom Letter 50 was addressed three weeks later and who is also mentioned in paragraph 5 of Letter 64(A); Cassien, otherwise unknown; Robert, age 30, to whom Letters 38 to 48 were written; Etienne, about whom there is no certain information; and Isidore, whose age is unknown but who made perpetual vows on June 7, 1705. From the *Catalogue* we know that Brothers Hubert, Clément, and Robert persevered until death. It is probable that the other three Brothers left the community before 1714, the date when the *Catalogue* was begun.

Brother Charles, Michel Crest, mentioned in paragraph 21, was born April 5, 1674, in the Diocese of Grenoble and entered the Institute in 1700. He was at this time a member of the community of Rethel, teaching there in the school, which was the first one to be established by Adrien

Nyel outside Reims in March 1682. Previously Brother Charles had belonged to the community of Laon. The chronicle of that community indicates that one day he met in the street one of his students who had absented himself from class. He tried to take hold of the boy and get him to come back to the school. However, the young man escaped and, running away, fell under the wheel of a cart loaded with wheat. The wheel rolled over his stomach, apparently without doing him any damage. In order to encourage the Brothers to thank God for the "miracle," Charles told them that several people had seen angels holding the wheels of the cart so that they would not harm the boy. Such a story was fuel for much gossip among the Brothers.

In paragraph 3 De La Salle refers to the decision that Brother Hubert must make regarding the vows. The first vows pronounced by any of the Brothers had been made on Trinity Sunday about ten years previously, probably in the year 1686. The exact year is not altogether clear from the accounts in the early biographers (CL 2: 28–31). Nor is it perfectly clear what kinds of vows were made. The 12 principal Brothers gathered by De La Salle wanted to take perpetual vows of obedience, chastity, and perhaps also poverty, but De La Salle persuaded them to take only the vow of obedience, or possibly obedience and stability, and only for three years. It seems probable, however, that even though the commitment was for three years, the Brothers renewed these vows annually. It was not until 1694 that perpetual vows were made.

It seems clear that some Brothers never did take vows, but also that over the years De La Salle became more ready to permit the Brothers to take perpetual vows after a varied and sometimes brief period. For example, Brother Barthélemy entered the novitiate on February 10, 1703, at the age of 25, and pronounced perpetual vows two years later on June 7, 1705.

In order to free the Brothers from having to spend time out of class preparing meals and shopping for supplies, De La Salle received into the Society young men who were not suited for teaching. They became known as serving Brothers and wore a special brown robe. De La Salle refers to these Brothers in paragraphs 17 and 25. As far as possible, there was one serving Brother in the larger communities. Brother Isidore, mentioned in paragraphs 25, 29, and 32, seems to have been one of these Brothers, but he also spent time in class. More is said about the serving Brothers in Letter 12 and the commentary following.

To ensure that the Brothers remained steadfast to their commitment to teaching in the poor schools, De La Salle collaborated with them in including certain restrictions in the rules of the community. The robe of the Brothers was to be different from the clerical soutane, and they were to perform no function in the church except that of serving low Mass. They were also forbidden to study Latin or to make use of it if they had already learned it. De La Salle feared that close association of the Brothers with the clergy would gradually turn them away from their classroom duties. In his *Mémoire sur l'habit,* written about 1690, De La Salle had mentioned specifically the school at Laon as a place where some slackness had crept into the Brothers' attention to their class duties because of too much freedom in this regard. De La Salle saw now the possibility of this happening once again at Laon should the Brothers take a prominent part in the Eucharistic procession on the feast of Corpus Christi alluded to in paragraph 24.

The opposition of De La Salle to the Brothers' participation in this procession is all the more significant in light of the enthusiasm with which all the people of the town entered into the ceremony. It seems almost everyone walked in procession: waxmakers, fishmongers, greengrocers, butchers, bakers, coopers, vintners, cobblers, hosiers, tailors, tilers, weavers, drapers. All the pious associations followed these groups, then the doctors and lawyers; these, in turn, were followed by the Franciscans, the Minims, the Capuchins, the monks of Saint John and Saint Vincent, the parish priests, the canons, and finally the bishop and the officers of the town and town council. It is easy to see how the Brothers might have become involved.

LETTER 9
To Brother Hubert

AM; AMG; EC 35; BL I.26

Paris
January 30, 1708

1   I am surprised, my very dear Brother, that you wrote me a letter dated the 24th, as you had already written one on the 19th and are due to write at the beginning of the month. You see, you are overanxious.

2   It is true that there is no pleasure in living in a house where there is no fidelity to the Rule, but, until such time as I can change the Brothers, you must try to bring some to it. As you know, fidelity to the Rule depends very much on the man in charge.

3   True, Brother Alphonse can be difficult at times, but you must try to get him to be more amenable. Let me know precisely what his faults are, and I will bring him back to his duty.

4   I think that you are not prudent enough or submissive
    enough in what you say, and it is difficult to have God's
    blessing when you act in this way.

5   I am pleased that you love the practice of the Rule, and I
    will help you as much as I can to bring about its obser-
    vance, but I am not in a position nor so much in control
    of affairs as to be able to make transfers before Easter.
    However, from now on I will give it thought before God.

6   It is quite wrong not to be strict with yourself in dismissing
    those unruly thoughts that wander through your mind,
    and not to be attentive to prayer.

7   I am surprised that, after telling me in your first letter
    that you are willing to stay where you are as long as I wish
    and that you leave yourself entirely in my hands to do
    with you as I wish, and this is the best disposition for you
    to be in, five days later you write quite the opposite to
    me.

8   You must be very changeable. This is a temptation and
    you must learn to recognize it as such and humble yourself
    for showing such weakness. Let the knowledge you have of
    it bring you to the resolve never to follow your whims.
    This is very important for you.

9   Often have recourse to God, and you will find that he will
    help you not only in the matter of observance of the Rule
    but also in submission and achieving constancy of mind.
    These are all things that you should try to acquire and for
    which you must often pray to God.

10 I will have to work with you and you must try to live dif-
    ferently; in particular be more assiduous at prayer and in
    following the spiritual exercises. This is what you must
    work hardest at and what you have not given enough care
    to.

11 If it is necessary for someone to go out, send another
    Brother and you stay at your place at the spiritual exer-
    cises. Give me an account of the number of times you
    have been absent and for what reasons. Please do not fail
    to do this in your monthly letter, for the chief care that a
    Director should have is to be the first at all the exercises.

12 You go to the kitchen and spend time talking with Broth-
    er Alphonse. This gives rise to familiarity and to his lack
    of respect for you. You are not straightforward in what
    you tell me. If someone has to go to the kitchen, send one
    of the Brothers, and you remain at the particular exercise.

13 You will have order in your class only insofar as you refrain from moving about and talking. Take care not to strike the students with your hand or with anything else.

14 It is a serious fault to laugh during meals. When you have fallen into such a fault that could give scandal, do you accuse yourself of it? You know that according to the Rule you should not fail to do so.

15 I don't know if you say your vocal prayers as slowly as we do here. This is important if you want to pray with attention.

16 If Brother Antonin has no confidence in you, it is because you do not win it by your reserve, your seriousness and your fidelity to the Rule. You do not show sufficient prudence or fidelity to the Rule, and this draws down on you the disdain of the others.

17 Often pray that your community may be faithful to the Rule, and for your Brothers when they don't do as they ought or when they are troubled; and ask of God the understanding you need for your guidance on these occasions.

18 I pray that God will give you the grace to edify them very much, and

> I am, my very dear Brother,
> Devotedly yours in Our Lord,
> DE LA SALLE

———— ◆ ————

Brother Hubert received this letter at Guise, having just been transferred there from Laon. The school at Guise was another of the school foundations made by Nyel in 1682. It is evident that the community there was not at all faithful to the Rule and that Hubert was very unhappy with the situation. His uneasiness is shown by the number of letters that he wrote. As he was still a young man of 25 years, he must have found it difficult to bring his community back to the faithful observance of the Rule.

Brother Alphonse, Pierre Marie, mentioned in paragraph 3 and born in the Diocese of Chartres on November 5, 1677, entered the Institute on June 27, 1700. It seems he was a serving Brother at this time in Guise. In 1717 he was in the community of Rethel where he signed the record of Brother Barthélemy's visit there on December 13, 1717. He died in Rethel on December 13, 1727.

There are allusions in this letter to the rules De La Salle had drawn up for Directors. De La Salle in paragraph 3 refers to the Director's responsibility to inform the superior of the Brothers' faults. In paragraph 14 he reminds Brother Hubert that the Directors were not to laugh outside of the time of recreation, and if they did so, they were to ask a penance from the superior.

Speaking of the speed with which the vocal prayers were said in community, De La Salle in paragraph 15 seems to indicate that the prayers in the novitiate where he was staying were said much more slowly. Brother Félix-Paul in his commentary on this letter remarks that while the prayers said by the novices were not as numerous, the prayers took the full quarter of an hour as required by the Rule.

Brother Antonin, Gervais Dubrecq, mentioned in paragraph 16, was born in Paris on March 18, 1685, and entered the Institute on May 17, 1705. He was in Rouen when Brother Barthélemy made his visit there on March 27, 1717. He was in Marseilles in 1727, made perpetual vows in 1734, was Director of Laon in 1745, and died in Reims on November 14, 1756.

LETTER 10
To Brother Hubert

AM; AMG; EC 36; BL I.52

April 18, [1708]

1   I am replying to both your letters, my very dear Brother, the second of which I have just received.

2   I thank God that he has given you the honesty to let me know in all simplicity the fault you were guilty of in writing to your mother and to M. Lalement. You see quite well that it is a serious fault and that it gives a very bad example. You must try to die to the world, which must also be dead to you.

3   In the future be exact in doing nothing without permission and acknowledging right away and simply the faults that you have committed. It is not enough to say in a general way that you have made mistakes at Guise that you have not made elsewhere; you must state what these faults are.

4   Since your confessor thinks it advisable for you to stay at Guise, then you must remain there. It is only three months until the school holidays, when we will settle matters.

5   I am very glad that you tell me what is on your mind and that you are at the same time obedient and generously trusting.

6   Tell me, then, in what respect and in what way have you never been so unfaithful to the Rule as you have been at Guise.

7   Pay great attention to the first sound of the bell out of love for God. This is an important matter.

8   The Brothers should not, it seems to me, go to the parish catechism on school days.

9   Take care that silence is kept in the community, I pray you.

10   I do not understand why you are so negligent of the Rule during recreation time. You must take every means to correct yourself in this regard. You know how important it is to spend the time of recreation properly and that it is this fidelity to the Rule that draws down God's blessing on a community.

11   It seems to me that it is not your job to do the cooking, but Brother Antonin's.

12   The spiritual exercises must not be missed. There are few of them and you two and Brother Isidore should be assiduous in making them.

13   When defects are hardly ever pointed out at the advertisements, it is often a sign that there is little fidelity to the Rule in the community.

14   You must be more careful to correct the Brothers' faults.

15   Don't let the Brothers argue or answer back when you give them directives.

16   Indeed, you must test their obedience and see that they practice it faithfully.

17   You should encourage Brother Antonin to be frank and to tell you everything with simplicity.

18   I don't know what you mean by "stuffing." Is it something sold already made up, like meat-turnovers?

19   Encourage your Brothers not to do anything through self-will. Insist on this.

20   See that spiritual reading is not omitted.

21   Take care that you apply yourself well to the practice of prayer. You know that on this exercise depends the blessing that God bestows on the others and that it draws down his graces on us.

22   Let me know in detail why your conscience is not at peace.
I am, my very dear Brother,
Devotedly yours in Our Lord,
DE LA SALLE

In this letter and the two subsequent letters to Brother Hubert, there are a number of references to the account that each Brother was expected to give of his conduct and even of matters of conscience in his monthly redditional letter to his superior.

In the *Recueil* De La Salle included a directory for the Brothers to give an account each week to the Brother Director of the community, and a directory according to which each Brother was to give an account to the Brother Superior of the Institute. Both of these directories refer to matters of conduct and to matters of conscience. In his meditation for the Third Sunday of Lent, De La Salle speaks of the need to "lay bare the depths" of one's soul to one's superiors. However, the Decree, *Quemadmodum,* issued by Pope Leo XIII on December 12, 1890, forbade superiors to induce their inferiors directly or indirectly to make a manifestation of conscience, while it left to inferiors the liberty of doing so freely and spontaneously.

At the time that these letters were written, this manifestation of conscience was practiced in many religious congregations. The Brothers, in addition, had freely chosen De La Salle as their confessor and spiritual director.

The "parish catechism on school days" mentioned in paragraph 8 must refer to lessons given under the direction of the clergy in church on feast days which were also days when school was in session. For some reason De La Salle was reluctant to have the Brothers participate in this program. He addressed a similar issue with Gabriel Drolin in Letter 18.

LETTER 11
To Brother Hubert

AM; AMG; EC 37; BL I.32

July 20, [1709]

1   What M. Binet told Brother Hyacinthe about the plans of the Bishop of Chartres, the bishop himself told me. He wants to install us in the house of Saint Vincent's, which will be quite inconvenient, since it has neither courtyard nor garden and where, it seems to me, you will be very uncomfortable. Brother Hyacinthe says the opposite.

2   I think that you will have to pray to God and have the students pray; also have them continue the litanies. Every Sunday, feast day, and Thursday, the weekly day-off, send two of the Brothers to receive Holy Communion at Our Lady's Church, in the chapel of the Blessed Virgin. And let this be their intention, that the bishop's plan may not

be put into effect, and that what is done may be for the greatest good not only for your housing arrangements but also for the increase in the number of classes and students. Don't let anyone from the community enter into discussion on the matter. Leave the result in God's hands.

3 There was no need for Brother Hyacinthe to write to me before you did nor, in my opinion, for him to come here. A letter to me would have been sufficient. I had written the above before he arrived.

4 The day before yesterday I spoke to Father De Gergy, who promised that he would write the next day about the matter to the Bishop of Chartres. If the bishop makes any inquiries of you, tell him that since he will be coming here soon and the business does not have to be settled until October, I shall be honored to discuss it with him when he comes here, or to Saint Cyr.

5 It was wrong of you to ask for picture cards which cost a great deal of money, particularly at a time such as we are going through now when people are without bread. Please do not approach Brother Athanase for such things.

6 With regard to the remark of the Bishop of Chartres that I am being asked for Brothers in several places, it is true, but it is communities of two Brothers that are asked for and this does not suit us at all. I won't have them; they would destroy our Society.

7 Don't stand around talking to the Brothers so much, I beg you. Unless you take care, you will fritter away the time of the spiritual exercises talking to them, and that just must not happen.

8 I am well aware that you must have the Brothers make their manifestation of conscience and strive to resolve their difficulties, but there is no need for these long conversations in which numerous external matters are spoken of, even harmful ones, often without our even noticing it. Watch out for this; I will be on the lookout too. This is more important than you think.

9 Do not speak on the way to recreation nor on the stairs when going about the house.

10 You and all the Brothers need to be warned of your defects. For this purpose use the time for that exercise well. You are not to write, speak to anyone, or do anything else during it. At this exercise, as well as that of the accusation of faults, you should give your whole attention to what is said.

11 Either you or Brother René should take Wednesdays as your day for Holy Communion. I don't know how you both expect to go to Holy Communion on the same day and both leave the house for confession together. He should go to confession when the others go, and you also should make it a point to go the same day as the others. These private, personal devotions are not at all appropriate.

12 It seems that you are looking for a great deal of bodily comfort. Be on your guard about that and do not make any plans about external matters without proposing them to me beforehand. This is important, and don't too easily give heed to the proposals the Brothers make to you. You are too easygoing on that score.

13 I pray to God that your community may be orderly and faithful to the Rule. Work hard at this.

I am, my very dear Brother,
Devotedly yours in Our Lord,
DE LA SALLE

———— ✦ ————

The original manuscript of this letter carries neither the name of the Brother to whom it was addressed, nor the year in which it was written. However, written at the top of the manuscript appears the heading, "Chartres, 1709." Comparison with the handwriting of Brother Hubert on the formula of his profession in 1725 identifies these words as written by Brother Hubert. This affords reasonable certainty that the letter was addressed to him in 1709.

The three schools in Chartres were served by seven teaching Brothers and one serving Brother. The schools were Saint Hilaire, Saint Michel, and Saint Maurice.

The Bishop of Chartres mentioned in paragraphs 1 and 6 was Godet des Marais. He had been a student with De La Salle at the Seminary of Saint Sulpice. In spite of disagreements between them regarding the teaching of Latin (CL 7: 375) in elementary classes and the austerity of the community life of the Brothers, the two remained good friends. On this occasion the bishop wished to transfer the Brothers from their community house to a former priory to which was attached a junior seminary. De La Salle mounted a campaign of prayer against the project and, at the same time, arranged a meeting to discuss the matter with the bishop. This meeting did not take place. Godet des Marais died in September of that year, and the transfer of the Brothers from their community to the seminary did not happen.

Brother Hyacinthe, Gentien Gastignon, mentioned in paragraph 1, was born November 1, 1669, and entered the Institute May 4, 1701, as a serving Brother. He was changed from Chartres shortly after this letter. It is possible that he found it difficult at his age of 40 to be under such a young Director. Brother Hubert was only 25 at the time. But Brother Hyacinthe persevered, becoming a teaching Brother in 1723 in charge of a school in Mende, and then Director of Saint Denis in 1740. He died in Chartres on April 13, 1751.

The reference in paragraph 5 to "people . . . without bread" refers to the famine of 1709 when the winter was so severe that winter crops froze and the ground was too hard for spring planting. The government commandeered whatever came to seed for the next planting. A loaf of bread that ordinarily sold for seven or eight sous cost 35 sous. This was a difficult period for De La Salle, who brought his novitiate from Rouen back to Paris, where the distribution of food was less stringent.

Brother Athanase, Jean Richer, mentioned in paragraph 5, made perpetual vows in 1699 and became Director of Chartres in 1705. He probably became procurator at Saint Yon in 1709. He is not listed in the *Catalogue* of 1714, so he may have died or left the Institute before that date.

The *Règles communes des Frères des Ecoles chrétiennes* of 1705 sheds some light on the community practices referred to in paragraph 11. In the *Règles* we read that all the members of the community were to receive Holy Communion ordinarily twice a week, on Sundays and on Thursdays, or on the feast day that might occur during the week. On the other days of the week, one or more Brothers were to receive Communion in turn. From De La Salle's remark about Brother Hubert's and Brother René's having adopted the practice of receiving together on Wednesdays, it would appear that René was a kind of Sub-Director. De La Salle did not want the two to be absent from the community together, which would have happened when they would spend the obligatory half hour in thanksgiving after Communion (CL 25: 23).

Brother René was the first Director of the school in Vans in 1711. He signed the record of Brother Barthélemy's visit to Laon on March 4, 1717, but he is not listed in the *Catalogue* of 1714. Perhaps the compiler of that listing of Brothers wanted his name forgotten. The history of the house of Laon speaks of a certain erstwhile good religious who left the Institute in 1720 at the instigation of the mayor of that town. This religious had some brief training in medicine and may have aspired to practice as a doctor. According to the history, he never did enter the medical profession, but he did try to become a hermit and was rejected by the clergy. He finally became some kind of guardian of property and, while fulfilling this job, was killed by some shepherds.

LETTER 12
To Brother Hubert

Copy; AMG; EC 38; BL II.5

October 2, 1710

1 I realize, my very dear Brother, that there are drawbacks in having serving Brothers take over the management of the domestic concerns of the community, but there are even more when the Director is involved in them.

2 We have had only too much experience of this in the past, my very dear Brother. If a Director becomes too concerned about day-to-day affairs, his whole community suffers; whereas, if a serving Brother loses the spirit of his vocation, he does harm only to himself.

3 It is said, for example, that since you have been at Chartres, you have not made one half hour of spiritual reading. What would the Brothers be doing at that time?

4 A Director must never be absent from the spiritual exercises. You have no business in the kitchen. Here, where we have a big community, nobody puts a foot in the kitchen except the one who looks after the sick. All the more reason why, in a community of four, the Director should not do so.

5 Your spiritual exercises and your school require all your care. If you involve yourself in anything else, you are acting in opposition to the designs of God.

6 A serving Brother must always speak politely and respectfully, and you should see that he does so.

7 It is not useless to mention your problems; effort will be made to resolve them. But it is often of no help just to tell me what I ought to do.

8 It is true that you have only one soul to save, but you will save it through obedience and through overcoming your dislikes.

9 You must not get upset about having to reprimand your Brothers. You are only doing your duty. You ought to have given a stiff penance to those two Brothers who joined forces against you.

10 Certainly, in order that there be good order in the community, the Director and the Sub-Director have to get on well together and be united. I will take steps to see that this is the case.

11 But the Brothers complain that you act only through whim, since Brother Joseph is no longer there. It is said that this is because the serving Brother has the management of the finances. You may be quite sure that it will remain that way in your house and everywhere else. If there are houses where this is not the case, they are few in number, and that situation will not last much longer.

12 It is not right for the bursar, when he goes out, to take all the money he wants without asking for it. He is not even to say, "I want so much." He should ask how much he is to take.

13 You must be very careful that the bell is rung on time. This is very important, especially the bell for rising in the morning. You do not mention if you turn the clock back outside the prescribed time.

14 Please see to it that there is no loud talk and that the rules are kept during recreation. It is your responsibility to see to this and to keep an eye on Brother Norbert during this time. You do not tell me your reason for failing to be present at the beginning of recreation.

15 You should never omit the community walk on the weekly holiday unless it is raining. Mere clouds or other trifles must not interfere with it.

16 Brother Athanase did quite wrong in writing to you and others. He asked me if he should withdraw what he said and stated that it was his great anger that led him to write.

17 So, you are ready to let the Brothers lose their vocations because you are not courageous enough to reprimand them, and you let Brother Quentin do as he pleases. Through your easygoing attitude you will bring him to the state where he will leave. Do not let him do anything without permission.

18 And do not let Brother Norbert criticize the rules during recreation. There is something about him that does not inspire his students to piety.

19 Brother Quentin is always asking to study penmanship. He doesn't need it.

20 If Brother Quentin wishes to make vows, he is to be allowed to do so. Perhaps, however, it will be wise to try him out a little more.

21 It has been suggested to me to send Brother Anselme to Paris. If it doesn't inconvenience you, I will take him there with me.

22 See that Brother Norbert carries out his responsibilities.

23 Brother Quentin readily falls to complaining if anyone will listen to him.

24 You must not miss your Communions. You can easily see that that would give bad example to your Brothers.

25 There are not two masters in the house, for in all religious communities there is the one who has charge of spiritual matters and the general direction and another who looks after the domestic arrangements.

26 Brother Hyacinthe is satisfactory where he is. Surely you can see that it is you who are being too difficult and that you want to do everything except your duty, which is to direct the school, lead the spiritual exercises, and look after the serving Brothers.

27 Brother Quentin will never agree with Brother Norbert even if it were to be only for a year.

28 You musn't let Brother Norbert do just as he pleases.

29 You must not be out of the house during the time of the spiritual exercises. It is a serious fault on your part to be out during this time as you have been in the past.

30 Do not give lessons in penmanship to Brother Hilaire.

31 When you saw that he did not carry out his penance, you should have shown no displeasure, but prayed to God for him, remained calm and, at some other time, tried to win him over and induce him to acknowledge his fault and perform a suitable penance.

32 You follow your natural inclinations too much on occasions like this. That is why God does not bless what you do.

33 You expect patience from your Brothers; then you must show patience yourself, and let them see that you are not acting through whim or following your inclinations at such times as these.

34 Brother says that when he happens to have some money, you expect him to give it to you to buy whatever you please. In that respect you are more demanding than I am or others are, and this is not wise.

35 He doesn't have to give you the money, but he has to buy all that is needed. That is the way it should be. You are to hand the money over to him. If he doesn't buy what is needed, let me know, and I will certainly see that he does so.

36 Take care that all the Brothers carry out their obligations. You must deal with them with discretion.

37 If you write most of your letters in haste, is that wise? A little more prudence and love of God would better suit you.

38 Praying that God may give you his Spirit,
    I am, my very dear Brother,
    Devotedly yours in Our Lord,
    DE LA SALLE

———— ✦ ————

The original manuscript of this letter has been lost. The copy in the archives of the Generalate was transcribed from the original by the secretary of Brother Agathon, Superior General at the time of the French Revolution. The copy does not state to whom the letter was addressed, but the fact that Chartres is mentioned, together with the names of the Brothers referred to in the letter, indicates that Brother Hubert was the recipient as the Director of the community at Chartres. It is interesting to know that, in spite of all the defects that De La Salle pointed out to Hubert in each of his letters, Hubert continued to act as Director until he became blind, dying at the age of 76.

From a community of seven Brothers serving three schools in 1709, Chartres became a community of four serving only one school, Saint Hilaire, in 1710. This resulted from the limited financial resources of Bishop Merinville, successor to Bishop Godet, who was installed in May, 1710. The four Brothers were Hubert, the Director; Norbert, the Sub-Director; Hilaire, the serving Brother; and Quentin.

Brother Norbert, André Desbouves, born on December 6, 1677, in the Diocese of Soissons, entered the Institute in 1700, the same year as Hubert. He was six years older than Hubert and had been in this community at Chartres for five years, so he may have felt uncomfortable under Hubert as Director. Later he became Director of the school in Calais and attended the Chapter of 1717, but was described in the *Catalogue* as being "dismissed" in 1720 (CL 3).

Brother Hilaire, Edmond Rivois, born on April 10, 1682, entered the Institute on July 10, 1704. He was a serving Brother at Saint Yon in 1708 and replaced Hyacinthe (see Letter 11) at Chartres. Later he returned to Saint Yon as doorkeeper and tailor, took perpetual vows in 1734, and died at Saint Yon on May 17, 1739.

Brother Quentin is known only from this letter. He was obviously young and did not have vows. He was restricted to the first class, in which reading but not writing was taught. He wanted to practice penmanship, but De La Salle insisted that he did not need to be involved in that.

Brother Anselme mentioned in paragraph 21 is not counted as a member of the community because he was on his way to Paris. The

An engraving by Froment of a composition by Hanoteau in Armand Ravelet's *Saint Jean-Baptiste de La Salle,* 1938, depicting the country house of Vaugirard, which became the second cradle of the Institute. The Founder himself lived there from 1691 to 1698, a period which corresponds to the consolidation of what he called the "Society of the Christian Schools" and which included the writing of the Rule, the training of the novices and Brothers, and the taking of first perpetual vows.

Catalogue does not give his family name and mentions only that he joined the Brothers in 1706, made vows for three years, and then left the Institute.

After the near collapse of De La Salle's young Society of Brothers in 1690–1691, there was an influx of novices in 1692. It was at this time that De La Salle decided to accept young men into the Society who did not show aptitude for teaching, and so he introduced two types of Brothers, those destined for class and those whose duty would be to provide for the temporal needs of the community. The latter were called *Frères servants* and wore distinctive brown robes. These Brothers were always referred to as *serving Brothers,* never as *lay Brothers,* because all the Brothers were laymen in a canonical sense.

References in paragraphs 11 and 25 indicate that De La Salle had been introducing a new development into the direction of the communities. The Brother in charge of domestic affairs was taking on the position of bursar or procurator, and the responsibilities in the community were separated. In the community of Chartres, at least, the Director who had been in complete control did not take kindly to the new arrangement. Evidently this new division of authority did not succeed as De La Salle had hoped. It was modified and later discussed at the General Chapter of 1717.

Also during that Chapter the position of the serving Brothers was defined and incorporated into the common Rule. Initially, there was meant to be no distinction between the two groups of Brothers other than employment; one group was destined for class and the other for temporal work. A serving Brother could become a teaching Brother, as did Brother Hyacinthe of the Chartres community. In 1723 he was the Director of the community and school at Mende.

Unfortunately, the serving Brothers came to be regarded as an inferior class of Brothers. At the time of the restoration of the Institute after the French Revolution an effort was made to eliminate this distinction. The Twelfth General Chapter (1810) decided that the serving Brothers would wear the same garb as the other Brothers (instead of the shorter brown robe they had previously worn), and be permitted to make the fifth vow of teaching the poor gratuitously (which previously they had not made). However, the Rule published in 1923 still contained a chapter entitled "Of the Manner in Which the Serving Brothers are to Behave." No reference to serving Brothers was made in the Rule published in 1947.

Letters 13 to 32
To Brother Gabriel Drolin

Although there is some doubt about the actual date, Brother Gabriel Drolin was most probably sent by De La Salle to Rome during the summer school vacation of 1702. Brother Gabriel was then 38 years old, and with him went Brother Gérard Drolin (very likely Brother Gabriel's natural brother), who, however, remained in Rome only a short time, returning to Paris during 1703. Brother Gabriel stayed on in Rome for 26 years, until 1728, when he was recalled by Brother Timothée, the second Superior General to succeed De La Salle.

Drolin was a native of Reims, baptized in the Church of Saint Jacques on July 22, 1664, and so was a youth moving into manhood at the time that De La Salle became involved in the schools for the poor of that city. He joined De La Salle as early as 1684, and his is the first name in the *Catalogue* of 1714 listing all the Brothers at that time.

De La Salle soon discovered that if the schools were to be effectively Christian, there would have to be a change in the approach of the teachers to their work. At the outset the teachers quite naturally looked upon their work as simply a means of gaining a livelihood, nothing more. In De La Salle's view their way of life outside of school needed to reinforce their teaching in the classroom. He therefore took measures to remove the gap that existed between the aims of the schools and the behavior of the teachers by arranging that the teachers stay with him in his own house, have their meals together, pray together, and study together. This was something that the teachers had not bargained for and before long they withdrew. But others who looked on the work of the schools as an opportunity to do something for God soon joined De La Salle.

The new group of teachers began to realize that should the schools fail, they would be without work and support for their lives. De La Salle preached trust in Divine Providence, but his words fell on deaf ears. It was all very well, the teachers said, for De La Salle to preach abandonment to Providence when he had his private wealth to fall back on and his canonry at the Reims Cathedral to provide him with security. They had nothing. De La Salle finally decided to resign from his position as canon and to dispose of his wealth in favor of the poor, thus putting himself on the same level as the teachers. Many of his friends, and the teachers also, wished that he would use his wealth to give financial support to the schools for the poor. But, following the advice of the saintly Father Barré, he took the occasion of a famine in the northern part of France to give his money away for the relief of the starving.

Canon Blain, one of the earliest biographers of De La Salle, submits that after the withdrawal of the first teachers, new candidates were inspired by God to give up their prospects for the future in order to follow the example of De La Salle and devote their lives to the Christian education of poor children. Certainly the action of De La Salle in resigning his canonry and divesting himself of his considerable fortune aroused plenty of interest and controversy among those of his social class in Reims. Gossip spread through the city describing De La Salle's quixotic action. It was while this was going on that Gabriel Drolin offered himself at the age of 20 to De La Salle to assist in his new work. Blain says that Drolin had studied for the priesthood before associating himself with De La Salle, and he may have been one of those to whom Blain refers as

> inspired to give up everything; . . . among them some who were engaged in their theological studies and who abandoned them in order to join him [De La Salle] in spite of their parents and in spite of the advice of the worldly wise who made determined efforts to make them change their minds. . . . They courageously renounced their chances of promotion to sacred orders and the hopes that were theirs of advancement in the state more honorable than that of school teachers. (CL 7: 224)

So Drolin joined De La Salle in the first exciting days of the new foundations, when the teachers decided that they should wear a distinctive robe, follow a way of life that included regular periods of prayer and spiritual reading, plan methods of teaching their students effectively, and adopt the name of Brothers in order to make clear their relationship toward one another and toward their students. He was also very close to De La Salle some five or six years later when the infant Society was near ruin. De La Salle then chose Gabriel Drolin and one other, Nicolas Vuyart, to join with him in pronouncing on November 21, 1691, an irrevocable vow "never to leave . . . the Society . . . even if we are obliged to beg for alms and live on bread alone." Vuyart was later to leave the Society under rather sad circumstances, but Drolin remained faithful to this heroic vow in spite of all the difficulties he encountered during his long, lonely years in Rome.

The correspondence of De La Salle with Gabriel Drolin that has been preserved tells us much about the sort of man Drolin was, about the difficulties with which he had to contend in his efforts to establish himself in a school in Rome, and also much about the character of De La Salle himself (Appendix B). We get the idea that De La Salle did not really understand the problems that Drolin had to face. The Founder was at times impatient with the lack of progress being made in the execution of his plans to have the Brothers established in the city of the popes, even though Drolin tried to explain the difficulties he encountered in his efforts to be accepted as a teacher who was a layman in the highly organized, clerically dominated, and closely guarded system of schools there.

Originally, the schools of Rome had been established to provide an education for prospective candidates for the priesthood and were at first under the direction of cathedral chapters. Later, they were controlled by the rector of the university, La Sapienzia, who had authority over all advanced education. The university was also responsible for the establishment of an elementary school in each of the 14 wards of the city. The teachers of these elementary schools, nominated by the rector and paid from the excise duty on wines, were bound to accept any poor children who presented themselves, but they could require fees from the rich to supplement their meager salaries. The result was that often the poor were neglected and their places were given to students who could pay. In addition to these schools, private elementary schools were also opened under the aegis of the rector of the university. These were, of course, schools where fees were charged, and so they were not available to the poor. Moreoever, in the middle of the seventeenth century, the salaries of the teachers of the regional schools were suppressed. As a result even these schools demanded fees. The teachers now came under the control of a regional supervisor. The schools had to accept some poor students, who were obliged to pay a nominal contribution each Saturday.

To get a teaching post in one of these schools, it was necessary to obtain a license from the rector of the university. No school could be opened within a specified distance from an already established school. By the beginning of the eighteenth century, the cardinal-vicar of Rome had taken steps to place more control of the schools in the hands of the parish clergy. It was into such a situation that Gabriel Drolin came in 1702. By 1704–1705 he had managed to be accepted as a teacher in the regional schools, but he could not maintain his position beyond August 1708.

A third type of school, the papal school, had come into existence during the course of the seventeenth century. Pope Alexander VII had established about 30 of these schools, taught by widows of good standing, whose salary was assured from private papal funds. These schools were under the jurdisdiction of the papal almoner and were solely for girls until early in the eighteenth century, when boys were admitted. Drolin obtained his license to teach in one of these schools provisionally in 1709 and permanently in 1712.

We might wonder what Drolin thought of De La Salle's frequent promises to send a second Brother to help him. From his letters to Drolin, De La Salle seems always to have been on the verge of sending a companion to him, but something always turned up to prevent his doing so. At one point the Founder had actually named the Brother he proposed to send, but Drolin replied that he did not want that particular man. Even De La Salle's own proposed visit to Rome was canceled at the last minute.

Thus, Drolin was alone in Rome for 26 years, never having the companionship of another Brother. In spite of all the problems and the frustrations he encountered, he remained faithful to the vow he had taken with De La Salle never to abandon the Institute.

The Sequence of Letters to Brother Gabriel Drolin

Before 1704
It seems fairly certain that De La Salle wrote three or four letters to Drolin prior to 1704, but these have not been preserved.

From 1704 to 1707
Between August 13, 1704, and April 1, 1707, De La Salle wrote 14 letters to Drolin that have been preserved. It seems clear that during this period at least three additional letters were not delivered to Drolin. There is evidence, then, that during these 32 months De La Salle wrote at least 17 letters in response to 16 letters written by Drolin.

From 1707 to 1710
Between April 1, 1707, and February 14, 1710, a period of 34 months, no letters of De La Salle to Drolin have been preserved. De La Salle may actually have written very few letters to Drolin during this period for various reasons:

✦ Father Divers, the procurator general of the Vincentians in Rome, through whom De La Salle's letters were being delivered, was replaced. At this time Father Divers fell into disfavor with the church authorities in Rome. He left Rome in April 1708. In fact, he arrived in Paris in July of that year and may have given De La Salle some assurance of Drolin's favorable situation in Rome.

✦ During the winter of 1708–1709, the communities in France were in great difficulty because of the scarcity of food. To cope with this situation, De La Salle may have had to spend a great deal of time and energy, thus reducing the number of letters he wrote during this period.

✦ De La Salle did write two letters in 1709 to Drolin, one in August and one in November (see Letter 27), but these letters were never delivered, possibly through some fault of Brother Ponce, to whom De La Salle had entrusted responsibility for their delivery.

From 1710 to 1712
From February 14, 1710, to December 16, 1712, five letters of De La Salle to Drolin have been preserved. Possibly eight others were never

delivered, and, therefore, during a period of 34 months, De La Salle apparently wrote 13 letters, a number almost comparable to the period from 1704 to 1707.

From 1712 to 1718

The period 1713–1714 was a time of crisis in the life of De La Salle. He may have felt that his assistance to the Institute, especially in Paris, was of little value or possibly that he was not even welcome among the Brothers. At this time De La Salle was turning over much of the administration of the Institute to Brother Barthélemy in anticipation of the Chapter of 1717. Also, there is a hypothesis that Drolin destroyed some letters which were of a confidential nature concerning his role in Rome, since the Society of the Brothers was a congregation which had not yet been officially approved. In Letter 16, for example, De La Salle advises Drolin to burn the letter after he has read it.

In a letter dated December 5, 1718, De La Salle states that he had written Drolin several times without receiving any answer, indicating that he believed that his letters had been intercepted. He knew that such was the case with Drolin's letters to him.

LETTER 13
To Brother Gabriel Drolin

Copy; AMG; EC 13; BL II.1

Paris
August 13, 1704

1 It was only a week ago, my very dear Brother, that I received your last letter, dated February 19.

2 On reading your letter I could not understand how you could have put yourself into the position you say you are in, just teaching reading and writing to little girls, and assuming a worldly spirit.

3 You must not try to cut down on expenses by doing what is contrary to your Institute practices.

4 It would have been better if you had done what you said in your last letter you are allowed to do; and it would be good if you do that as soon as you receive this letter. For, I beg you, do nothing that is not in accord with your Institute, whatever the cost, otherwise God will not bless you.

5 Investigate thoroughly this canon who spoke to you, to see if he is a man to be relied on and if what he told you is

not just idle talk. If the gentleman wishes to write to me, I will look into the matter to see if we can depend on him.

6   As for yourself, stay where you are and do as you have proposed to me.

7   It seems to me that being in that part of the city, where you can give instruction to poor children who lack it, is better than being in a house even to instruct the poor who can find others to teach them.

8   I know that M. Théodon is remaining there and that his wife is leaving at once. She is quite happy to buy material and have a robe made for you.

9   I do not know the value of the 40 écus that you tell me you have received. Please, when making out your accounts for me, do so in the French livres and sous so that I can understand.

10   Mlle Théodon says that she will take you a New Testament in the vernacular. You can just as easily get one as she can.

11   If you wish, and if you haven't one, I will give her one for you, if she doesn't leave too soon. Please do not buy a Latin one or claim to know Latin.

12   Like you, I am afraid that my letters have been opened. Mlle Théodon says that she left one that she had forgotten lying around for three weeks or a month.

13   Ask God in prayer to do with you as he wishes.

14   You must abandon yourself completely to his guidance and you must do nothing without seeking advice.

15   Perhaps M. Langlois could handle your letters to me and mine to you.

16   Above all else, do not do anything that is not in accord with your Institute.

17   I beg of you, get yourself settled at once if you have not already done so.

I am, my very dear Brother,
Devotedly yours in Our Lord,
DE LA SALLE

———— ◆ ————

This letter is preserved in copy only. The original was given to a Father Baume on December 7, 1783, by Brother Agathon, Superior General, and has been subsequently lost. It is strange that Brother Agathon should have given this letter away, since that same year he issued an instruction to the

Brothers forbidding them to give away or allow to be given away without written permission anything whatever that had been associated with De La Salle.

There was considerable delay in the delivery of Drolin's letter mentioned in paragraph 1. It had been sent from Rome on February 19 and arrived in Paris only in the first week of August. Letters from Paris to Rome were confided to a courier who took about two weeks to get to Rome. The return journey took about the same time. So the very shortest time lapse between the sending of a letter and the arrival of a reply was about a month. The French postal service was run by businessmen who profited from the payments made for each letter delivered. When the letters were sent to foreign countries, the organization of the service and the payments became more complicated, since agreements had to be arranged among the various countries. Overall, the papal service was cheaper than the French service. When the Brothers had established themselves in Avignon, a papal city, De La Salle was able to avail himself of the papal postal service by sending his mail from Paris first to Avignon and then arranging for the Brothers to have it forwarded to Rome. Drolin made use of this service for his return mail to his Superior. On occasion, however, De La Salle and Drolin took advantage of the kindness of friends to have their mail delivered.

Ordinarily, it was the receiver of the letter who paid the cost of its delivery. However, on occasions, De La Salle paid the cost of the postage in advance. When this was done, the word *franc* was written on the outside of the letter to show that the recipient was not to pay on delivery.

The M. Langlois mentioned in paragraph 15 was most probably the director of the French postal service in Rome, and would have been admirably placed to assist Drolin with sending mail to Paris and receiving it from that city. In the parish registers of Rome during this period, the name *Langlois* appears with the mention of his position in the French postal service.

De La Salle's insistence in paragraph 11 that Drolin must not purchase a Latin New Testament recalls the strict rule in force among the Brothers against the study of Latin or even the use of it, other than in the responses at Mass. The prohibition against Latin was one of the means that De La Salle took to remove from the Brothers the temptation to abandon their difficult lives as teachers for the more comfortable life of a parish priest. De La Salle apparently was not aware that in the papal states at that time vernacular editions of the Bible were forbidden.

In this letter we meet the first of the many French people who befriended Drolin during his first years in Rome, namely, Jean-François Théodon and his wife. He was a sculptor, several of whose works were to be found in Saint Peter's and in the Gesù. Mlle Théodon, after the death of her husband, founded a religious congregation, the Sisters of Saint

Martha. The Sisters of this congregation adhered to the Jansenist faction in the religious controversy of that period. Henri Daniel-Rops, in his *The Church in the Seventeenth Century,* maintains, however, that their involvement with Jansenism was moderate: "They worked as peasants and sustained the spirit of the sect in their humble life of prayer."

In paragraph 9 De La Salle says that he does not know the value of the 40 écus that Drolin received. De La Salle's confusion arose from the fact that there was a twenty percent loss on French money in the rate of exchange in Rome. The écu was worth three francs in France, but cost five francs in Rome. In his letters, De La Salle uses *francs* and *livres* interchangeably, though it seems that the *franc* was the French term and *livre* a Roman as well as a French term. De La Salle had evidently sent Drolin 250 francs, which he calculated would be worth more than 83 écus, not the 40 écus (200 livres) that Drolin said he had received.

One way to understand the value of a livre in France in De La Salle's day is to recognize that the ordinary annual fee that the Brothers needed for their maintenance was 200 livres, excluding minimal housing but including food, perhaps some clothing, and household goods, such as candles and kitchen fuel. This, too, was the amount that De La Salle paid for the annual support of his sister, Marie, when she went to live with their grandmother in 1672. It is also the annual income De La Salle arranged for himself when he gave away his patrimony in 1684. If we estimate that $2,000 is a minimum needed for comparable maintenance today, then the value of a livre in today's currency is probably ten dollars.

In his search for appropriate employment in a school, Gabriel Drolin had been offered a post as teacher in an orphanage attached to the Hospice of Saint Michael. Since De La Salle envisaged the possibility of the Brothers of his Institute eventually establishing themselves in a number of schools in Rome, he did not want Drolin to restrict his freedom by accepting such a post. De La Salle also questioned the advisability of relying too much on the canon mentioned in paragraph 5 who made the offer, until Drolin found out more about him.

LETTER 14
To Brother Gabriel Drolin

AM; AMG; EC 14; BL I.5

[October 1704]

1   I have received your three letters, my very dear Brother, one through M. De La Bussière, that of September 9 through the post, and the third, dated September 16, through the parish priest of Saint Hippolyte.

2   As I do not know the value of Roman currency, when you mention an amount in your letters, indicate its value in French currency.

3   I do not understand why you say that you have taken up residence where you are to cut down expenses. What saving can you make, since you probably have to act as if you weren't living there anyway?

4   How has this helped you while you have been living there?

5   I do not know if it is because you fear putting yourself entirely in the hands of Providence. Never think that I will abandon you.

6   M. Théodon is said to be coming back soon, but I do not know how true that is.

7   I am sending you a note asking him to advance you 50 livres to get yourself settled and to provide for your needs when you do.

8   Therefore, I beg you to do so at once, for the longer you delay the older you get, and after all this there will be nothing to show.

9   Although you have been living in a house for a year or two years, as you are now, what progress have you made when all is said and done?

10 You will have to make up your mind to come back or to get something under way where you are.

11 You will, no doubt, receive this letter a few days before the feast of the dedication of Saint Peter's. Make a novena for this intention from the vigil until the end of the octave and then make a start on something.

12 Place more trust in God.

13 I will be responsible for the rent of the places you lease until such time as Providence makes provision.

14 It is about two years since you went to Rome, so you must get something done and live in accordance with your vocation.

15 It is not my intention to starve you or let you starve to death.

16 M. Brodard of Rethel has left me a bequest of 2,000 livres. I do not benefit from this yet because it will come to me only on the death of his sister, who is 85 or 86 years old. Apparently there will not be long to wait.

17 We are very poor because the parish priest of Saint Sulpice gives us very little now.

18 As regards those written statements that you are asked to provide, please take care that they don't do us harm. This is very risky.

19 The best thing would be if you could have a school where you are now teaching catechism.

20 The sooner you can get out of your present situation and be employed according to your vocation the better it will be.

21 For the love of God, work toward this.

　　I am, my very dear Brother,
　　Yours devotedly in Our Lord,
　　De La Salle

———— ✦ ————

Judging from the copy of Letter 13 that has been preserved, the original was addressed to "My very dear Brother Gabriel, of the Society of the Christian Schools, Rome." Letter 14, however, carries the address "Monsieur Gabrieli Drolini, à Rome." This change was probably done at Drolin's request. If he had been known in Rome as a member of a religious congregation, he would have found himself in a very difficult situation. Ecclesiastical law in Rome at that time obliged all religious to live in their recognized religious houses, and there were stringent regulations about their residence in the Holy City. Not only did Drolin not have a recognized religious house to live in, but he was a member of a group that was not even officially recognized by the Church outside some few dioceses in France. Also, under penalty of the law, the Brothers were forbidden to constitute themselves as a Society until such time as they were officially registered to do so under *lettres patentes*. This explains why in paragraph 18, De La Salle warns Drolin about the "written statements" (*mémorials*), which he no doubt had to present to the authorities of the regional schools giving his status and credentials for the position of teacher.

From the opening words of Letter 13, we know that the delivery of Drolin's February letter had been delayed for some months. In this letter we see how Drolin dealt with the frustration of this delay. He took the precaution this time of sending three copies of his letter, one through the postal service, a second through the hands of M. De La Bussière, and a third through the parish priest of Saint Hippolyte in Paris.

M. De La Bussière, referred to in paragraph 1, another of Drolin's French friends in Rome, had given him living accommodations in return for teaching his two daughters, an arrangement which De La Salle frowned on. De La Salle urges Drolin to make every effort to get employment in one of the regional schools. Since he promised to send the money for the rental of a classroom, it is evident that some progress had been made.

M. Brodard of Rethel, mentioned in paragraph 16, is one of those

These seals of the Institute of the Brothers of the Christian Schools are preserved in the archives of the Generalate, Rome, Italy.

This is a copy (actual size) of a wax seal used by De La Salle on three "obediences" dated 1707, 1708, and 1709.

This is a copy (actual size) of a wax seal on an "obedience" dated 1711 and bearing the signature of De La Salle.

This is a copy (actual size) of a seal that appears on the first page of Institute publications after 1726. It appears in varying shapes — as rectangle, circle, oval, or ellipse.

This seal of the Institute was adopted by the General Chapter of 1751: a shining silver star on a blue shield with the inscription, "Signum Fidei" (Sign of Faith). This copy is from the first page of a circular of Brother Agathon, 1787.

A modern version of the 1751 seal

laymen who took a great interest in the project of the Christian Schools and provided for them generously. Rethel was the first town outside of Reims where De La Salle established a school. In February 1682 an agreement was reached in Rethel through the efforts of Father Vincent Cercelot whereby De La Salle bought a house of residence for his teachers, while the township provided for their annual stipend of 100 livres each.

Earlier in the year 1704, the Writing Masters had won their case against De La Salle and the Brothers of Paris. De La Salle had to pay a fine of 100 francs and the 17 Brothers, 50 francs each. In addition to this difficulty, the parish priest of Saint Sulpice, Father Joachim Trotti de La Chétardie, alluded to in paragraph 17, withdrew his support for the Founder and the Brothers and refused to pay them their stipend. For De La Salle, then, the prospect of the bequest of the 2,000 livres which he mentions in paragraph 16 was very acceptable.

This letter was sealed with an image of Saint Joseph and the Child Jesus, which was the first seal of the Institute.

LETTER 15
To Brother Gabriel Drolin

AM; AMG; EC 15; BL I.4

Paris
December 23, [1704]

1   In reply to your last letter, my very dear Brother, I have to say that I do not know why you hesitate so much after all my letters. As for myself, I cannot encourage you more than I have done.

2   You should be encouraging me, and if you yourself have no great enthusiasm for this work, which seems to be the case, then you will not succeed.

3   I do not expect you to cost us nothing, but I do think and I have thought that, after taking the matter in hand for six months or a year at most, you would no longer be an expense to us. I was counting on this very much.

4   I do not think that you should involve yourself in Brother Gérard's dispensation from his vows. He is one of the most fickle people I know. He is not suited for the world and would have been well suited for the Trappists.

5   I am very sorry that I dissuaded him from joining them. He never knows what he wants to do.

6   You have already explained to me the expenditure that
     you will have to undertake. Do so whenever you need to.
7   I will help you in every way I can, but I do think that, for
     the undertaking to succeed, the initiative must come from
     you and not from me. What I have to do is back you up.
8   As you are aware, I have already spent 400 francs on you
     and don't see any result from it.
9   Please see that this situation does not continue.
              I am, my very dear Brother,
              Devotedly yours in Our Lord,
              DE LA SALLE

     Give thought to what you must do and pray to God about
     it.

                    ──────── ✦ ────────

On the occasion of this letter, De La Salle reverted to addressing it to
"Brother Gabriel Drolin." This suggests that it was carried to Rome by
a dependable person, perhaps M. De La Bussière. There is no indication
on the manuscript of any payment of postage being made.

   From the tone of the letter, it can be seen that De La Salle is very
disappointed that Drolin has not been successful in obtaining a teaching
post in the regional schools, as Drolin had led De La Salle to believe. The
Founder seems to be rather hard on his disciple who, from what we can
infer, has been making every effort to get such a post.

   Brother Gérard, mentioned in paragraph 4, was probably Drolin's
brother. The formula of perpetual profession of obedience and stability
of a Brother Gérard Drolin, dated December 6, 1697, is housed in the
archives of the Generalate. His name does not appear in the 1714 *Catalogue*
of members of the Institute. In other letters De La Salle refers to Drolin's
brother as having left the Institute.

LETTER 16
To Brother Gabriel Drolin

AM; AMG; EC 16; BL I.8

                                                    Paris
                                          February 11, 1705

1   It's a long time, my very dear Brother, since I received any
     news from you.

2 Please let me have some news and send your letter by way of Avignon, addressed to De La Salle, c/o very dear Brother Albert, Free Schools, near Saint Symphorien, Avignon.

3 The schools are making fine progress in Avignon. We will have four Brothers there and a house big enough to lodge 20 persons.

4 I presented three of the Brothers to the Archbishop of Avignon, who is the special nuncio to France. He received them very kindly, and graciously gave them his blessing before they left.

5 Please keep this secret and never speak about it to anyone; even burn this letter. You talk about things too much.

6 I do not know if you will ever get anything done in your present place.

7 You have to be led by the Spirit of God and motivated by great zeal. It seems to me that you have not enough of one or the other for such an undertaking.

8 But God be blessed and his will be done.

9 Let me know if you are still in the same employment and are seeking nothing more.

10 Be careful that you do not become too accustomed to the worldly spirit and manners, which you ought to hold in abhorrence, for you will find them hard to give up later on.

11 I pray Our Lord will fill you with his Spirit and will do with you what he wills.

12 In the future send all your letters by way of Avignon when you have to write to me, so that they may be safe and confidential.

13 My good wishes to M. De La Bussière.
> I am, my very dear Brother,
> Devotedly yours in Our Lord,
> DE LA SALLE

14 Please get precise information about the Institute of the Fathers of the Pious Schools: what their rules are, their method of government, how widespread they are, if they have a Superior General, what powers he has, if they are all priests, if they collect fees. Find out all you can about them, and let me know in the fullest possible detail.

———— ✦ ————

Evidently De La Salle is writing this letter before he has received an answer to his previous one, three months earlier. As such, the tone of the letter is helpful for interpreting the tone of the previous one. It is significant that De La Salle is sharing news and even confidential information. There are three references to confidentiality in this letter. De La Salle is anxious not to let his work be known prematurely, especially to official channels in Rome.

This letter was sent through M. De La Bussière to be delivered to Drolin under the name of M. Santenot. No satisfactory explanation has been given for the use of the pseudonyms, Gabrieli Drolini and Santenot, though the most acceptable one seems to be the need to avoid any investigation by the ecclesiastical authorities into Drolin's membership in a religious group not yet officially approved. The choice of Santenot as an alias has defied explanation, and there is no hint of explanation given in any of De La Salle's correspondence. Letters 16 to 28 are all addressed in this name. Whatever the reasons may have been, Drolin was known in Rome by his real name, often Italianized, as is shown in the register of the parish of Saint Lorenzo, where he lived, and in the list of teachers in the regional schools for the year 1706.

We find in paragraphs 2, 3, and 4 of this letter, the first reference among all extant letters, to the establishment of the Institute in Avignon, the city of the popes. The inclusion of these references to Avignon suggests that Drolin already knew of the projected foundation for which Brother Gérard, Drolin's own brother and original companion in the Roman venture, had paved the way on his return journey to Paris (CL 7: 396).

The person who negotiated with De La Salle for opening a school in Avignon was Jean-Pierre Madon de Chateaublanc, the pope's treasurer. Contrary to Blain's account, which was also accepted by Battersby, it was the wife of Lord De Chateaublanc who instigated the action of her husband to found a free school for the poor in the parish of Saint Symphorien. This foundation was accomplished, according to Blain, in 1703. In his references in paragraph 3, De La Salle speaks of several schools in Avignon and indicates that they are doing well. De La Salle gives Drolin more news about Avignon in his next letter.

The Archbishop of Avignon was Laurent Fieschi, who is mentioned again in Letters 17, 18, 19, and 24. It seems probable that De La Salle hoped to have his help in obtaining papal approval for the Institute.

Brother Albert, referred to in paragraph 2, had acted on De La Salle's behalf with regard to the opening of the schools in Avignon, Marseilles, and Valréas. He is also mentioned in several other letters and was regarded by De La Salle as one of his most capable Brothers. Since his name does not appear in the *Catalogue* of 1714, we may infer that Brother Albert either died or withdrew from the Institute before that date.

The Institute of the Fathers of the Pious Schools (Piarist Fathers), founded in Italy by Saint Joseph Calasanz, had met with considerable opposition from the teachers of established schools and from the regional school teachers. De La Salle had met with similar opposition in Paris from the Writing Masters and the Masters of the Little Schools. De La Salle firmly wished his Institute to become well established in order to forestall any attempts to alter its structure and organization. He had already experienced such efforts on the part of well-meaning persons in Paris and other cities of France. There is no indication that he ever received from Drolin the information he requested about the Piarist Fathers.

LETTER 17
To Brother Gabriel Drolin

AM; AMG; EC 17; BL I.9

Paris
April 27, 1705

1   I am told that your letter arrived here on Easter Sunday while I was in the country, my very dear Brother. I received it on the following Saturday.

2   It brought me a great deal of joy, for not only has it been a long time since I received any news from you, but also because you tell me that at last you are carrying out the work proper to your vocation.

3   It is no use examining how you have let opportunities slip by because you did not notice them.

4   You were wise to set yourself up in a place far removed from the Pious Schools.

5   You have made a good decision to continue to have your meals at De La Bussière's house. Please give him my good wishes.

6   You have also done well in not living there entirely.

7   If you need any school books, like the classroom prayers (I don't know whether or not you have any), we have had them reprinted recently and can easily send you them by way of Avignon.

8   With regard to what you say about the position of papal school teacher, follow Father Divers' advice.

9   It would be better, perhaps, to pray earnestly to God and wait for the best opportunity to present itself.

10   I am far from taking you to task. All that I have been impatiently waiting for is that you should carry out the work that is yours.

11 I am surprised that you say that you never got much support from me because there is nothing I haven't tried to do and am not ready to do to support you.

12 I am quite sure that you have no intention of following the example of Brother Nicolas, and that is the reason I have placed so much confidence in you.

13 It is not time for you to push yourself forward so strongly in Rome; it is enough that you have made a start.

14 A house suited to our Brothers' needs has been bought at Avignon. It can house 20 Brothers. The vice-legate loves the Brothers and sends his page to their school.

15 I intended to send you the man who established the school, but you did not want him.

16 His Grace, the Archbishop of Avignon, who is special nuncio to France and who has come to know me since our establishment at Avignon, has been named Archbishop of Genoa and is to leave immediately for Rome, where he is to receive the cardinal's hat.

17 He told me he would look after the interests of the Institute and do what he could for our Brothers. Before they left him, he gave them his blessing.

18 Try, I beseech you, to overcome the worldly spirit to which you have quite a tendency, by devoting yourself to prayer and to the spiritual exercises and by restricting the number of visits you make. In trying to have the spirit of your Institute as deeply as possible, you will draw down on yourself God's graces in abundance.

　　　I am, my very dear Brother,
　　　Devotedly yours in Our Lord,
　　　DE LA SALLE

———— ✦ ————

If De La Salle had felt despondent at the lack of progress that Brother Gabriel Drolin had been making, as exhibited in his previous letter, he now reveals his joy on hearing of his disciple's achievement. Drolin had recently gained the post of teacher in the school in the parish of Saint Lorenzo, in the Campo Marzo, one of the poorest and most densely populated districts of Rome. This meant, in effect, that he was teaching a class annexed to the regional school of that area and under the auspices of the regional school supervisor. This school was entirely gratuitous as far as Drolin was concerned, although he had to collect a nominal weekly payment from the students on behalf of the school authorities. De La Salle objects to this financial arrangement in his next letter.

De la Salle

f. Nicolas Vuyart

f. gabriel Drolin

Above are the signatures of the three who made the "heroic vow" of November 21, 1691, whereby they promised by a vow of association and union to establish the Society of the Christian Schools, "even if we are the only three left in the Society and even if we are obliged to beg for alms and live on bread alone."

With funds received from Paris, Drolin rented one room for his class and one for his own sleeping quarters, while still taking his meals at De La Bussière's home. In paragraphs 5 and 6, De La Salle expresses his approval of this arrangement.

Drolin must have felt that De La Salle had lost faith in him, and he was somewhat annoyed by the remarks his Superior had made in his previous letter. After several years of looking in vain for a teaching post, Drolin protested that he had no intention of deserting the Institute as Brother Nicolas Vuyart had recently done. Vuyart had made a vow (together with De La Salle and Drolin) in 1691 to continue as a member of the struggling Institute of Brothers no matter what should happen. Later, while Vuyart was the Director of a training school for rural teachers in the parish of Saint Hippolyte in Paris, the parish priest had bequeathed the school to Vuyart in order to assure its continuance. This arrangement had been made with the approval of De La Salle. However, on the death of the priest, Vuyart, considering himself the proprietor of the school, refused De La Salle entrance to it. He continued to maintain the school but deserted the Institute. Since, other than paragraph 12, there is no mention of this incident in De La Salle's correspondence, it is reasonable to assume that Drolin knew of Vuyart's actions from his communications with other Brothers in France, and perhaps even from some communications with Vuyart himself, who had been Drolin's confrere during the difficult times of 1691.

Father René Divers mentioned in paragraph 8 was procurator-general to the Holy See for the Vincentian Fathers (Lazarists) in Rome. He may have been Drolin's confessor. In any case, when Drolin was discouraged because of his difficulties in securing a teaching position and supporting himself in Rome, it was Father Divers who encouraged him not to give up his efforts. Father Divers also introduced him to friends who helped him until he eventually secured a teaching assignment. De La Salle sent Letters 21 to 27 to Drolin through Father Divers until the priest had to return to France in 1708.

De La Salle mentions in paragraph 15 that Drolin had rejected the Brother whom De La Salle had proposed to send to Rome to be with him. This inclusion seems to indicate that an earlier letter written by De La Salle making this specific offer has not been preserved.

The Archbishop of Avignon, Laurent Fieschi, of whom De La Salle speaks in paragraph 16, was nominated to succeed to the Archdiocese of Genoa, which had become vacant in December 1704. De La Salle had knowledge of the appointment prior to the official announcement by the ecclesiastical tribunal on May 14, 1705. His reference to Fieschi's receiving the cardinal's hat was, however, premature. That did not take place until May 1706. It was Fieschi and his former secretary, then a bishop in Rome, who later promoted Drolin's efforts to gain a post in one of the papal schools.

LETTER 18
To Brother Gabriel Drolin

AM; AMG; EC 18; BL I.10

Paris
August 28, 1705

1   I was indeed very surprised, my very dear Brother, at not receiving news from you for so long.

2   In the future please write more often, and it seems to me that it will be best if you do so every month.

3   Brother Michel and Brother Jacques died of typhus, one after the other, at Chartres, since I last received a letter from you. Please pray to God for them.

4   I am very pleased that you are no longer hampered by being at M. De La Bussière's house. But tell me, how do you live and on what?

5   You say that you do not like being in debt. It would be nice to know if you are in debt, and how much you owe, to whom and why. That's just what you don't tell me.

6   I do not at all approve of your teaching Latin. You know quite well that it is contrary to our Institute practice. We must at all times remain firm in the practices of the Institute, otherwise we lose everything and God will not give our work his blessing.

7   I don't like these Saturday offerings of money received like this from the students. Although you get nothing out of it, it has a false ring about it in our schools.

8   If you need a class prayer book, know that we had books reprinted last year with all the necessary rubrics for use.

9   If there are any others you want, we can send them to you by way of Avignon. But I think we could have our books printed in Avignon, where they have been given official approval, and then have them sent on to you.

10 You must let me know how Christian doctrine is taught in Rome.

11 Like you, our Brothers in Avignon tell me that they suffer from the intense heat.

12 I am happy that you are now at peace and that you neither make nor receive visits.

13 Make sure that you take advantage of this time and of such a wonderful opportunity to try to give up worldly ways and to adopt a simple demeanor and the manners and way of acting in keeping with the Spirit of God.

14 With regard to the teaching of catechism, it seems to me that the right thing and the important thing is to teach it in your school.

15 Is it forbidden for a school teacher to teach catechism to his students in class?

16 I do not like our Brothers teaching catechism in church. However, if it is forbidden to do so in the school, it is better to do it in the church than not at all.

17 As for myself, I do not like to make the first move in any endeavor, and I will not do it in Rome any more than elsewhere. I leave it to Divine Providence to make the first move and then I am satisfied.

18 When it is clear that I am acting only under the direction of Providence, I have nothing to reproach myself with. When I make the first move, it is only I myself who am active, so I don't expect to see much good result; neither does God usually give the action his special blessing.

19 I am told that the Archbishop of Avignon, now of Genoa, is soon to be a cardinal.

20 The Bishop of Vaison is asking for the Brothers. You know him.

> I am, my very dear Brother,
> Devotedly yours in Our Lord,
> DE LA SALLE

———— ✦ ————

After waiting for some months to hear from Gabriel Drolin, De La Salle suggests that he write to him monthly, the customary practice among the Brothers, introduced during the critical years 1690–1691 and later incorporated into the Rule.

As usual the Founder includes news of the happenings in France, this time in paragraph 3, the sad news of deaths in the Chartres community during the typhoid epidemic that struck the city. Three members of the community died, together with the Brother who had been sent from Paris to act as infirmarian. Two who died in February 1705 were probably reported to Drolin with a request for prayers in an earlier letter, since lost. This letter is one of the very few examples we have of the death announcements sent to the Brothers by De La Salle. A second example is mentioned in Blain's life of De La Salle: "Pray for Brother Henry, who died in sentiments of quite extraordinary piety, July 1, 1699" (CL 8: supplement, 76).

In Rome the teaching of catechism was reserved to the Archconfraternity of Christian Doctrine, established by Pope Pius V in 1571. The instruction was carried out in the churches under the supervision of the parish clergy. For De La Salle and his Brothers, the teaching of catechism was an integral part of the daily school program and fundamental to their concept of the Christian School. De La Salle was uncomfortable with this Roman practice of separating religious instruction from the ordinary school situation and indicates as much in paragraphs 14, 15, and 16. He also expresses dissatisfaction in paragraph 7 with the collection of the weekly contribution of money from the poor students.

In this letter, as in Letter 17, De La Salle offers to send copies of the text which he wrote, *Exercices de piété qui se font pendant le jour dans les Ecoles chrétiennes*. The first edition of this work received approbation on March 21, 1696. Subsequent requests for approbation were made and granted in 1697; November 2, 1702; and April 13, 1705. Permission was given in 1705 under Royal Privilege to print a number of works by De La Salle, including *Les Devoirs d'un Chrétien envers Dieu et les Moyens de pouvoir bien s'en acquitter, divisé en deux parties; Instructions et Prières pour la Sainte Messe, la Confession et la Communion, avec une Instruction méthodique par demandes et réponses pour apprendre à se bien confesser;* and *Cantiques Spirituels, sur plusieurs points de la Religion & de la Morale chrétienne*. Several of the songs in *Cantiques Spirituels* were sung to the common melodies of the day. The song *Charmante Gabrielle*, which is still popular today and to which was sung *Protestation d'un Chrétien à Jésus-Christ*, does not appear in the edition published in 1705 but is found in that of 1760 (CL 18: 61 and CL 22).

LETTER 19
To Brother Gabriel Drolin

AM; AMG; EC 19; BL I.11

Paris
September 4, 1705

1   My astonishment at not receiving a letter from you for five months, my very dear Brother, has led me to include this letter to you with one to M. De La Bussière. I fear that you have not received the letter before the last one I wrote to you.

2   I did not know when M. Théodon would be coming back nor do I know if he has arrived.

3 I was not aware that you had left M. De La Bussière's house and did not think that you would have done so without mentioning it to me beforehand. For, if you rely on me entirely right now, you will place me in an awkward position, since I am less able to help than I have ever been; much less, in fact, because I am very short of money.

4 I have established our novitiate in a suburb of Rouen in a fine house which used to be occupied by some nuns. Our Brothers have schools now in Rouen, where Brother Ponce is stationed. This is why I am short of money.

5 You ought not to have gone into debt without getting my approval beforehand.

6 I told you that all you could expect from me as regards getting you settled would be some help for six months or a year at most. Since then I have negotiated the arrangements at Rouen, and it has drained me of money.

7 All I can do is let you have a bill of exchange for 50 francs through Avignon, drawn on M. De Chateaublanc, the papal treasurer. He made the arrangements there for our Brothers. There are five of them there now and he has bought a house for them.

8 At the Archbishop of Avignon's residence, you can find out where M. De Chateaublanc pays the papal revenues in Rome and who is his correspondent there.

9 I shall send the money at once, though it will inconvenience me, for over the next three months I can expect no money; on the contrary, I shall be in arrears.

10 Please do not go into debt without my approval, for I am not at all happy about debts. I do not want any and have never wanted or allowed any in our communities. There is nothing I detest so much. That is why you will never be able to count on me again when it comes to debts, for I will not listen to the least suggestion.

11 As far as expenditure goes, I want to look ahead not behind me. Take no steps, make no decisions, without asking my advice beforehand. I will answer you at once.

12 I have just now received your letter. The Avignon route is convenient for us.

13 I don't know if the former Archbishop of Avignon, now of Genoa, has become a cardinal, as I was told he would when he arrived in Rome.

14 I know it is better to live in more difficult circumstances, withdrawn from worldly concerns, and I am glad that you

are in such dispositions. Still, when you decide to do this, you must put yourself entirely in the hands of Divine Providence, or, if you have not enough virtue for that nor enough faith, then you must take the necessary means before you carry out your plan. If you do neither, you are not acting as a Christian nor as an intelligent man.

15 Take care not to give bills of exchange to anyone without my instructions to do so, for I will not meet the payments. I am no longer in a position to do so. I have to adjust my accounts day by day. You will receive your money without having to pay exchange.

16 I do not know what you mean when you say that you will make an effort to see if you can do something for me in the near future. Please explain this to me, for I would very much like to have a clearer understanding.

17 I am glad that you have got over the measles.

18 In his letter of August 29, Brother Albert tells me that the Diocesan Censor has returned all our books with his approval. I will write to him to let you have two copies of the class prayers and prayers for Mass as soon as I know your address.

19 We have had the class prayers reprinted with full rubrics for use in a way that will suit teachers and students.

20 We are going to open a school in Marseilles; and after Brother Albert has been there until Easter, I will be able to send him to you to give a little help in your endeavors if they are not going well. He is really good at that. In the first six months he would work wonders.

21 Pray often to God for this intention from now until then, asking him to guide what we are doing in Rome and elsewhere, according to his will.

22 I thought that the explanation I gave you around Christmas time was clear.

23 We have Brothers at Dijon and at Brest. I don't know if I mentioned this to you.

24 Please go often to Saint Peter's as a sign of your complete submission to the Church.

I am, my very dear Brother,
Devotedly yours in Our Lord,
DE LA SALLE

This building in the Rue Berbisey, in the parish of Saint Peter in Dijon, France, housed the school which the Founder opened in 1705.

This letter was written only a week after Letter 18, which was a reply to one received from Drolin after a lapse of several months. In paragraph 4 of Letter 18, De La Salle expressed his satisfaction that Drolin was no longer living at De La Bussière's house. In Letter 19, however, De La Salle states, in paragraph 3, that he did not know that Drolin was no longer lodging with his benefactor and is worried that he will not be able to send Drolin enough money to support him. The apparent contradiction may be explained if in the first instance Drolin was still taking his meals with De La Bussière, but now in the second instance he is no longer doing that. (See paragraph 7 of Letter 21.)

The property of Saint Yon on the outskirts of Rouen, mentioned in paragraph 4, was to be used primarily as a novitiate. The lease of this property was, at least in part, responsible for De La Salle's present shortage of money. He had to pay 100 livres every three months.

Brother Ponce, mentioned in paragraph 4, was the Director of the community at Rouen, and formerly the Director of the Brothers at Saint Sulpice in Paris. His excessive severity while at Saint Sulpice and his harsh treatment of a young Brother in that community had been, to a great extent, responsible for the hostility toward De La Salle and the Brothers shown by the parish priest, Father De La Chétardie. Brother Ponce's name is also coupled with De La Salle's in the lawsuits brought against the Brothers of Paris in 1705. Later, Brother Ponce was sent to Avignon and became De La Salle's representative in southern France. Canon Blain writes scathingly of Brother Ponce's eventual withdrawal from the Institute, which involved his theft of funds from the community where he was the Director.

After obtaining permission through Royal Privilege for the printing of several publications that he had prepared for school use, De La Salle submitted them for ecclesiastical approval to the Diocesan Censor in the papal city of Avignon. In doing so De La Salle was conforming to the requirements of the Holy See. De La Salle mentions this ecclesiastical approval in paragraph 18.

As usual, De La Salle gives a few tidbits of news concerning the expansion of the Brothers' work. The school in Marseilles did not open for several months, but the one in Dijon had opened in June 1705. (See Letter 35, addressed to M. Rigoley, founder of that school.) Nothing is known of any foundation of the Brothers in Brest at this time, although De La Salle mentions in paragraph 23 that there are Brothers there.

De La Salle once again in paragraph 20 offers Drolin the services of Brother Albert to help in establishing himself in Rome, although he indicates in Letter 17 that he is aware that Drolin does not wish to accept the offer.

LETTER 20
To Brother Gabriel Drolin

AM; AMG; EC 20; BL I.12

Paris
October 28, 1705

1 I do not know, my very dear Brother, whether or not you received the letter I wrote in reply to your previous one. I addressed it as you directed. Keep sending your letters by way of Avignon.

2 I am sending this one in care of M. De La Bussière to avoid making a mistake and for greater safety. Give me another address next time if this method is not suitable, or let me know where you live.

3 You do well to wait on the guidance of Divine Providence.

4 I told you not to run up debts for me because I do not want to hear them even mentioned and you must not expect me to pay for any at all, neither by bill of exchange nor by any other means. I have never wanted debts and will not have any at all.

5 When you need something, let me know in advance. You know what I told you in the past; please count on that.

6 You should not have left M. De La Bussière's house without consulting me and without knowing where you would live.

7 I told you what I could do; you must depend on what I say.

8 I want to be quite clear about what I am undertaking.

9 God placed you in M. De La Bussière's house. You should have stayed there until you found employment that enabled you to live independently.

10 I mentioned that I would see that you were given the 50 francs that are at Avignon. It seems that there will be no exchange to pay.

11 I am going to send to Avignon some books of class prayers which we had printed with the rubrics. They can be sent on to you from there.

12 I have seen M. Théodon only once. He has not been well.

13 In your last letter you indicate that you are sending his receipt. However, I have not received it, and it was not in your letter.

14   It is of no use drawing bills of exchange on my account, for I would not be able to honor them.

15   I am well aware that it is advantageous to live withdrawn from the world, but you have to have life's necessities, and you need to know where you can get them before you leave the world.

16   I addressed my last letter simply to M. Santenot. Find out if it went astray or not.

17   See if God shows his approval of your work, and notice if Divine Providence is assisting you or if it seems that Providence wishes to help you.

18   I would very much like to know in what part of the city you are living.

19   Pray to God for us and believe me, my very dear Brother,
       Devotedly yours in Our Lord,
       DE LA SALLE

———— ✦ ————

The postal service between Paris and Rome was often quite irregular and subject to unexpected delays; however, De La Salle's letter addressed directly to M. Santenot got through without problems, contrary to the fears De La Salle expressed in paragraph 1. The fact that he did not send it in care of his friend De La Bussière caused him some misgivings.

To understand the repetitions of concerns in De La Salle's successive letters, it is necessary to realize that his letters and Drolin's do not actually follow one after the other in perfect order, since they often crisscrossed en route.

The sentence in paragraph 15 — "I am well aware that it is advantageous to live withdrawn from the world, but you have to have life's necessities, and you need to know where you can get them before you leave the world" — was judged very severely by the theologian who examined De La Salle's writings during the preliminary stages of the process of beatification which led to De La Salle's being declared "venerable" in 1838. The theologian believed that this comment showed that De La Salle lacked complete confidence in Providence.

In response to this theologian, who played the role of the devil's advocate, the theologians who were promoting the cause of the beatification, Rosatini and Mercurelli, resorted to an entirely different interpretation of De La Salle's use of the word "world." They proposed that De La Salle was advising Drolin to stay in the world of the De La Bussière home, but not become involved with the secular (worldly) activities there. Apparently this argument, more adroit than accurate, went unchallenged.

LETTER 21
To Brother Gabriel Drolin

AM; AMG; EC 21; BL I.13

Paris
February 11, 1706

1 I could easily see that you were not feeling quite yourself, my very dear Brother, when you wrote the letter prior to the one I am answering, but I tried not to give you cause for that.

2 I am very happy to learn from your last one that your annoyance has lessened. It would have been entirely appeased, I think, when you received my last letter.

3 You will do well to cash the note for 100 francs that I got for you as soon as you can.

4 With regard to what you say I mentioned in my letters, I wrote under two different sets of circumstances. First, when you were doing nothing else but taking care of M. De La Bussière's children and, second, when you were trying to get employment in a school while still living at his house.

5 In the first case, I kept urging you to get out of the situation since I considered it to be at odds with your vocation.

6 In the second, I wrote to you that you should take it for granted that I could assist you for no more than six months or a year. I don't know whether I said a year or a year and a half, but that is really as far as I would have gone.

7 So I looked on it as providential when M. De La Bussière invited you to take your meals at his house, for I had little chance of helping you financially. And I have even less chance now than ever.

8 You should not have left the place Providence had provided for you without finding out if I approved and was in a position to provide for your livelihood and for how long, and without our having first agreed together on a definite plan.

9 However, I will do all I can for you, though I certainly have no money to spare at the moment and have a debt of about 900 livres.

10 I am distressed to see you living in such poverty as you do. Please tell me what I can do to remedy this situation.

11 You can see the situation I am in; nevertheless, your position appears to be very embarrassing and I feel it deeply.

12   I would very much like to know if you are making any
further progress.

13   If you have to pay exchange on money sent from Avignon
to Rome, I prefer to have the 100 francs sent to me here
and to pay for M. De La Bussière's bill of exchange in
Paris. In that way it will cost us nothing for exchange, and
you will get the full 100 francs. Let me know what must
be done.

14   I delayed sending you a reply because I had not noticed
the little note enclosed with your letter and thought that
my previous letter would have put your mind at rest.

15   It is now two weeks since we opened classes at Marseilles.

16   You must not think of giving up until we have decided
together what we will have to do.

17   If within a short time you cannot make any headway, then
all that will be left will be to put all our trust in God and
leave in his hands the care, the guidance, and all the
necessary arrangements. I will then take steps during the
summer to see that our undertaking does not fail and to
free you and myself from a very difficult situation.

18   Pray often to God for this intention and for all our concerns from now until Pentecost.

19   I have heard that Cardinal De Janson is coming back to
France and that the Abbé d'Estrées is to take his place.

20   Please do not write to all the various people that you do.
This useless exchange of letters is not appropriate to our
style of life.

21   In union with you in Our Lord and in his love,
      I am, my very dear Brother,
      Devotedly yours,
      DE LA SALLE

———— ◆ ————

This is the first of the series of Letters 21 to 26 sent to Brother Gabriel
Drolin in care of Father Divers, the procurator general of the Congregation of the Mission in Rome. Father Divers had arranged accommodation
for Drolin in an establishment kept by the Vincentian Fathers for young
men preparing for the priesthood. It was Father Divers who also helped
him in some way to obtain a teaching post in a papal school, and who,
in addition, acted as his confidant and spiritual director, encouraging him
when, as we see from paragraph 16 of this letter, he was on the point of
giving up and leaving Rome.

We gather from the first several paragraphs that Drolin had reacted
with some annoyance to De La Salle's criticism of his withdrawal from De

La Bussière's house and to the fact that he had not received sufficient money to pay for the lease of his newly acquired school. Evidently, Drolin had told De La Salle that he had acted just as De La Salle had so often advised him to do. De La Salle attempted to mollify him. In fact, De La Salle adopted a less critical tone in his reprimands from this point onward. One cannot help feeling sympathy for Drolin, who had been working so long with so little success and under such difficult circumstances alone in a foreign country. At the same time we can understand De La Salle's problems with financial difficulties. Less than a week before he wrote this letter, the Court of Justice in Paris had reaffirmed the decision previously handed down in favor of the Masters of the Little Schools against De La Salle and the Brothers teaching in that city. On February 10, De La Salle was notified of the decision which carried with it the imposition of heavy fines, the 900 livres mentioned in paragraph 9. This, in addition to the commitment for the lease of the new house at Saint Yon in Rouen, made it increasingly hard for him to subsidize Drolin in Rome.

This letter, with De La Salle's careful explanation in paragraphs 4 to 7 of his understanding about Drolin's relations with De La Bussière, clarifies the situation of Drolin during his early years in Rome. From January to September 1704, Drolin was teaching the De La Bussière children (Letters 13 and 14), no doubt in compensation for his room and board. Beginning in October 1704, Drolin was negotiating with the regional authorities for a teaching position (Letters 15 and 16). Letter 17 of April 1705 indicates that Drolin had secured a position in late 1704 or early 1705, but that he was also considering a position in one of the papal schools. In any case, De La Salle considers that Drolin is now employed according to the purposes of the Institute. However, in paragraphs 8 to 12, De La Salle inquires about the security of Drolin's position as teacher in the regional school. In fact, Drolin had to leave that employment in August 1708, but in October 1709 he was able to obtain the position in a papal school on a tentative basis, then permanently in 1712.

LETTER 22
To Brother Gabriel Drolin

AM; AMG; EC 22; BL I.14

Paris
April 16, 1706

1   I received your last two letters, my very dear Brother, one dated February 23 and the other, March 2. I did not get the first one through M. De La Bussière, however, but through the French post.

2   I saw to it that M. Théodon got your enclosure.

3   I am happy that you have enough confidence in Father Divers to tell him to whom you write and why.

4   I find it hard to believe that he knew of the letter to the Governor of Calais and of its contents. Please do not write letters that are as useless as that one was.

5   You should have sent me the copy of your authorization to conduct a school right away, without waiting till I got the information from other sources. Thank you for sending it to me in your last letter.

6   I am not at all annoyed about the letters that you include with those you send me. That is not what I meant to speak to you about. I meant that you should neither write nor receive all those useless letters that are not at all in accord with our way of life.

7   I have instructed Avignon to honor M. De La Bussière's bill of exchange.

8   I'll try to see that you are satisfied with me.

9   We have Brothers in Marseilles where they began a short time ago. They have about 200 students and that in one school only. There are schools in four parts of the town, all of which the Brothers will eventually have.

10   It is to be hoped that as our Brothers approach nearer and nearer to you, God will finally bless and increase your school.

11   We shall try to provide you with the means and shall shortly see what can be done in this regard.

12   Pray often for me; I am in great need of your prayers. I will also pray for you and will try to help you and bring you relief in every way I can. Have patience a little longer.

    I am, my very dear Brother,
    Devotedly yours in Our Lord,
    DE LA SALLE

---- ✦ ----

Drolin had become acquainted with the Governor of Calais, the Duke of Béthune, when he was assigned to that city in 1700. Since the Duke spent most of his time at his town house in Paris where De La Salle was a welcome visitor, De La Salle became aware of Drolin's letter, as he mentions in paragraph 4.

It is not difficult to imagine how De La Salle managed to hear, as he mentions in paragraph 5, of Drolin's success in at last getting authorization to teach in the regional schools in Rome. Drolin was no doubt so delighted in finally obtaining what had so long eluded him that he would have told all his acquaintances, who evidently got the news to De La Salle before Drolin sent his letter off to Paris. De La Salle seems not to have been lacking multiple sources of information.

In paragraph 9 De La Salle mentions the situation of the Brothers in Marseilles. In March 1704 a deacon had been engaged to direct a school in the parish of Saint Laurent in Marseilles. However, the report of the success of the Brothers in Avignon so impressed those responsible for this new parish school of Saint Laurent that they began negotiations in 1705 with De La Salle for the services of the Brothers. Brother Albert, as we learned from Letter 19, was delegated to act on De La Salle's behalf. In January 1706 the Archbishop of Marseilles gave such a favorable report on the Brothers that the deacon was dismissed, and the Brothers from Avignon were welcomed a few days later to take charge of the school. The founders of the school officially thanked Brother Albert for his efforts on April 6, Easter Monday, 1706. De La Salle had intended to send Albert to join Drolin after Easter that year, but once again his decision had to be delayed. (See Letter 19, paragraph 20.)

LETTER 23
To Brother Gabriel Drolin

AM; AMG; EC 23; BL I.15

Paris
May 12, 1706

1   It was only yesterday that I received your letter, my very dear Brother.

2   Three days ago, I gave a bill of exchange drawn on the Brothers of Avignon for the 100 livres that you owe M. De La Bussière. I am sending you the receipt so that you can hand it to M. De La Bussière; get his and send it to me.

3   I thought that there would be no exchange to pay on the 100 livres. It is a great loss every time. Perhaps we could save ourselves this or at least a good part of it. You should have warned me about it beforehand.

4   I am not happy that you presented a written statement to the papal almoner; it was probably not the right thing to do.

5   As I wrote to you, you may be sure that I have not abandoned you.

6   If you don't get any payment, let me know at once, and, in that case, you have only to inform Brother Albert in Avignon to draw a bill of exchange for ten écus in your favor. But if you receive payment, you are not to do this, for he will find it quite difficult to send you the money.

7   If I had received your letter four days earlier, I would not have sent you this bill of exchange. I would have instructed Avignon to forward you the money.

8   Do you think I would let you starve?

9   We have to see how to make out between now and October, when I shall certainly bring about a change in your situation.

10   You must take care that the owners of your house do not take possession of your goods.

11   Still, it is not right that you appealed to your sister.

12   The post leaves every week. Why don't you write to me? Why did you let five weeks go by without writing?

13   Please do not act like that any more, and do not take any further steps except in case of emergency when you cannot wait for my reply.

14   I shall pray to God and have many others offer prayers for you and your needs.

    I am, my very dear Brother,
    Devotedly yours in Our Lord,
    DE LA SALLE

15   You didn't send me the date of your authorization to teach. You merely put: "Dated, etc." Please send it to me with full detail, both copy and signatures.

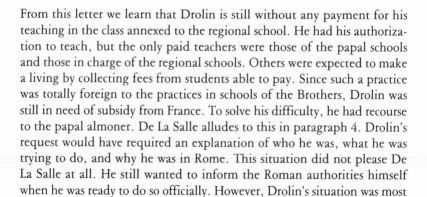

From this letter we learn that Drolin is still without any payment for his teaching in the class annexed to the regional school. He had his authorization to teach, but the only paid teachers were those of the papal schools and those in charge of the regional schools. Others were expected to make a living by collecting fees from students able to pay. Since such a practice was totally foreign to the practices in schools of the Brothers, Drolin was still in need of subsidy from France. To solve his difficulty, he had recourse to the papal almoner. De La Salle alludes to this in paragraph 4. Drolin's request would have required an explanation of who he was, what he was trying to do, and why he was in Rome. This situation did not please De La Salle at all. He still wanted to inform the Roman authorities himself when he was ready to do so officially. However, Drolin's situation was most unenviable. He was in danger of having his household goods confiscated to pay the rent, as indicated in paragraph 10. His appeal to his sister for help mentioned in paragraph 11 met with De La Salle's disapproval also. Still, his sister must have assisted him, for in paragraph 5 of Letter 26, written nearly a year later, we find De La Salle confessing that he had not yet repaid the money owed to Drolin's brother-in-law.

The postscript about the missing date of Drolin's authorization to teach in the regional schools reveals the care that De La Salle, true son of a lawyer, gave to legal matters. He was concerned not only with the exact date, but also with the signatures on the document. If he had been planning to prepare an appeal to the Holy See for the approval of the Institute, this information would have been useful.

LETTER 24
To Brother Gabriel Drolin

AM; AMG; EC 24; BL I.17

Paris
June 21, 1706

1 Since my letter of April 16, I think that you have received two letters prior to this one, my very dear Brother.

2 In the first I mentioned that I had given a bill of exchange drawn on the Avignon community to M. Marteau. He would take only 100 livres for it, although I pressed him to accept 107 livres.

3 I sent you the receipt he gave me and asked you to give it to M. De La Bussière and get one from him to say that you are out of debt in view of the amount paid to M. Marteau.

4 I asked M. De Chateaublanc to let you draw a note for ten écus. Please let me know through whom you draw it and how you go about it.

5 I do not know what expenditure you undertook and now regret. Rest assured that I will not let you lack what you need.

6 Carry out your work in school quietly without precipitous action, otherwise I think that you will not have God's blessing.

7 You see what has come of all your written appeals. Don't seek an audience with His Holiness; you would ruin everything. We will have to take other measures. God will show us the way.

8   Don't let slip the opportunities that come your way, but don't be overeager.

9   You tell me that all you are asking for is rent for your school and your room. What do you live on? Make sure that you don't give up.

10   I am pleased that Msgr. Fieschi has become a cardinal.

11   Isn't the Abbé De La Trémouille the same Abbé De Noir-moutier whom I knew as the vicar general of Laon, the hunchback, who has been in Rome for some time now?

12   In five or six months, when the Brother from Avignon comes to Rome, there will be a more suitable opportunity to seek an audience through the good graces of Msgr. Fieschi, who was the Archbishop of Avignon, not to mention that the vice-legate of Avignon is going or has already gone to Rome to be Governor there.

13   But I am not in favor of these human means, and they are not the sort of means used by the saints.

14   You speak as though I am very insensitive and as if I am not prepared to give you anything. I wonder if it is because you are not receiving my letters.

15   I arranged for the last one to be given to you by M. De Chateaublanc of Avignon.

16   I don't think that your life is as hard as you make it out to be.

17   M. Leroy, who lives in this region and tells me that he has dined with you, said that you kept wine in your cellar and good wine at that.

18   A Breton priest, who had obtained a parish while in Rome and has returned to his own province and who tells me that he spent several years at Saint Sulpice, says that he lived near you. He has led people in his region to believe that when he left you in Rome, you were a deacon. I don't know what he means by that.

19   I do not understand what you mean when you say that you gave a bill of exchange for 107 livres to M. De La Bussière and that you have given instructions that my note be paid without saying to whom it is to be made out. Tell me what you mean by all that. Surely you can follow what I wrote at the beginning of this letter.

20   The Brothers at Avignon tell me that they have honored the bill of exchange from Rome. Please make sure that there is no misunderstanding in this whole matter.

21 I don't know why you tell me not to write by way of
    Marseilles. I have never yet written to you by that route.
22 My letters to you through Avignon should, I think, cost
    only four sous, since that is the cost from Rome to
    Avignon. Write often.
23 I beg Our Lord to shower his graces on you and
        I am, my very dear Brother,
        Devotedly yours in Our Lord,
        DE LA SALLE

———— ✦ ————

In a previous letter, Drolin had told De La Salle of his written request
to the papal almoner for financial assistance. This request had met with
no success. Drolin then stated that he was thinking of seeking an audience
with the pope. This course of action De La Salle simply forbade, for, from
his experience in obtaining civil and ecclesiastical approval for the Sisters
of the Child Jesus in Reims, he knew, as he suggests in paragraphs 7 and
12, of the importance of having friends at court even in the most deserv-
ing cases. The news mentioned in paragraphs 10 and 12 that Msgr. Fieschi
and Msgr. De La Trémouille, whom De La Salle knew from Avignon and
Laon, had been created cardinals and that the vice-legate of Avignon was
to be the Governor of Rome, must have seemed providential to De La
Salle. So he speaks once more of sending a second Brother to Rome, mentioning in paragraph 12 that his arrival will provide the suitable occasion
for a papal audience.

We have no information about the M. Leroy named in paragraph
17, but the Breton priest mentioned in paragraph 18 is Father Suiro. He
had been in Rome to compete for one of the parishes in Brittany, nomina-
tion to which was reserved to the Holy See. Applicants for such benefices
entered some form of competitive examination, the winner being awarded
the position of parish priest.

Brother Gabriel Drolin is named in the *Status Animarum* of San
Lorenzo of 1705 as *Sigr., Gabriele de Rolini, subdiacono, Mro di scola*.
The Breton advanced him to the diaconate. Since Drolin was, by this time,
wearing a long robe rather than the short one of the Brothers, he was no
doubt presumed to be a cleric in Rome, where the schools were normally
conducted by clerics. In later letters we will find that De La Salle is concerned that his disciple might actually be entering Orders and thereby acting in contradiction to the established practice of the Institute of the
Brothers.

LETTER 25
To Brother Gabriel Drolin

AM; AMG; EC 25; BL I.19

Paris
November 26, 1706

1   I have received your letter of October 16, my very dear Brother.

2   I don't think that I had heard from you since July 24. That is a very long time.

3   I am very sorry to hear of your accident.

4   I am very glad that you drew the bill of exchange on Avignon, for I told them many times to send you that money. I don't know why they didn't do so.

5   It is true that they told me they cannot easily find the means nor the opportunity to transfer money to Rome. No doubt they will get the amount to you.

6   You were quite right to stop the negotiating you were do-ing, and I am happy that you still have a good number of students. But does no Italian say anything about the gratuity of your school? Doesn't that fact bring you to public notice at all? Doesn't anyone ask you what you live on? Or who enables you to run a school free of charge like that?

7   I didn't know anything about the lawsuit against the Lazarists.

8   In actual fact, the cost of postage from Rome to Avignon is only four sous by the papal postal service. That is what is always marked on the letters of yours that I get. I am giving instructions that this is to be sent by the papal ser-vice. You must let me know how it turns out.

9   Give M. Leroy, of Paris, my regards.

10   I would very much like to know what that Breton did that brought such dishonor on him. I really would.

11   I am acquainted with His Eminence Cardinal De La Tré-mouille. He is a fine man without any affectation at all.

12   I met here the former vice-legate of Avignon, who gave up his post during August. I believe he has gone back to Rome. He is a priest who has great esteem for our schools in Avignon.

13   Thank you for letting me know in detail how you spend your time.

14 Pray for us in a special way as soon as you get this letter of mine and from Christmas Day until Sunday, the day after New Year's, make a novena to Saint Peter for a special need that is urgent and important for our Society. If you receive my letter too late for this, but I don't think you will, begin and end the novena later.

15 We have a community near where your brother lives. I have had them give him the post of sacristan there because he wasn't working out his salvation in the world; he is too easygoing. At present, he is quite steady and prudent. He comes to confession to me.

16 This is my usual address, Rue Saint Honoré, because we have a school in the parish of Saint Roch.

    I am, my very dear Brother,
    Devotedly yours in Our Lord,
    DE LA SALLE

——————— ✦ ———————

From the information of the opening paragraphs of this letter, it would seem that some of the correspondence between De La Salle and Drolin through Avignon had been intercepted or had otherwise gone astray. This situation became noticeably worse later on. There is no indication, however, to show whether De La Salle did or did not write during the five months since the letter of June 21. If he did, that correspondence has not been preserved.

The months of August and September 1706 immediately preceding the date of this letter were particularly painful for De La Salle because of the difficulties raised by the Writing Masters. Father De La Chétardie, the pastor of Saint Sulpice, did nothing on this occasion to oppose them, though in November of the previous year he had intervened on behalf of the Brothers in a similar dispute with the Writing Masters, but only after a long delay. At that time he had arranged that the Writing Masters return the classroom furniture that they had previously confiscated. This time, however, the Brothers prevailed on De La Salle to withdraw them from the schools in Saint Sulpice parish. They returned at the beginning of October, but with the understanding that only poor students could be admitted (CL 8: 43).

De La Salle's questions in paragraph 6 about the Italian reaction to Drolin's school being free of charge make clear the special character of gratuity maintained by the schools in France. It was precisely at this time, the fall of 1706, that this character of the Christian Schools was a legal issue of critical significance. The Writing Masters, who charged a fee in their schools, lost several students who transferred to the Brothers in the parish of Saint Sulpice largely because of the good reputation that the Brothers' schools had earned. The Writing Masters sued De La Salle for admitting students for a fee, contrary to the express purpose of the schools. He, in turn, challenged them to find a single instance in his schools of a student who paid any fee. Thus gratuity was not only the special character of the Christian Schools, but even the necessary condition on which they were allowed to exist. However, the situation for Drolin in Rome was quite different, and the Italians were not at all curious about his free school or his means of livelihood.

Although De La Salle had established his novitiate at Saint Yon in one of the suburbs of Rouen, he desired to establish in or near Paris a house large enough to serve as the center of the Institute. According to Georges Rigault, the author of *Histoire générale*, a detailed history of the Institute, De La Salle commissioned Brother Thomas, the Institute's pro-curator, to look for a suitable property. Brother Thomas had remained on close terms with Father De La Chétardie, even while that priest carried out his vendetta against De La Salle. Brother Thomas found a property which De La Salle considered particularly suitable and persuaded De La Chétardie to approve of it and to provide for its immediate lease. Prob-ably this search for a community house for the Brothers was the special intention which De La Salle, in paragraph 14, recommended to Drolin's prayers.

An interesting insight into De La Salle's character is derived from his reference in paragraph 15 to the help that he had arranged for Drolin's brother by providing him with needed employment in a place where he would receive some support from the Brothers. This former Brother was not managing well since he had withdrawn from the Institute, and De La Salle recognized that he probably needed encouragement and personal support as much as he needed employment.

LETTER 26
To Brother Gabriel Drolin

AM; AMG; EC 26; BL I.21

Paris
April 1, 1707

1   It is about a week, my very dear Brother, since I received your letter.
2   I was quite upset to hear of your illness but am happy that God has brought you back to health.

Letter 26, to Brother Gabriel Drolin

3 I have also been very unwell for six weeks and could not walk, but I am much better now.

4 I was quite surprised at not hearing from you. It caused me a lot of anxiety.

5 As yet I have not repaid your brother-in-law the money you mentioned to me. I will do so as soon as possible.

6 It will be necessary to wait a little longer. What I want to do is send you a Brother at the end of this coming summer because I am most anxious to let you have a rest and a better chance to apply yourself to prayer.

7 Still, I don't know what prevents you from doing this.

8 I know that most of the cities of Italy are neither large nor populous, and M. Bonhomme, who is here, tells me the reason.

9 Often pray that God will bless this work of his.

10 Brother Albert has established another school at Valréas in the Comtat, in the Diocese of Vaison.

11 The Bishop of Vaison, whom you know, is very pleased with the Brothers and has given them his house in Valréas to live in.

12 A short time ago, Brother Ponce opened a school in Mende, an episcopal town in France, just as you enter Languedoc. He has fallen ill there.*

13 Pray to God for us, and believe me, my very dear Brother,
    Devotedly yours in Our Lord,
    DE LA SALLE

Your last letter was not dated.

———— ✦ ————

We have no indication what illness Drolin was suffering from, and we can assume only that it was the result of the accident referred to in Letter 25, paragraph 3. Certainly Drolin's continued worry over his difficult financial situation, his lack of the companionship of community, and his overwork would have contributed to whatever illness he had. He tells De La Salle that all this was undermining his spiritual health too.

In a rare moment of self-revelation, De La Salle confides in paragraph 3 that he also had been unwell for some six weeks, although he does not mention the cause of this illness. One of De La Salle's biographers, Canon

———

*The numbering of paragraphs of the Letters in this volume follows the numbering of EC; in this case, however, EC numbers the last three paragraphs 11, 11, 12.

The school building at Mende

Blain, however, gives some detail of the incident that confined De La Salle to bed for so long. One evening as De La Salle was returning to his community, he stumbled in the snow and fell on an iron stake fixed into the ground as a doorstop. The iron stake struck a large swelling already on De La Salle's bad knee. The pain was so great that De La Salle fell almost unconscious in the snow and mud, and he was quite unable to rise. Two passersby at first thought that he was drunk, but helped him up and left him leaning against a wall. There he waited until he was able to continue his way. He finished the short distance to the community house in about an hour. On his arrival home he was carried to bed where he stayed for about six weeks (CL 8: 456).

As usual, De La Salle gives Drolin news of developments in France. In paragraphs 10, 11, and 12, he writes of two foundations in the south of France, at Valréas and Mende, under the direction of Brothers Albert and Ponce. The Brothers remained only eight months in Valréas since the Municipal Council required them to teach Latin, which was contrary to the practices of the Institute. (For another reference to the foundation in Mende, see Letter 56 to Brother Mathias.)

The M. Bonhomme referred to in paragraph 8 has not been identified with any certainty. The name of a Father Bonhomme, chaplain of the church in 1712, appears in the register of the parish of Saint Louis of the French in Rome.

LETTER 27
To Brother Gabriel Drolin

AM; AMG; EC 27; BL I.33

Paris
February 14, 1710

1   I was delighted, my very dear Brother, to receive your letter of November 7, forwarded to me a few days ago by your brother.

2   I wrote you two letters, one in August and the other near the end of November, which Brother Ponce tells me he handed to the courier himself. I addressed them both to M. De La Bussière to be handed on to you.

3   If I am not to send them in care of him, let me know and give a definite address, whether to you personally or in care of someone else, but please make sure it is safe.

4   I am delighted that you now have a papal school. That is what I have been hoping for.

5   I have asked Brother Ponce to call on the Bishop of Ca-vaillon for me, if he is in residence, and offer him my thanks for his kindnesses to you.

6   I must see to it that you have another Brother to keep you company.

7   I am pleased that you have left M. De La Bussière's, and I am now writing to thank him for the kindness he has shown you and the hospitality he has extended to you. I will tell him also that I will not forget him but will pray for him and also have prayers offered to God for himself and his family.

8   It is good to know that you have been on retreat in order to try to regain fully the spirit of your vocation and that of prayer. I pray that God will grant you this grace.

9   I know that it is a great misfortune to have to be in con-tact with the world, and it is much to your advantage that you have, to a great extent, broken that contact. Make every effort, also, to disassociate yourself from those can-didates for ordination.

10   You may be assured that I will not fail to pray to God for you.

11   It is a great joy to me that you are now in excellent health.

12   I know that you have plenty to do and am happy that you have a great number of students.

13   I know, too, that there is a great deal of corruption where you are and that you have to be very careful and watchful over yourself not to get caught up in it. Blessed be God that he has given you the grace to keep free from it up till now.

14   We have Brothers in Grenoble, Alès, Mende, and Mâcon, I think, since the last time I heard from you.

15   Pray for God's blessing on our Institute, and trust me, my very dear Brother.

        Devotedly yours in Our Lord,
        DE LA SALLE

———— ✦ ————

Letter 26 was the last of the letters addressed to M. Santenot, in care of Father Divers, procurator general of the Congregation of the Mission. Divers had become suspect in Rome because of his ambiguous stance in the religious controversies current in France at that time. He left Rome on April 7, 1708. This situation could explain in part why we have no record of letters to Drolin from De La Salle from April 1707 until early in 1710.

From this Letter 27 we learn that De La Salle had written to Drolin at least in August and November 1709 in care of De La Bussière. Letter 27 was evidently sent by the same method also. The letters of August and November, which Brother Ponce forwarded through the papal postal service, were probably not collected by De La Bussière, since he would have used the French postal service.

During this long period of silence, Drolin had gone through a time of considerable difficulty. He had had no word from De La Salle, his financial difficulties continued to increase, apparently without any improvement in sight. To add to his problems, Drolin lost his position as a teacher in the regional school system, perhaps because of his association with Father Divers. He acquired temporary lodging, however, in a house belonging to the Priests of the Mission, in which aspirants to the priesthood lived and made their retreat in order to obtain certification of their suitability for ordination.

Contact with the young men preparing for ordination seems to have induced Drolin to consider receiving the subdiaconate himself. His name appears in the *Liber Ordinationum* of the vicariate of Rome, dated May 5, 1709. No doubt he took this step in the hope that he might more easily regain his post in the regional schools. As we learn in Letter 28, De La Salle became aware of Drolin's action from a third person whom he does not name. De La Salle may well have had some awareness of what Drolin was doing when he wrote this letter, but since it was not mentioned by Drolin in the letter delivered through his brother, Gérard, De La Salle does not refer to it directly. He may be doing so indirectly in his remark in paragraph 8 about Drolin's being on retreat.

Ironically, Drolin could have been on this retreat in preparation for the tonsure. De La Salle may have known this, but speaks of the retreat as aimed at regaining "fully the spirit of your vocation . . . I pray God will grant you this grace." In paragraphs 9 and 10 De La Salle adds, "Make every effort, also, to disassociate yourself from those candidates for ordination. You may be assured that I will not fail to pray to God for you." His earlier remark in paragraph 6 about sending Drolin "another Brother to keep you company" indicates De La Salle's continual concern to support Drolin not only in his ministry but also in his vocation. Perhaps De La Salle intended that these comments would serve as a gentle reminder to Drolin of Drolin's commitment to remain a Brother. Such subtlety may not have been lost on Drolin, for in his next letter to De La Salle, he seems to accuse the Founder of not being completely frank with him. De La Salle denies this accusation in paragraph 25 of Letter 28 when he replies, "It is not true that . . . I tell you only half the facts; I tell you things just as I think them to be."

Paragraphs 4 and 5 suggest that Drolin's appointment to a papal school was due to the good offices of the new Bishop of Cavaillon, Bishop Guyons de Crochans, the former secretary of Cardinal De La Trémouille. He was named bishop while still only tonsured. In order to fulfill the requirements for ordination to the priesthood, the newly appointed bishop resided with the Priests of the Mission in the same house as Drolin, receiving successively minor orders, subdiaconate, diaconate, priesthood, and then ordination as bishop. De La Salle received news of Drolin's new appointment in a letter received from Drolin's brother, Gérard.

Negotiations for the opening of a school by the Brothers in Grenoble, mentioned in paragraph 14, got under way in March 1706. The opening was delayed because of the death of the bishop and did not take place until 1708, after the installation of the new bishop. The school at Alès was opened in October 1707, and the school at Mende, mentioned in paragraph 12 of Letter 26, was opened in March of the same year. No information has come to light on the foundation at Mâcon. It is not mentioned in the list of 22 schools and communities in the deed of conveyance given by De La Salle to Brother Barthélemy, dated November 14, 1718 (CL 26: 313).

LETTER 28
To Brother Gabriel Drolin

AM; AMG; EC 28; BL I.34

May 12, 1710

1   Your letter bore no date. I was much consoled, my very dear Brother, on receiving your last letter.

2   You say that you have not had any letters from me except the one you received dated February 14. But I must say that this was the third I have written since last August or September, because I am always anxious to hear from you.

3   Indeed, I was upset that the failure to get letters from me caused you to falter in your love for piety.

4   It would have been very distressing if you had abandoned your school, since it has appeared up to now that God wanted it.

5   You must, of course, teach catechism to your students every day.

6   I don't understand why you say it is difficult for you to have your students assist at Mass because you are alone.

7   The best reason you advance for having a second Brother with you is that you are no longer a young man and that it is time another was trained to the customs and the language of the country.

8   I follow your reasons against this and it is difficult to find an easy solution. In the first place, since the rate of exchange is very high at present in France, we lose a great deal in exchange. Again, conditions here are so wretched that it would be difficult to provide anything at all to cover the expenses. Twelve pistoles together with exchange would come to more than 24 here, but, as you point out, this would be for one year only. So, it is not a very easy question.

9   I do not know what you mean by saying that you are not completely faithful to the Rule. Have you made some change in your robe or your lifestyle? Let me know in what way.

10   Of course, when there are two of you, both will need to be seen following the same Rule. You would do well to discuss the matter with the cardinal vicar's secretary.

11   I do not understand why you say you are paid your monthly stipend of a pistole as if to a private individual and not as to a school teacher. I think that you mentioned to your brother that the papal coat of arms is over the entrance to your school and that it is one of the papal schools.

12   That is what I have thought for some time, and that the reason why you are living near the Capuchins is that your school is in that area.

13   It would be fine if you had such a school and the certification as well.

14   I will take steps to send you a second Brother during the coming holidays. Try to take the measures needed for this.

15   I shall send you two copies of the school prayers. There are some at Avignon; Brother Ponce could send you some. I would very much like you to write to him from time to time.

16   I have not yet thought about traveling to Rome; I could do it at present only with great difficulty.

17   I do not fail to pray for you and for the success of your work.

18   I am upset that you must have so much contact with the world. It is easy for me to see that because of this your piety has diminished. Take up the practice of prayer once and for all, I beg you.

19   Several of your letters and mine must have vanished somehow or other. I feel like writing to one of the Capuchins to see if you would get my letters more quickly.

20 A week ago I asked Father Divers, who came to see me, if he would write requesting that you be told that I had written many letters to you and was worried about not getting any news about you. He told me that he would write a week ago today and that I should write to you direct.

21 You acted wisely in not going where they wished to place you. That would have ruined everything. You are right in saying that the work of eight years would have been wasted.

22 I did not receive the letter that you wrote at that time.

23 So, what you receive from the Pope is only a sort of alms. Let me know what this is all about.

24 I am told that you intend to take the tonsure. Tell me how the matter stands. You know, of course, that that is contrary to Institute practice.

25 It is not true that when I write to you I tell you only half the facts; I tell you things just as I think them to be.

26 You must try to increase the number of your students.

27 I am glad that you go from time to time to make retreats at the house of the Society of the Mission.

28 You told me in your previous letter that you had at least 60 students.

29 I am delighted that you have broken contact with those priesthood candidate friends of yours. Try to do the same with the others as soon as possible.

30 I pray God to fill you with his spirit, and I am, my very dear Brother,

   Devotedly yours in Our Lord,
   DE LA SALLE

———— ✦ ————

Drolin evidently gave De La Salle two reasons in favor of sending a second Brother to Rome and two reasons against such a step. De La Salle's response in paragraphs 6 and 7 addresses the first two reasons. He indicates that he does not understand why Drolin has difficulty taking his students to Mass by himself, and he agrees that Drolin is not getting any younger and will need time to train the Brother who may be sent. But he addresses in paragraph 8 only the first of the reasons against sending a Brother, that is, the expense of his upkeep, and we do not know the second reason that Drolin advanced. Perhaps it was the lack of a Brother with the right qualifications or the scarcity of Brothers altogether.

From De La Salle's remarks in paragraph 11, it is clear that Drolin has not been accepted as a permanent teacher in the papal school system, but only provisionally on half-stipend. Drolin was also having difficulty teaching catechism during school time, as indicated in paragraph 5. (As noted earlier, it was the practice in Rome that the Archconfraternity of Christian Doctrine taught catechism in the parish church on Sundays under the direction of the parish priest.) Nor does it seem, according to paragraph 6, that Drolin was able to carry out the prescription of the Brothers' Rule that required the students to be taken to Mass each day during class hours. From the comments in paragraphs 9 and 18, it is clear that Drolin must have also confessed to De La Salle that he was less than faithful to the Rule, frequenting worldly society, and failing to spend sufficient time at prayer. Lacking any form of community support for so many years, the wonder is that Drolin persevered in his vocation at all.

It would appear that Drolin made no mention that he had had his name placed in the *Liber Ordinationum* of the vicariate of Rome. In paragraphs 24 and 29, De La Salle invites him to give a clear statement of his position with regard to the receiving of Orders. He reminded him that such a course of action was contrary to Institute practice from its earliest years (CL 11: 52: *ceux qui composent cette communauté sont tous laïques*). In fact, Drolin's signature was attached to the document prepared by the Brothers at their General Assembly of 1694, in which, recording the election of De La Salle as Superior, the Brothers stated that, "after him [De La Salle] for the future and for all time, no one will be either received among us or chosen as Superior who is a priest or has received Holy Orders . . ." (CL 7: 348; CL 3: 10). No doubt De La Salle's reminder brought back to Drolin memories of that noteworthy assembly.

Paragraph 9 indicates that De La Salle was insistent on Drolin's wearing the religious garb of the Brothers as it was worn in France. (See also paragraphs 5 and 6 of Letter 31.) He had defended this custom against those who had wished to interfere and have the Brothers wear a clerical soutane. He wished his Institute to be established in Rome as an Institute of Brothers who were unmistakably not priests. However, he seemed to be unaware of the prevalent attitude in that city that all teachers should be at least in minor orders. He refers in paragraphs 10 and 14, as well as paragraph 5 of Letter 29, to his promise of a second Brother as a means of persuading Drolin to resume wearing the Brothers' robe.

(De La Salle's remark in paragraph 25 about telling "only half the facts" receives attention in the commentary on Letter 27.)

LETTER 29
To Brother Gabriel Drolin

Letter 29 was written from Marseilles, where De La Salle stayed after his visit to the other schools of the Brothers in the south of France. He indicates in paragraph 12 that he was on his "way back to France" — actually Paris — where his presence was required by the impending lawsuit brought against him by the Clément family for allegedly taking illegal advantage of a minor, the Abbé Clément.

In 1708 the Abbé had approached De La Salle, expressing the desire to establish a training school for teachers who would work in the village schools. He wished it to be staffed by Brothers. After considerable hesitation De La Salle was prevailed upon to arrange for the young Abbé the purchase of a suitable property at Saint Denis outside Paris. This was done partly with funds that De La Salle held on behalf of his Institute. Still, De La Salle suggested that a newly formed community of priests be asked to staff the training school. The Abbé would have no one but the Brothers, and so they began to teach in the new school at Easter, 1709.

The Abbé's father endeavored to have his son annul the contract he had entered into, but without success at first. In early 1711 De La Salle set off for his visits to the south of France, but he was soon recalled to face charges leveled against him by Clément senior for having taken fraudulent advantage of the young Abbé who was still a minor. The case was decided against De La Salle, who refused to defend himself and limited himself to writing an explanation of some papers and letters of the Abbé's that had come to the notice of the judicial authorities. Leaving his defense in the hands of his lawyer and others he trusted, De La Salle set out for Languedoc and Provence, mistakenly thinking that Brother Barthélemy and the Brothers of Paris were siding with his adversaries. Legal judgment was finally brought against De La Salle (CL 8: 72–78).

For De La Salle this episode began a two year self-imposed exile during which he saw the destruction of his work in Marseilles. He was recalled by the Brothers of Paris, Saint Denis, and Versailles on April 1, 1714.

Letter 29: To Brother Gabriel Drolin
AM; AMG; EC 29; BL I.37

Marseilles
August 24, [1711]

1   I am sending you this letter, my very dear Brother, by the hand of Count Miaczinski, son of the Grand Treasurer of Poland, who is on his way to Rome with his manservant to study for the priesthood.

2   Although he is the eldest of his family, he wishes to give up a secular career and do his theological studies.

3   Please, on the day he arrives, look for an inn where he will be comfortably accommodated. He is a very religious gentleman with whom I have a very special friendship. He can be of great service to you.

4   I wrote to you from Avignon. I think that you will have received my letter and have answered it.

5   We will soon be able to send you another Brother, but, I do beg you, do not give up the Brothers' robe.

6   Do not make any decision on this matter based on what the Lazarist Fathers say to you. Those in Paris would be quite happy to destroy our Institute. I am very glad that I can write this to you in confidence.

7   Please write to me from time to time and do what you can to bring about all possible good for our community. The count will be of great help to you.

8   Let me know just how things are with you. Since the Pope has six schools in Rome, it would be very desirable if they were all in the hands and under the direction of our Brothers.*

9   Do all you can for Count Miaczinski. He will be very useful to you and to us also.

10   We have just opened schools at Versailles, Boulogne-sur-Mer, and Moulins. Pray that God may increase them more and more.

11   I pray that God will shower his graces on you, and I am, my very dear Brother,

> Devotedly yours in Our Lord,
> DE LA SALLE

12   I am on my way back to France.

13   Tell me how you are received by Cardinal De La Trémouille.

14   I had dinner with the Bishop of Cavaillon and thanked him for his kindness toward you.

———— ◆ ————

Count Miaczinski, mentioned in paragraph 1, son of the Grand Treasurer of Poland, had sought refuge in France after his father had taken part in an uprising against King Augustus II of Poland. When a victorious rival seized the throne in 1709, the family fled to France. The young count received the tonsure on August 28, 1712, and the first two minor orders

---

*The numbering of paragraphs of the Letters in this volume follows the numbering of EC; in this case, however, EC numbers the last four paragraphs 8, 10, 11, 11.

on July 26, 1713, but his name does not appear in the *Liber Ordinationum* nor in the parish register of Santa Susanna in 1714. General Joseph Miaczinski, possibly a relative of his, was guillotined during the French Revolution on May 25, 1793.

During the 15 months that had elapsed between this letter and Letter 28, one other letter had been sent to Drolin. What happened to it we do not know, except that it was sent by way of Avignon. Nor do we know when it was written. In his previous letters, however, De La Salle had urged Drolin to adhere to the Institute practice of monthly letters to the Superior, but now we find him suggesting that Drolin merely write from time to time. It is not immediately clear why De La Salle has relaxed in his desire to hear from Drolin on a monthly basis, except that he may now have more confidence in Drolin.

De La Salle may have entrusted more responsibility to Drolin in whatever preliminary steps De La Salle had planned for an official approach to the pope for approval of the Institute. Having in mind such a plan may be why he repeats in paragraphs 3, 7, and 9 that Count Miaczinski can be of service to Drolin. These steps may also be implied in De La Salle's request in paragraph 7 to "do what you can to bring about all possible good for our community." There are some hints of this in earlier letters, too, as in Letter 19, paragraphs 16, 20, and 21, and Letter 24, paragraphs 7, 8, 10, and 12. François-Elie Maillefer, in his biography of his uncle, De La Salle, states that, at the insistence of the Brothers, De La Salle consented to try to gain papal approbation for the Institute. His intention of sending two Brothers to Rome had an appeal for papal approbation as its eventual purpose. Maillefer goes on to say that Drolin forgot about this assignment. Nevertheless, he was still in Rome and was the only Brother there in 1725 when Pope Benedict XIII granted the Bull of Approbation.

Though De La Salle was very concerned that Drolin may have worn a clerical soutane instead of the Brothers' much shorter robe, which reached only to the middle of the leg, the Bull of Approbation specifically made mention in its Article XVIII of the long religious robe which reached to the ankles. Drolin may have had something to do with that!

The references to Cardinal De La Trémouille and to the Bishop of Cavaillon, Guyons de Crochans, in paragraphs 13 and 14 suggest that De La Salle was not only thanking the bishop for his help to Drolin, but may also have been arranging a meeting with the cardinal, who was the ambassador of France to the Holy See. The bishop had been the cardinal's secretary, and it is significant that De La Salle had dinner with him, although there was no Brothers' school in his diocese. Apparently, De La Salle maintained good relationships with members of various associations of a pious and political nature, which gave his foundations a certain amount of protection and supplied him with information not generally made public. The *Edition Critique* suggests the hypothesis that Drolin's pseudonym, "Santenot," was a secret identity in one such association, whose mailing address could be used for De La Salle's letters to him. This arrangement could have been made by De La Salle to send Drolin information of a confidential nature about Drolin's role in the project of securing papal approbation for the Institute. It may have been letters of this nature that Drolin burned as he was instructed to do in paragraph 5 of Letter 16, the first letter De La Salle wrote to him under the name Santenot. (For the contrary opinion that De La Salle did not intend that Drolin secure papal approbation see CL 11:92ff.)

De La Salle's remark in paragraph 6, that the Lazarist Fathers (Vincentians) were working for the downfall of the Brothers' Institute, is difficult to understand. It may have been that, like some of the Sulpicians, these particular Lazarists had disagreed with De La Salle's concept of the organization and government of the Institute. In actual fact, however, members of that congregation had played a prominent part in the foundation of the schools in Versailles and Boulogne-sur-Mer. There was some difference of opinion between the parish priest of Versailles and De La Salle about the transfer of one of the Brothers, but aside from this one incident, De La Salle's remark in this letter remains unexplained, as does his reference to the lawsuit against the Lazarists in paragraph 7 of Letter 25.

LETTER 30
To Brother Gabriel Drolin

AM; AMG; EC 30; BL 1.38

[Marseilles]
[July 1712]

1   I had hoped to come to visit you, my very dear Brother, and was ready to do so in the company of a certain Father Ricordeau, Canon of the collegial church of Troyes, who went to Rome a month ago. But a matter cropped up here suddenly and delayed the trip, for it was urgent. However, the matter did not come to anything of significance.

2   I will find it difficult to send you another Brother before I have begun a novitiate in this province. I intend to establish one immediately, since men from this province are needed because of the difference between the language here and that of the rest of France.

3   You are right in not accompanying the count all the time.

4   I am pleased that he has paid you in full.

5   Let me know if, when I come to see you, I can bring him some books and how much they will cost, because I do not want to have to wait afterwards for payment.

6   As soon as the novitiate is established, I will go to see you and talk things over with you.

7   I replied by return post to all your letters and to those referring to your baptismal certificate. I mentioned that I was told that, to get the certificate, they had to know the year and the date of birth, at least the year.

8   That is what I said in my reply to you. You must have received my letter. If you give me this information, I will have it sent on to you at once, for the District Registrar is the only one who keeps the register for this.

9   I am sending you all the picture cards that can be found in the house.

10 I am, my very dear Brother,
        Devotedly yours in Our Lord,
        DE LA SALLE

11 Father Ricordeau is under suspension. Why, I don't know. Perhaps that is why he has gone to Rome. He did not tell me this, and I asked you to help him only because he wanted me to do so. If he is still in Rome, don't do anything for him except with great prudence.

12 I did not give him letters of introduction except to you, because I did not want to put myself in an awkward position, as I know neither his business nor what he plans to do.

———————— ◆ ————————

The previous letter, Letter 29, closed with De La Salle's announcement of his return to Paris, where he was required to face charges in the Clément affair. He was now back in Marseilles, but he makes no mention to Drolin of his unhappy experience with the court case or of his suspicion that the Brothers in Paris were against him. Blain tells us that, feeling himself surrounded by people who desired his defeat, he left Paris when he was informed that the decision of the court was against him and a warrant for his arrest was forthcoming (CL 8: 79).

After he had left, the Brothers in Paris received two writs issued against him outlining the penalties imposed by the court. They were made out to him as "Priest of the Diocese of Reims and Superior of the Community of that City." According to Blain, the omission in these writs of any reference to the communities of Paris was to make it appear that De La Salle was not acceptable to the Brothers there and to enable Father De La Chétardie, the one to whom Blain refers as "the great enemy," to gain control of these Brothers.

Brother Barthélemy innocently forwarded these writs to the Founder simply to inform him of what was happening in his absence. But by this time De La Salle's suspicions had deepened, and receiving these documents further discouraged him. He now assumed that Brother Barthélemy and the Brothers in Paris no longer supported him, and he broke off all correspondence with them. These were the circumstances under which De La Salle moved through the communities in the south of France until he came to Marseilles, from which place he wrote Letter 30. As usual he made no mention to Drolin of the unpleasantness that he had suffered (CL 8: 79–80).

The urgent matter mentioned in paragraph 1 that cropped up suddenly to prevent De La Salle from going to Rome was the prospect of founding a second school in Marseilles in the parish of Saint Martin. After promising negotiations had begun, however, the pastor of the parish changed his mind, and the school was not established. As De La Salle mentioned in paragraphs 2 and 6, he was also detained in Marseilles by the work of establishing the novitiate which was to open shortly.

Drolin, no doubt, needed his baptismal certificate, referred to in paragraphs 7 and 8, in order to qualify for a full license to teach in a papal school.

Little is known about Father Ricordeau named in paragraph 1. No mention has been found in the archives of the Diocese of Troyes of his being under suspension. It is thought, however, that he might have been the scapegoat for the cathedral chapter in its opposition to the bishop, who wanted to reduce the revenues of the canons in order to increase his own.

There is no indication in the original manuscript of the date or the place of origin of this letter. However, paragraph 3 of Letter 31 tells us that it was given to a priest of Saint Martin's parish, Paris, to take with him on his journey from Marseilles to Rome. We are also told in the opening paragraph of Letter 30, that Father Ricordeau had already been gone a month from Marseilles. A letter found in the French embassy in Rome reads, "The favorable opportunity of the departure of Father Ricordeau, Canon of the church of Saint Stephen in Troyes, Champagne, gives me the honor of sending you this letter . . ." It is dated June 8, 1712. Hence the presumed date of Letter 30 is July 1712.

LETTER 31
To Brother Gabriel Drolin

AM; AMG; EC 31; BL I.39

Marseilles
December 16, 1712

1 I think, my very dear Brother, that you should not have loaned or advanced so much money to the count. That is not befitting, especially for people like us. In fact, you should not have loaned him anything at all.

2 All that I can say about it, now that it has been done, is that you should discuss things before you do them, not after they have been done. If you had asked me beforehand, I would have said not to loan him anything.

3 There have been only three letters since Father Ricordeau left and I have answered them all. The first I answered and sent through the assistant priest of Saint Martin's, Paris; the second through the post; and this is the reply to the third. I have answered all your letters since I have been in Provence.

4 I have high hopes of sending you another Brother, but it will not be until after Easter.

5 Is it true that you wear a long robe and a long mantle as reported by Father Ricordeau, who has arrived back on the papal galleys?

6 If that is the case, how do you expect a companion Brother to dress? For you must both dress alike and wear the garb of the Institute.

7 I am told that you also wear a narrow brimmed hat. The Lazarist Fathers don't wear a different hat when they go to Italy.

8 I would be very happy if a second Brother were to help you withdraw from frequent contact with the world and if the papal stipend went to him also.

9 I consider what has been done in Rome to be of great importance, but we must wait until the novitiate that I began here four months ago has been well established before I can either come to visit you or send you someone who is a native of this region.

10 I think that you should not too easily break off your association with the count.

11   Father Ricordeau told me that he sold you for nine livres a sash that he bought for 11 livres.

12   He is not a man that you can altogether depend on. He was suspended. Was his suspension lifted while he was in Rome? I think that is why he went there.

13   I was not anxious to get involved with him. He was even annoyed that I was not prepared to give him letters of recommendation, but I was careful not to. He would not tell me why he was going to Rome, and I knew that he had been suspended by his bishop, for whom I have a great deal of respect and esteem. I think someone told me that he had said Mass here.

14   There is another priest for whom I found a place. He lived for a time in one of our communities. He was suspended for having gone off to war though he was a priest. He is now 54 or 55 years old.

15   If he asks to have the suspension lifted either through a Roman banker or personally, I would like you to let it be known in the appropriate quarters that this should not be granted without my reasons against it having been heard first.

16   He belongs to the Diocese of Rouen. It is neither to his advantage nor to the Church's that he be reinstated. His name is Celisier, I think. He is from Rouen itself. He has changed his name and kept the one he used during the war, De Saint Georges.

17   Father Ricordeau tells me that one of the teachers of the papal schools is very old and that a Brother could easily take over his school. He says, too, that there are only three papal schools in Rome. Is this true?

18   He also says that you haven't as many as 30 students and that you are not devoted to your classes.

19   It is a fine thing you have been doing, going to teach catechism to the poor Frenchmen in the two hospices that you mentioned. It would be good to continue this practice.

20   It was quite wrong of Father Ricordeau to say that the Brothers in Troyes almost came to blows.

21   He says that you had him to dinner only once, though you say seven or eight times. I had him to a meal only once on his way to Rome and not at all on his way back. He was most anxious to come here often for that purpose.

22 How was it that my name was mentioned to the Queen of Poland?

23 My coming to Rome will be deferred for a long time.

24 Please pray to God for us, and
    I am, my very dear Brother,
    Devotedly yours in Our Lord,
    DE LA SALLE

25 The count is asking me for 200 francs' worth of books and other things. But I can neither bring nor send anything unless I can be sure of receiving payment on my arrival.

———— ✦ ————

The distress caused by the unhappy circumstances surrounding the lawsuits connected with the Abbé Clément and the training school for rural teachers must have been relieved by the welcome given the Founder on his way south to Marseilles. He must have been especially delighted by his reception in that city, probably at the end of May 1712. The Brothers had already been teaching in the parish of Saint Laurent since 1706. Now they were asked to establish a school in the parish of Saint Martin. De La Salle's proposal (Letter 30) to set up a novitiate so that young men from Provence could be trained as Brothers was greeted with enthusiasm.

A third school in the city was planned for the Brothers, that of Our Lady of Accoules. This spontaneous acceptance of De La Salle and the Brothers was contrary to his experience. His biographers, Blain and Maillefer, both tell us that he was uneasy with the enthusiasm with which his plans were received and with the facility with which they were put into practice. He was to find out shortly how appropriate his forebodings were and how much he would suffer in the south of France. At the time of his writing this letter, however, everything and everyone smiled on him and his Brothers.

The first letter De La Salle wrote "since Father Ricordeau left," as he says in paragraph 3, was Letter 30, July 1712; the third is this Letter 31. The second may never have reached Drolin; in any case, it is not among those known to be extant. When De La Salle remarks in paragraph 3 that this is "only" the third letter he has written during the period, it may be that Drolin had written others to De La Salle that were not answered, probably because De La Salle never received them.

Obviously, Drolin's financial situation has improved to the point that he could lend money to the count, as he writes in paragraph 1. The devil's advocate at the process for the beatification of De La Salle accused him in this incident of lacking Christian charity in the way he wrote to Drolin about lending money to the count. The advocate for the cause defended De La Salle for two reasons: that De La Salle and his communities in France were very poor; and that Drolin, as a religious, could not act independently of his Superior, and since he was local superior of a "community of one," he was bound to dispose of the community's goods with prudence.

The way Drolin dressed was a constant concern to De La Salle, and he raises the topic in paragraphs 5, 6, and 7. The length of the robe is discussed in the commentary on Letter 28. As for the hat, the dimensions of the Brothers' hat were described in the 1718 *Règle du Frère Directeur d'une Maison de l'Institut*: "six inches wide and four-and-a-half inches high," with a brim of six-and-a-quarter inches. The Chapter of 1720 reduced the width to five-and-a-half inches. The turned-up, wide brim is the origin of the tricornered hat that became part of the Brothers' garb at the end of the eighteenth century.

Father Celisier, mentioned in paragraph 14, 15, and 16, may be the soldier-priest whom Blain described as having been converted by De La Salle and as having subsequently lived for two years in one of the communities of the Institute (CL 8: 341). Blain praises the charity of De La Salle in helping this priest, but the devil's advocate, during the process of beatification, questioned De La Salle's charity in opposing the move to have the priest reinstated. The advocate for the cause defended De La Salle, saying that he was inspired by his great zeal for the holiness of the ministers of the Lord.

There is no record from the history of the Troyes community of the altercation among the Brothers mentioned in paragraph 20. However, De La Salle does not deny that it happened.

No doubt it was the count who spoke to the Queen of Poland about De La Salle, a question which he raises in paragraph 22. She was living comfortably as an exile in Rome. Later she went to live in France, where she died in 1716.

LETTER 32
To Brother Gabriel Drolin

AM; AMG; EC 32; BL I.41

Saint Yon, Suburb of Rouen
December 5, 1716

1   It has been against my wishes that I haven't written to you for so long, my very dear Brother. I wrote to you several times without receiving a reply. I think that my letters were intercepted, as I know some of yours have been.

2   I have had many disappointments during this time. At present I am living in a house in a suburb of Rouen. It is called Saint Yon and we have our novitiate here.

3   I assure you that I have a great tenderness and affection for you and often pray to God for you.

4   You can write to me as often as you wish. I have confidence that the Brother who is now in charge at Avignon will faithfully forward your letters to me. He is a very discreet man. I will answer them.

5   For nearly ten months now, I have been ill in this house, where I have been living for a year.

6   The vacillations of the Archbishop of Paris are causing concern among the bishops. I don't know what is thought of this in Rome.

7   I have been greatly encouraged by your last letter, and the assurance of your wholehearted affection gives me much joy.

8   Please let me know how you are getting along.

9   I was hoping to send you, during the holidays, a Brother who has been in Rome, knows a little of the Italian language, and is a prudent man and a good teacher. But we have employed him elsewhere in the belief that his usefulness in that position would be a matter of great importance.

10 The Brothers are preparing for an assembly from Ascension Day to Pentecost Sunday to settle many matters that concern our rules and the government of the Institute.

11 I pray you to give your consent to the decisions that shall be made at this assembly by the principal Brothers of our Society.

12 I believe that you are still teaching your classes. Please let me know how many students you have.

13 Your nephew came to see me, saying that he wished to be a Brother and that he had been to see you. He said that you were going to become a priest. As he is of changeable temperament, I sent him away to think it over. I haven't heard from him since.

    I am, my very dear Brother,
    Devotedly yours in Our Lord,
    DE LA SALLE

———— ✦ ————

This letter is the last letter of De La Salle to Drolin that has been preserved in Drolin's collection, and almost certainly the last that he actually

Letter 32, to Brother Gabriel Drolin. The sheet was originally folded, somewhat like a modern aerogram, and sealed with wax. The outside address appears above. The body of the letter is on the facing page. The final sentences were actually written on the reverse side.

Ça été bien malgré moy, mon très cher frère, que je ne
vous ay point écrit depuis si longtemps. Je vous ay écrit
plusieurs fois sans avoir reçu réponse de vous. Je crois
que c'est qu'on a intercepté mes lettres comme j'ay sceu
qu'on en a intercepté de vous à moy. J'ay eu beaucoup
d'affaires fâcheuses depuis ce temps et je suis présentement
en une maison d'un faux bourg de St .... nommée
St Yon où est le noviciat. Je vous assure que j'ay bien
de la ..... affection et de l'affection pour vous et que je prie souvent
Dieu pour vous. Vous pouvez me croire que je vous ..... le
J'espère que les fins qu'elle a aujourd'huy ..... tenue et feu ....
m'envoyer mes lettres ou il est fort sage et je vous y prie de my
depuis près de Dieu mais j'ay été informé ..... la ..... maison
dans laquelle je suis depuis un an les affaires de mes
..... depuis Paris causent du trouble parmy les évêques
je ne sçay ..... en passe à Rome. J'ay été bien consolé
de vos dernières et la continuation de vos affection et de
votre bon cœur me fait bien du plaisir. Faites nous sçavoir
je vous prie comment vont vos affaires. Je pense que nos ...
vous envoyer un frère qui a été à Rome et qui sçait ...
peu le latin et qui est fort sage et bon maître mais nous l'avons
employé ailleurs parce qu'on y que ce frère ..... dont il serait dans ce ...
soit d'une grande conséquence. Les frères se disposent pour
faire nos affaires tout depuis la ..... jusqu'à la ..... tenue pour
régler beaucoup de choses touchant les règles et la ..... de
..... je vous prie ..... votre ..... pour tout
ce qui se ..... dans cette assemblée par les prières et ..... de

Société. Je crois que vous continuez toujours vos ...
faites moy le moins ..... connaissant comment ... agit ...
votre ..... et ..... ont ... me disant qu'il voudrait ...
fort et qu'il avait été ..... croira que vous ..... à le ...
comme il est léger. Je l'ay renvoyé pour y penser et il n'en
n'ay point, ... des nouvelles depuis. Je suis en N. S. mon
très cher frère tout à vous DE LA SALLE

à St Yon fauxbourg de Rouen
le .. décembre 1716.

wrote to him. On Trinity Sunday, May 23, 1717, the Assembly of the Brothers elected Brother Barthélemy as Superior General and, from that day, De La Salle considered that he no longer had the right to address letters to Drolin as he had been doing up to that time. The next letter to Drolin came, in fact, from Brother Barthélemy.

There appears to be a number of reasons for the lack of communication between De La Salle and Drolin over the four years between Letter 31 of December 1712 and this letter of December 1716. During almost the entire year of 1716, De La Salle had been ill and confined to the house at Saint Yon. Several letters that he wrote by way of Avignon had been intercepted, as had been some of Drolin's to him. During 1713 and well into 1714, he was convinced, quite mistakenly in fact, that the Brothers of Paris, and in particular Brother Barthélemy, no longer wanted him as Superior after the painful lawsuits instigated by the father of the Abbé Clément. This conviction had led him to break off correspondence with the Brothers in Paris. His feeling of inadequacy as Superior was strengthened by the debacle that followed his efforts to establish the Brothers firmly in Marseilles.

Blain and Maillefer tell much the same story of the hostility that arose against the Founder in Marseilles, although the motivation to which each attributed it is different. In Maillefer's view, the hostility was due to the opposition of influential people to what they considered De La Salle's inflexibility in regard to the Brothers' Rule that, in their judgment, was too severe. When the Founder showed himself unprepared to accede to their insistent demands that he mitigate the Rule, a vicious libel was spread about him, "filled with calumnies designed to make him despicable in all eyes" (CL 6: 209). The offer of the second school there was withdrawn, and not only was support also withdrawn from the novitiate, but a deliberate campaign was mounted to empty it of novices. In addition, there was some personal opposition to him on the part of some of the Brothers. There seemed now no chance of the Brothers' taking charge of the third school, that of Our Lady of Accoules. Blain tells much the same story but he attributes the withdrawal of support for De La Salle to the hostility of the Jansenist clergy of Marseilles, aroused by De La Salle's refusal to have any part in their opposition to the orthodox Catholic position.

In the face of increasing hostility which seemed about to destroy his work, De La Salle withdrew from Marseilles to spend some time in retreat outside the city. It was his hope that, in his absence, some degree of calm might prevail. Reports were spread, however, that he had deserted the Institute and that several Brothers had followed him by leaving also. Some of the Brothers of the surrounding districts began to give credence to these rumors and informed De La Salle that it seemed that he had come to Marseilles only to destroy the Institute there. Thinking that his presence was the cause of all the trouble, he decided to withdraw altogether and journey to Rome. He was about to embark for this journey when the Archbishop of Marseilles met him and persuaded him to stay and take over the school of Our Lady of Accoules. His adversaries, however, were able to prevent this. De La Salle therefore left Marseilles and Provence early in 1713 and traveled west.

The first community that De La Salle called on was that of Mende in Languedoc. Here, according to Blain, he was rebuffed at the door of the community house by two Brothers who had been most opposed to him earlier in Marseilles. According to Blain, the Brothers refused him admittance, saying that if he wished to stay he would have to pay board and lodging. Sent away by his own Brothers, De La Salle was given hospitality by the Capuchin Fathers. He was also looked after by a community of women who were devoted to the Christian education of girls in the district of Mende.

The historian Rigault suggests, however, that the Brothers of Mende were hard pressed for accommodations, that they informed De La Salle of this and that he then found a place with the Capuchins. The fact that he stayed in Mende for about two months would lead us to believe that Blain's version is incorrect. If Blain's account were true, De La Salle's presence over two months would have been a constant source of embarrassment to him and the Brothers. After his stay in Mende, De La Salle went to Grenoble, riding a horse which was a gift from the superior of the community of women.

While in retirement in Grenoble, where he was made most welcome by the Brothers, he learned the good news that the situation in Marseilles had improved and all was at peace again. Fearing that his return to Marseilles might only inflame hostilities anew, he remained in contact with the Brothers there by letter and through some trusted persons to whom he delegated his authority.

His time in Grenoble was spent mainly in prayer and retreat, though he did send one of the Brothers to Paris to report to him on the situation in that city. He also devoted considerable time to the composition of works of piety for the Brothers and their students and to the revision of a school catechetical text. The peace and tranquility that De La Salle enjoyed at Grenoble came to a sudden end when, in April 1714, he received a letter from the Brothers in Paris ordering him to return and resume the general direction of the Institute.

For some time De La Salle suspected that the mail between himself and Drolin was being interfered with. In paragraph 1 of this letter he states it as a fact that letters from Rome had been intercepted. The culprit seems to have been Brother Ponce, Director of the Avignon community and representative of De La Salle in the south of France. According to Blain,

Ponce took advantage of the unrest in Marseilles to leave the Institute after having appropriated for himself the community funds. In paragraph 4 De La Salle assured Drolin that it would now be safe to write by way of Avignon as the new Director was a trustworthy man. He was none other than the Brother who later succeeded Brother Barthélemy as Superior General, Brother Timothée.

Archbishop Louis de Noailles of Paris, mentioned in paragraph 6, was known for his vacillating attitude toward the Bull *Unigenitus*, issued by Pope Clement XI in 1713 to condemn Jansenist teachings contained in *Le Nouveau Testament en Français avec des réflexions morales sur chaque verset*, written in 1699 by Pasquier Quesnel. His wavering resulted in the appeal to a General Council against the pope's action. The pope's answer to this appeal was another Bull, *Pastoralis Officii*, condemning the "appellants" and even excommunicating them. At one period things came to such an impasse that the establishment of a Gallican Church, independent of Rome with De Noailles as its head, was openly discussed. In October 1715, when about to leave Paris to take up residence in Saint Yon near Rouen, De La Salle refused to pay a visit to the archbishop. His fidelity with regard to the pope became even more clearly defined when his name was confused with that of his younger brother, Canon Jean-Louis de La Salle, on the list of appellants (CL 8: 222–223; see Letter 132).

In paragraph 2 of this letter to Drolin, De La Salle sums up all these troubles of 1712 to 1714 in the simple statement, "I have had many disappointments during this time."

The Brother whom De La Salle in paragraph 9 was thinking of sending to Rome at this time was probably Brother Irénée. The position of great importance which this Brother eventually assumed was Director of novices. (See Letter 119 for more information about Brother Irénée.)

On the day before De La Salle wrote this letter he had called a meeting of five Brothers to sign an agreement to send Brother Barthélemy to visit the houses of the Institute to secure approval for holding a General Chapter regarding the rules and the government of the Institute. Reference is made to this assembly in paragraphs 10 and 11. The five Brothers were François, Director of the boarding school at Saint Yon; Dosithée, Director of the schools in Rouen; Ambroise, Director of the house of detention at Saint Yon; and Charles and Etienne, both teachers at Saint Yon. This signed agreement of delegation was taken by Barthélemy on his visits to the communities of Chartres, Moulins, Mende, Les Vans, Alès, and then to Avignon, where he stayed from January 8 to 10, 1717.

Letters 32(A) and 32(B)
From Brother Barthélemy
to Brother Gabriel Drolin

The following two letters were written to Drolin by Brother Barthélemy, De La Salle's successor, elected during the Assembly referred to in paragraph 10 of Letter 32. Letter 32(A) was evidently written at the request of the Founder, while Letter 32(B) is a personal announcement to Drolin of the death of De La Salle.

LETTER 32(A)
From Brother Barthélemy
to Brother Gabriel Drolin

AM; AMG; EC 32(a); BL IV.Ap.2

Paris
February 18, 1718

My very dear Brother,

1   May the grace and peace of Our Lord Jesus Christ be with us. It is with great pleasure that I write this letter to you, having heard from our dear Brother Joseph that you had written to him, anxious as you are about our dear Father, M. De La Salle, from whom you had not heard for a year. That is what our dear Brother Joseph has told us on your behalf.

2   I must tell you, my very dear Brother, that M. De La Salle is very worried that you did not answer his last letter which I myself posted at Avignon and for which I paid four sous postage, following our dear Father's instructions.

3   He had hoped that you would give your consent to all the decisions of the Assembly that took place last May and in which the assembled Brothers thought it proper to entrust to me the general direction of the Institute. In assembly and by secret ballot, we also chose our dear Brothers Jean and Joseph as Assistants.

4   Our dear Father considered it advisable to resign from his position as Superior, for he thought it necessary for the good of our Institute that the Brothers should take over its general direction while he was still alive and could guide

them by his wise advice and counsel. Our dear Brothers did not think that they should bring any more pressure on him to resume the superiorship which he had laid aside several years ago.

5   He has instructed me to greet you on his behalf with great affection and to ask you to let us know if you want us to send you another Brother during the coming holidays to assist you. We will try to choose for you a good, competent man to help you and continue your work after you.

6   The Institute continues to make good progress. We have bought a house for 15,000 livres for our novitiate in Rouen, and it seems very likely that we will soon have a foundation in Canada. For this we hope to have a commission from the Prince Regent. He has already granted 3,000 livres annually for the support of the teachers in our school and for teachers whom we will be sending later and whom we expect to train in France or in Canada. If this matter can be brought to a successful conclusion, it will very much strengthen our position here in France.

7   We ask you, my very dear Brother, to be good enough to visit the Church and the tomb of Saints Peter and Paul, to receive Holy Communion and to recommend to the care of these two great apostles the affairs of the Institute, and to pray especially for the true conversion of him who is, with all possible esteem and affection, in Jesus and Mary, my very dear Brother,

Your very humble and devoted servant,
Brother Barthélemy

8   I do not fail to remember you daily in my poor prayers and beg you to do the same for me.

9   Our dear Brother Jean Jacot humbly sends you his best wishes and recommends himself to your prayers.

This letter was evidently written by the newly elected Superior General at the request of De La Salle, who was anxious about Drolin's apparent failure to give his consent to the decisions of the General Assembly of the previous May as De La Salle had requested. Meanwhile, Drolin, concerned about De La Salle, had written by way of Reims to inquire what the situation was. Knowing from the last letter of De La Salle about the General Assembly, Drolin would have realized that the Founder would no longer be Superior, but he would not have known to whom to write as the new Superior or where De La Salle would now be living.

Like De La Salle, Brother Barthélemy was not to carry out the promise mentioned in paragraph 5 to send another Brother to Rome to help Drolin. This was left to the next Superior General, for Barthélemy died a year after the Founder, on June 8, 1720.

The possibility of establishing a community of Brothers in Canada arose from the attempts of a certain Father Charron to obtain the services of four Brothers (paragraph 6). He had come to France in the hope of uniting the small congregation he had founded in Canada to an already flourishing congregation, possibly De La Salle's Institute. He failed to arrange the unification but did succeed in getting authorization to introduce six school teachers into the colony. According to Blain, Brother Barthélemy, with the approval of De La Salle and the consent of the Brother Assistants, agreed to Charron's request and selected four Brothers for this mission. Two days later, De La Salle was heard to say to one of the Assistants, "Good heavens, what are you doing? Such an action will cause you no end of trouble. The consequences will be disastrous." Brother Barthélemy overheard the remark but replied that it was too late since all arrangements had been made and the fares paid for the voyage. De La Salle repeated, "But, what are you doing?" The Superior General and his Assistants, impressed by De La Salle's repeated questioning of the proposal, broke off the negotiations. It later surfaced that Charron had intended to separate the Brothers and have them teach singly in country schools, a practice that De La Salle would have never countenanced (CL 8: 153).

Brother Barthélemy was not known personally by Drolin, who had set out for Rome before the new superior had even entered the Institute. Probably to let Drolin know that he had, as it were, a friend at court, Brother Barthélemy mentioned to him in paragraph 9 that Brother Jean Jacot, one of Drolin's confreres of the first days of the Institute, was now one of the Assistants and sent him his greetings. (For more information about Brother Jean see the commentary on Letter 1.)

LETTER 32(B)
From Brother Barthélemy to Brother Gabriel Drolin

AM; AMG; EC 32(b)

Rouen
April 13, 1719

My very dear Brother,

1   The grace and peace of Our Lord Jesus Christ be always with us. It is with great sorrow that I write to you this second letter to let you know of the death of our very dear Father, which took place on Good Friday at about four

o'clock in the morning, after he had received the last sacraments of the Church, much to the edification of those present. He had been ill all through Lent.

2 All Rouen mourns his passing and regards him as a saint. Crowds came to see his body on Friday and Saturday until his burial took place. I hope that you will send a short reply to my last letter.

3 The Archbishop of Rouen and the First President have graciously offered us their patronage. I commend myself to your good prayers and I am, with all my heart, in Jesus and Mary, my very dear Brother,

Your very humble and devoted servant,
Brother Barthélemy

4 PS: I consider it my duty to send you the first part of our very dear Father's will which concerns all the Brothers of our Society. It is the last instructions and directives he gave us.

5 "I commend to God first of all my soul, and next all the Brothers of the Society of the Christian Schools to whom he has united me. I recommend them above all things to have always an entire submission to the Church, especially in these distressing times and, in order to give proof of this, never to be at variance with our Holy Father the Pope and the Church of Rome, always remembering that I sent two Brothers to Rome to beg of God the grace that their Society may always be entirely submissive to the Holy See.

6 "I also recommend them to have a great devotion to Our Lord, a great love for Holy Communion and the exercise of prayer, and a special devotion to the Most Blessed Virgin and to Saint Joseph, the patron and protector of their Society; to acquit themselves of their work with zeal and unselfish generosity; to maintain an intimate union among themselves and unquestioning obedience to their superiors, which is the foundation and support of all perfection in a community."

7 Our very dear Father wrote a number of letters in defense of the Constitution of Our Holy Father, Pope Clement XI, which did a great deal of good.

———— ◆ ————

There is no record that Brother Barthélemy wrote to Drolin again after this notice of De La Salle's death. The extract from the Founder's will quoted in paragraphs 5 and 6 contains his dying recommendations to his disciples, written just four days before his death.

The First President mentioned in paragraph 3 was Nicolas Pierre Camus Le Pontcarré, of the Parliament of Normandy, who had been a friend of De La Salle and associated with the Lasallian foundations in Rouen. He was on such good terms with the Brothers that he considered it his privilege to withdraw to the gardens of Saint Yon for a quiet walk whenever he wished.

The small school directed by Gabriel Drolin developed very slowly despite the good work of his successors. There were many financial problems and numerous difficulties arising from the fact that it was located so far from the country of its originators. It was not until 1727 that another Brother was finally sent to be a companion for Drolin. Brother Timothée, Superior General, sent Brother Fiacre, Jacques Nonnez, to spend a year with Drolin in order to work with him and eventually replace him in 1728. Brother Thomas, the procurator, had also come with Brother Fiacre, but only on a temporary mission, probably as a representative of the Superior.

Brother Fiacre was soon joined by Brother Silvestre, François Regnauldin, but the school did not flourish. In fact, at an audience on May 2, 1736, Pope Clement XII stated that it was not necessary that there be any increase in the number of Brothers in Rome, because the children of the papal city were well cared for by the Piarist Fathers. In 1743, however, the school was settled on the Via della Purificazione with financial help from the boarding school in Marseilles and from then on became quite successful. Thus the Brothers in Italy today can trace their history uninterruptedly to the initial heroic work of Brother Gabriel Drolin.

Letters 33 and 34
To Father Deshayes

Father Deshayes was a member of a group of men called the Congregation of the Jesuit College, a name derived from the location where they held their meetings and exercises of piety. One of their charitable activities was the upkeep of the school at Darnétal, with which Adrien Nyel is thought to have been connected in 1670.

LETTER 33
To Father Deshayes

AM; AMG; EC 112; BL I.6

Rue Charonne, Faubourg Saint Antoine, Paris
September 26, 1704

Dear Father,

1   I learned from Father Chardon this morning that you had written to him asking for some of our Brothers for Rouen, that you would like to have two and want to know how much will be needed to maintain them.

2   I am quite ready to send you two.

3   As regards the cost, you know we are not very hard to please, but we cannot send you one only.

4   If you would kindly let me know what part of the town they are wanted for and what stipend you hope to give them, I will be very much obliged.

5   I think that we will easily come to an agreement and that the Brothers I send will give satisfaction.

> With respect, I am, Father,
> Your very humble and obedient servant,
> DE LA SALLE

------ ◆ ------

Since the Brothers conducted schools only under the aegis of the parish priests where their schools were located, Father Deshayes' first approach was made to Father Chardon, not to De La Salle.

Battersby maintains that Father Deshayes was a seminary companion of De La Salle at Saint Sulpice. Brother Félix-Paul, however, states that

Deshayes was born in 1660 and therefore would have been too young, only 12, when De La Salle was at Saint Sulpice.

LETTER 34
To Father Deshayes

AM; AMG; EC 113; BL I.7

Paris
November 18, 1704

Dear Father,

1   Yesterday I received the letter which you did me the honor of sending.

2   Please let me ask you for a clarification of one matter which you did not explain. It is this: Will the teacher you are requesting be required to lead the singing in the parish and assist the parish priest in his functions? As you know, our Brothers do neither the one nor the other.

3   Would you kindly also tell me how many parishioners there are in the two parishes in the district and if each parish has its own school teacher?*

4   I have been to Darnétal. I thought it was farther from Rouen.

5   I am much obliged to you for your kindness and I am, with respect, Father,

   Your very humble and obedient servant,
   DE LA SALLE

✦

In his previous letter De La Salle was under the impression that the Brothers were going to be teaching in Rouen, whereas it is clear in this letter that the establishment is intended for Darnétal, a large village about a mile from the city of Rouen. He learns that the school would serve two parishes, Saint Pierre of Carville and Saint Ouen of Longpaon. He also learns that the stipend for each teacher is only half of what he ordinarily requests,

---

*EC has the reading "*combien il y a à peu près de communions*," "approximately how many Communions there are." It is now considered that the more accurate reading of the manuscript should be "*combien il y a à peu près de communians*" which would give the rendering "how many parishioners there are."

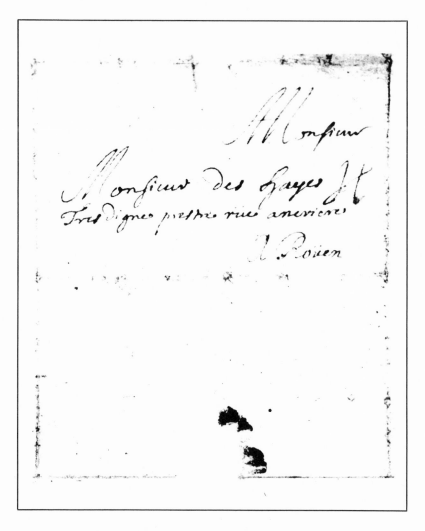

Letter 33, to Father Deshayes appears on the facing page. The wax that sealed the letter is visible below the outside address, which was written on the upper fold.

Monsieur

J'ay appris de m.^d Chardon ces matin que vous luy
aviès ceÿt pour apprendre de nos freres pour rien et que
vous en demandès deux et souhaitterés desireÿs ce qu'il
rendra. Je suis fort disposé a en donner deux pour ce qu'il
ne pria avoir sçauoir que nous ne sommes pas difficiles
et que nous n'en pourrions pas envoyer un seul. Si vous voulès
bien me faire sçauoir pour quel quartier on les demande
et ce qu'on souhaitte de leur donner vous m'obligerés tres fort
Je croÿs que nous connoissons aisément et qu'on sera content
de ceux que j'enuoyeray. Je suis auec respect.

Monsieur .

a Paris rue Lanoÿe
fauxbourg St anthoine
ce 16.e Septbre 1709

Vostre tres humble et tres
obeissant seruiteur
Delasalle

but he does not seem to make this an issue. He is concerned, however, that the Brothers not become involved in any of the clerical functions of the parish. This firm position has been explained in the commentary on Letter 8.

The Brothers took charge of the school in Darnétal early in 1705, some months before they took over the schools in Rouen.

LETTER 35
To M. Rigoley

M. Claude Rigoley, secretary and auditor general for the Province of Burgundy, had undertaken the project of the establishment of a free school to be conducted by the Brothers in Dijon. According to Blain, he was supported in this by his wife and family. In fact his wife's brother, Father Lanquet de Gergy, assistant to Father De La Chétardie at Saint Sulpice, was a good friend of De La Salle (Letter 11, paragraph 4). Blain states that he was a very devout man, who even at that time received Communion daily. He arranged to provide a house and a stipend of 400 francs for two Brothers. Unfortunately the house was not ready when the Brothers arrived in Dijon in June 1705, and Rigoley had to accommodate them in his own home. The inconvenience that this caused was accentuated by Brother Antoine's zeal in asking De La Salle for books and furniture for the new community house and school, all of which had to be stored by the Rigoley family. Judging by the list of needs drawn up by Brother Antoine, it is no wonder that the Rigoley family was disturbed.

Letter 35: To M. Rigoley
Copy; AMG; EC 114; BL II.2

Paris
July 10, 1705

Sir,

1   I received your last letter on my return from the country.
2   I am very sorry for the inconvenience that our Brothers are causing you by having to stay so long in your house. At the same time I deeply appreciate the charity and kindness you have shown them.
3   I can see that the first steps in the establishment of this school have caused you a great deal of trouble up to the present and still cause problems. It is because of your zeal for the instruction of children that you undertook this

enterprise and that you have continued to carry it out in spite of the difficulties it has caused you.

4   As regards the textbooks that I had sent for the classes, I would not have thought of doing so if Brother Antoine had not asked for them.

5   I am sorry that you are unhappy about that.

6   Would you please let them stay at Dijon until they can be sent elsewhere, if anyone else should need them?

7   I do not know, Sir, if you have noticed whether the house you rented has two adjoining rooms in which classes can be held. This is absolutely necessary for our Brothers.

8   If you have overlooked this precaution, I would ask you to ensure it by renting some nearby rooms between now and the time when our Brothers occupy the house.

9   With all possible respect and gratitude,
   I am, Sir,
   Your very humble and obedient servant,
   DE LA SALLE

———— ✦ ————

In paragraph 1 De La Salle alludes to the fact that he had recently traveled from Paris to Rouen in Normandy to inspect the property of Saint Yon, which he had leased from the Marchioness of Louvois for a novitiate. On July 11, the day after he wrote this letter, he signed the lease at the city residence of the Marchioness in Paris. The lease document bears the words, "The lessee declares that, having visited and inspected the property, he signs the lease with full knowledge and understanding."

In writing his letter to pacify Rigoley and apologize for the inconvenience caused by the Brothers' living arrangements and by Antoine's enthusiasm, De La Salle in paragraph 7 takes the opportunity to tell the benefactor that the Brothers' Rule required their classes to be in adjoining rooms (CL 25: 43).

LETTER 36
To Brother Paulin

There is doubt about the identity of Brother Paulin. The fact that the manuscript of this letter was found with letters addressed to Brother Mathias in Pernes near Avignon suggests that Brother Paulin was one of the Brothers who formed the first community in Marseilles in 1706. The injunction in paragraph 4, that he be ready to take triennial vows when the Founder came to Rouen, indicates that Paulin was a member of the Rouen community of 1705, which was lodged at the hospice of the poor of that city. The work that the Brothers were asked to do in addition to their class teaching in Rouen wore down their health. Fortunately for Paulin, he was transferred to Marseilles, where conditions at that time were much more agreeable. It is not known if Paulin was still in Marseilles when trouble broke out there in 1712. There is no record of him after 1710.

Letter 36: To Brother Paulin
AM; AMG; EC 52; BL I.51

October 25, [1705]

1 Alas, my very dear Brother, why are you worrying about your parents? I believe that they hardly think of you. Why do you work yourself into such a state of anxiety about them? Let them carry out their work and you do yours.

2 Say to yourself, as Our Lord said, that he who looks back is not worthy of him.

3 I am very glad that you are now resigned to God's will as regards your school. God will bless you because of your submission notwithstanding your former repugnance.

4 I very much want you to take triennial vows, my very dear Brother. Be ready to do so when I come to Rouen.

5 You must expect to have troubles all through your life, wherever and in whatever situation you may find yourself. That is why you need to be disposed to bear calmly all those that God sends you in the state of life in which he has placed you.

6 Please take care to be exact in regard to silence. It is one of the most important means of keeping a community faithful to the Rule.

7 Be specially wary of Brother Martinien; he is a regular chatterbox. Don't stay alone with him.

8 Disregard your desires, I beg of you, when they serve only your personal satisfaction. Have no other desire than to please God. That is why you are in this world and in your vocation.

9 You ask to be in the same community as Brother Barnabé because you know him. How can you make such a request? Don't you see that this is following nature altogether? Ask God to do his will in you and through you. Such a request will be much better for you.

I am, my very dear Brother,
Devotedly yours in Our Lord,
DE LA SALLE

Brother Martinien, the "chatterbox" (*bien causeur*) mentioned in paragraph 7, did not persevere. Another Brother took the same name in June 1711, so it may be concluded that this Brother Martinien left the Institue before then.

Brother Barnabé, Jean Jannin, mentioned in paragraph 9, did persevere. Born November 30, 1683, in the Diocese of Reims, he entered the Institute in July 1700. He was in Dijon at its foundation in 1705 and was Director there in 1717, when Brother Barthélemy made his visit to that community. He founded the community of Auxonne in 1723 and made perpetual vows at Saint Yon on September 22, 1727. He participated in the General Chapter of 1734 and died at Auxonne on September 18, 1740.

Although in paragraph 3 the Founder urged Brother Paulin to accept his position in the school at Rouen as the manifestation of God's will, it is hard to blame him for wanting to be transferred elsewhere. Blain reveals the drudgery imposed on the Brothers by the administrators of the hospice for the poor where the Brothers lodged:

> The Brothers had to get the poor out of bed and take them for prayers. At 8:00 A.M. four of them went to their districts to teach their students. On returning at midday they served at the table and kept order during the meal. After that they had their meal and when they had finished, each returned to his school. Back again once more, they followed the poor to the refectory and then finished their day with them as they had begun, with evening prayers. The fifth Brother stayed in the hospice to conduct school there. . . .
>
> The two Brothers who went to the school of Saint Maclou each had 100 students to teach, as did the one who taught at Saint Eloi's. The fourth at the Bouvreuil Gage had 150, while the fifth at the hospice had even more. They carried on with this work as best they could from May 1705 until June 1707. When one of them fell ill or was spent with exhaustion, De La Salle replaced him with another more vigorous Brother. But this could not go on for long. (CL 8: 23–24)

LETTER 37
To Brother Thomas

Brother Thomas has been referred to in many of the letters as the procurator of the expanding Institute of the Brothers. Usually the references have been in answer to complaints made about the difficulties he caused. Yet in his letter to Brother Barthélemy (Letter 125) in 1718, De La Salle indicates that Brother Thomas is still the bursar of Saint Yon and that he handles the financial business of the Institute in conjunction with the Superior General.

Brother Thomas, Charles Frappet, was one of the earliest followers of the Founder. He was born in Danthuine in the Diocese of Reims, on October 18, 1670, and entered the Society in August 1690. This was the time when De La Salle introduced serving Brothers into the Society. Thomas was admitted as one of these Brothers and eventually found his career in the management of the Institute's financial and business affairs. He organized the newly acquired property of Saint Yon in 1705. While De La Salle was absent in the south of France and again after his return to Paris, Thomas signed, in the Founder's name, investment policies on behalf of the Society. Other documents show him at Calais, 1717, at Rouen again in 1718, Troyes in 1720, and back in Paris in 1722. Maillefer mentions in the introduction to the second version of his biography of the Founder written in 1740, that Brother Thomas had badgered him until he got possession of Maillefer's first manuscript, written in 1723 (CL 6: 17).

In 1725, after the reception of the Bull of Approbation of the Institute, Thomas pronounced his perpetual vows as a teaching Brother. Blain attributes to him an important part in obtaining the Bull of Approbation and *lettres patentes*. However, Rigault, in his *Histoire générale*, corrects some of Blain's assertions.

On his return from Rome, Brother Thomas was stationed at Paris where he became Director in 1734, dying there on February 24, 1742.

The following two passages, constituting Letter 37, are preserved only by Blain. Blain refers to them as reminiscences of a Brother identified as Thomas. In passage (a) Blain presents Thomas as directly quoting De La Salle. Passage (b) appears in Blain's text as an indirect quotation, but is used as a direct quotation in Lucard's *Vie du vénérable Jean-Baptiste de La Salle,* 1874.

No date is given to these extracts, though they probably both belong to the period when the Brothers were beginning their work at Saint Yon, that is, 1705 to 1707.

Letter 37: To Brother Thomas
   EC 64; CL 8: 264

[1705-1707]

(*a*)   . . . In this way you will find an opportunity of winning the affection and esteem of the people of a city that has no love for you. You may suffer for a while, but it will not be for long. Besides, you may rest assured that God will always provide you with what you need if you serve him well. . . .

(*b*)   . . . You complain that your novitiate is very poor. I think
that the means God wishes to use to provide for your living is that you take children in as boarders, to teach them
well and bring them up well. . . .

———— ✦ ————

The city of Rouen was very much opposed to the establishment within
its boundaries of more religious orders, for this usually meant that the
city tax rates had to be increased and borne by the business people.
However, the establishment of a boarding school for children who could
pay would remove this fear from the municipal council and provide a service for the parents who could afford the fees.

Passage (b) of this letter was later used in a protest against the refusal
by the Minister of Education to allow the extension of the boarding facilities
at Passy in 1883. The argument seems to have been that Lasallian boarding schools were schools with long-standing traditions, and should not be
victimized by unwarranted attacks from lay associations of boarding school
teachers.

Letters 38 to 48
To Brother Robert

Brother Robert, Denis Maubert, entered the Institute in 1700 at the age of 24. From the remarks made in these letters, it seems that he carried out the functions of both a serving and a teaching Brother. In 1704 his name appears on the list of those affected by the court order forbidding the Brothers to teach in Paris. He evidently was able to return to Paris shortly thereafter, for he was indicted in another suit by the Writing Masters in 1706 and went to Laon with Brother Hubert (Letter 8) for a short period. Judging from Letter 38, probably written in 1705, it is possible that he was assigned under Brother Ponce to open the school and the community at Darnétal. Later he took over the direction of that school under the supervision of Brother Joseph, Director of the Rouen community. That seems apparent in Letter 40, written in 1708.

Robert was still at Darnétal in 1717 when Brother Barthélemy visited to obtain the community's adherence to the General Chapter of that year.

There are references to Robert in Letters 4 and 5 written to Brother Denis, who was also at Darnétal at that time. Brother Robert died at Meaux in 1734.

Six of these letters bear the name of Brother Robert. Another four appear in Ms. 22 and in Blain; part of Letter 38 is also in Maillefer. That all of these letters were addressed to Robert can be ascertained from internal evidence, according to the *Edition Critique*.

LETTER 38
To Brother Robert

Ms. 22, 26; AMG; EC 53; BL III.26; CL 8: 369 and 400

[1705]

1 I have received your letter, my very dear Brother, and am very happy that you have great peace of mind. I pray that God may keep you in that state.

2 I am also delighted that you say you are determined to persevere in the Institute to the end of your life, and my joy is much greater because of your desire to return to the novitiate.

3 This is a sign that you are really desirous of advancing in virtue. This gives me great pleasure.

4   You must love poverty, my very dear Brother. Although he could have been rich, Our Lord was very poor. So you must imitate this divine model.

5   But it seems to me that you want nothing to be lacking which will give you pleasure. Well, who wouldn't be poor under those conditions? Would not the great and powerful ones of the world give up all their riches to enjoy an advantage that would make them happier than the princes and kings of the earth?

6   Please remember that you did not join the Institute to enjoy every comfort and satisfaction, but to embrace poverty and its consequences. I say its consequences because there is no point in loving virtue unless you love all that comes with it and gives you the means of practicing it.

7   You say you are poor; how much pleasure it gives me to hear you say that! For to say you are poor is to say that you are happy. "Happy are you who are poor," Our Lord said to his apostles. I say the same to you.

8   How fortunate you are! You say you have never been so poor; so much the better. You have never had so many opportunities for practicing that virtue as you do now.

9   In this regard I could say to you what a great Pope once replied to a Jesuit who was explaining the great poverty of his community, which, he said, had never been so poor. "So much the better for you," he replied. "The poorer you are the better off you will be."

10 Take care while the community is being set up that you do not let yourself become negligent in the practice of the Rule.

I am, my very dear Brother,
Devotedly yours in Our Lord,
DE LA SALLE

———— ◆ ————

This letter appears as Letter 26 in Ms. 22 under the heading, "Poverty is to be loved." The letter is quoted almost in its entirety by Blain (CL 8: 369 and 400), and Maillefer also quotes some sections (CL 6: 68–71). Both biographers use citations from the letter to illustrate De La Salle's love of poverty.

At the time that he received this letter, Robert had been appointed to join Brother Ponce, the Director, in establishing the community of Darnétal and to open the school there. According to Blain, these events took place in February 1705. The community was indeed very poor, as their allowance was only 150 francs, whereas the amount was usually fixed at 200 francs per Brother.

LETTER 39
To Brother Robert

AM; AMG; EC 54; BL I.45

May 1, [1708]

1 Be faithful, my very dear Brother, to leave everything as soon as the bell rings, and see that the bell is given the correct number of strokes.

2 It is not right to shout at the mothers and chase after the children. You should be more prudent.

3 Please observe silence in your community.

4 In particular, take care not to talk to the children out of curiosity.

5 Don't get upset about remarks that are made in the streets, but be recollected. It is your duty to edify people.

6 The reason why you are experiencing apathy and have so many distractions during prayer is that you are too concerned about external things and you talk too much.

7 Take care not to do your reading out of curiosity. Spiritual reading is not meant for that; it is to prepare you for prayer.

8 You will get nowhere if you allow yourself to give way to discouragement.

9 See that your pupils attend class regularly; this is very important.

10 It is shameful to slap them. Be careful not to lose your patience.

11 I know the parish priest well and am sure that any advice he gives will be worthwhile.

12 I beg you to get on well with the Brother in community with you and see that your house is well ordered.

13 I am, my very dear Brother,
　　　　Devotedly yours in Our Lord,
　　　　DE LA SALLE

———— ✦ ————

This letter and Letter 40 are both dated by Brother Félix-Paul in his *Edition Critique* as having been written in 1708. In Letters 4 and 5 addressed to Brother Denis, both dated 1708, reference is made to the second member of the community at Darnétal, who slaps his pupils and by his rough manners in the streets is an embarrassment to Brother Denis. Letter 4 identifies this Brother as Robert. Both Denis and Robert were at that time under the supervision of the Director of the Rouen community, Brother Joseph. Brother Denis, who was in charge of the school, was ill at the time of this letter, so De La Salle gives some advice to Brother Robert on the management of the school.

LETTER 40
To Brother Robert

AM; AMG; EC 55; BL I.47

May 21, [1708]

1   You must not get annoyed with the Brother in community with you, but you must try to live peaceably with him.

2   If there is anything that upsets good order, you have only to mention it to Brother Joseph when he is in Rouen or, if he is absent, to Brother Barthélemy, so that they can rectify it.

3   Be faithful, moreover, in practicing obedience, for it is a virtue you should have very much at heart; it is the principal one you should practice in community.

4   Be exact in ringing the bell to the last stroke and always on time. This is most important.

5   Please answer the door promptly; this is a duty of a doorkeeper.

6   Take care not to be negligent in the matter of rising in the morning, for that fault is most displeasing to God.

7   And don't stand talking to the Brothers when you meet them in the street.

8   Do not let yourself give way to curiosity, which is a great obstacle to progress in virtue.

9   When you go to Rouen, give an account of your conduct to Brother Joseph or, if he is away, to Brother Barthélemy.

10   It is really important for you to carry out your penances in the refectory, for they will be very helpful to you in correcting your faults.

11   For the love of God be faithful to the practice of obedience.

12   Time is very precious. God will require an account of the time you have wasted.

Letter 41, to Brother Robert

13   Apply yourself well to spiritual reading, for it will be very helpful to you in preparing for prayer.

14   The apathy you experience in prayer and when receiving Holy Communion is due to the fact that you don't apply yourself and you don't think of spiritual matters outside the time for prayer.

15   Don't stay away from Communion; you need it.

16   Supervise the children carefully, for there will be no order in the school except insofar as you are watchful over them. That is what assures their progress.

17   Their improvement will not be brought about by your impatience, but by your vigilance and prudent behavior.

18   Do take care that they are well-behaved and devout in the church and at prayer. This is one of the first things you should make them learn.

19   I don't know why you say that, if you become ill, you will be shown the door. You will be cared for.

20   You must be careful when you write. Your letters cannot be read because you do not write three words coherently and because you forget some of them. Please be careful of this in the future.

      I am, my very dear Brother,
      Devotedly yours in Our Lord,
      DE LA SALLE

21   I am quite surprised that you were so indiscreet as to tell Brother Denis that I instructed you to write to me about his conduct. That was very wrong.

22   Please do not let such a thing as your speaking like that happen again. Surely you can see that this can only cause him anxiety and make trouble between you both and between him and me. This is more important than you think.

———— ◆ ————

From paragraph 18 of Letter 5 to Brother Denis, it is clear that Robert was a source of annoyance because of his behavior while walking in the town. In this Letter 40 De La Salle attempts to correct him and urges him to give an account of his behavior on these occasions to Brother Joseph or Brother Barthélemy.

Brother Joseph's place as Director of the community of Rouen and Darnétal was taken by Brother Barthélemy when Joseph was away on visitation. On the weekly day free from class, the Brothers from Darnétal went to Rouen to give their account of conduct. Brother Barthélemy was the Director of the novitiate at Saint Yon, near Rouen.

As was seen in Letter 5, Brother Denis, the man in charge at Darnétal, was not in good health, so De La Salle transferred him during the school holidays. Until that time, life in the community of Darnétal must have been very difficult for both the rough-mannered Robert and the impetuous and frivolous Denis.

LETTER 41
To Brother Robert

AM; AMG; EC 56; BL I.46

December 7, [1708]

1 You do not tell me, my very dear Brother, why you have not been receiving Holy Communion. You should have given me your reasons.

2 Take care not to let yourself give way to impatience and to outbursts of anger.

3 There must be union between you both, genuine courtesy toward lay people, and great patience with your students.

4 Be faithful to be present at the spiritual exercises and to go nowhere without permission.

5 It is better to omit some part of the spiritual exercises than to take time from class to carry out what is necessary, for you must not lose a minute from class.

6 Be very careful to speak softly in the house when you have to speak, and make sure that it is really necessary. You must never speak from a distance nor from the window.

7 Don't dwell on thoughts about your classwork during the time for prayer. Everything at its proper time.

8 Make sure you don't reduce the numbers of the students by your rebuffs, but teach them well so that they will not leave.

9 You must not take them on to a new lesson before they are ready. Be careful about this, otherwise they will learn nothing.

10 You will have to see about buying books, provided they are good ones and that I know what sort they are.

11 You must have some shirts made up and other linen articles if need be, but let me have a list of what linen items you have and what you require.

12 You are not to accept the least thing from the parents of students or from the students themselves.

13 See that you both keep the rules and are closely united, and show great respect not only toward your Brother but toward people generally.

> I am, my very dear Brother,
> Devotedly yours in Our Lord,
> DE LA SALLE

———— ◆ ————

Robert was now in charge of the school, and we find that De La Salle gives advice about the administration of both the community and the school. It is significant that in paragraph 5, De La Salle asks him to omit some part of his spiritual exercises rather than miss class to do something else that seemed to be needed. De La Salle considered classroom duties as important for the sanctification of the Brothers as spiritual exercises. He gives Robert advice to this effect because Robert seems to have needed encouragement to overcome his natural weakness in the face of his school work. In fact, in 1729 Robert took vows as a serving Brother.

The books mentioned in paragraph 10 were the first readers on three graduated levels. These would be purchased from local bookstores. It was only afterwards that the book which De La Salle wrote, *Les Règles de la Bienséance et de la Civilité chrétienne,* was used as the reader (CL 19).

De La Salle considered the gratuity of the schools to be one of the most important features of the Institute. In Darnétal the poverty of the community would have been a serious temptation for the two Brothers to receive gifts from both parents and students, and De La Salle forbids this practice in paragraph 12.

LETTER 42
To Brother Robert

AM; AMG; EC 57; BL I.49

February 26, [1709]

1 You can easily see, my very dear Brother, that you could have greatly scandalized the woman next door by speaking so angrily to her. You must always be prudent in what you say, especially when you are speaking to outsiders.

2 Show great charity also to the Brother in your community. Whenever you have anything to report, mention it to Brother Joseph so that he can set it right.

3   You will do well to send away people who come to speak to Brother during spiritual reading and during prayer.

4   Be sure not to eat other than at meal times; this is not to be tolerated. The hunger you think you have at such times is only a temptation.

5   Be exact in ringing the bell the prescribed number of strokes, for this is quite important in a community.

6   Take care never to tell untruths; that would certainly be a great fault. And don't give way to curiosity, for it is quite harmful.

7   Perhaps it is because you have done this that you find it difficult to apply yourself to prayer and to the other spiritual exercises.

8   Your whole concern during the student Masses must be to supervise the children.

9   Make sure that you don't strike the students, for it is a serious fault and you can't be too much on your guard against it.

10 You are quite right in trying to have your students make progress so that their numbers will increase, but also so that you may carry out your responsibilities.

11 Be satisfied with starting class on time.

12 Take care that your school runs well and that your community is faithful to the Rule.

     I am, my very dear Brother,
     Devotedly yours in Our Lord,
     DE LA SALLE

———— ◆ ————

In the 1706 manuscript copy of the *Conduite des Ecoles chrétiennes* are found the following instructions for the Brothers when they took their students to daily Mass: "They will exercise continual supervision over the students. . . . They will content themselves with simple attention to the sacrifice of the Mass" (CL 24: 91–92). De La Salle alludes to this conduct in paragraph 8.

     In one of his letters to Gabriel Drolin, De La Salle expresses his amazement that Drolin finds it difficult to take his students to Mass during school time. The Rule of 1705 laid down specifically that the Brothers were to take their students to Mass in the nearest church each day unless it was judged impossible by the Superior of the Institute for them to do so (CL 25: 35). In Letter 8, addressed to Brother Hubert, the Founder draws attention to this point of Rule and to the part to be played by the Brothers during the student Mass.

LETTER 43
To Brother Robert

Copy; AMG; EC 69; BL II.6

[March 1709]

1   You must make it your concern to overcome your thought-
    less behavior, my very dear Brother. It is a failing you
    need to be especially on your guard against because it is
    very harmful to you.

2   Take great care against routine in your actions. Develop
    the view of faith more than you apparently have.

3   Surmount your feelings of repugnance when you meet
    with humiliations, for these will turn out to be profitable
    for you if you accept them graciously.

4   Try to overcome the feelings flowing from what comes into
    your mind, and never let yourself argue about what you
    are told to do.

5   Be faithful to leave everything as soon as the bell rings,
    for that is important as is also attending to your spiritual
    reading, which is a great help to prayer.

6   Daily examination of faults is very necessary for you.

7   The distractions you have during prayer are caused by your
    thoughtless behavior. So, please overcome it.

8   Don't be anxious about your confessions. In this matter act
    with simplicity. The anxieties you experience with regard
    to your confessions, and your Communions also, are temp-
    tations from the devil.

9   Take care that your students say their prayers devoutly.

10 Don't leave your place in class or listen to any excuse as far
    as that is concerned.

11 Exercise restraint when you are administering punishment,
    and don't do it when you feel moved to impatience.

12 Talk with Brother Joseph about what you propose for
    reading during breakfast.

13 It is a good idea to enter into yourself, reflect on your fail-
    ings, and then humble yourself for them.

14 The more repugnance you feel for something, the more
    willing you should be to do it.

15 It is good to do what you are ordered notwithstanding the
    dislike you feel for it.

16 Take care not to communicate by signs in the house; it is
    a serious fault.

17 Follow the method of assisting at Holy Mass.

18 The more completely silence is kept in your school, the more order there will be. For this reason see that silence is kept.

19 I would like you to pronounce your triennial vows on Trinity Sunday.

> I am, my very dear Brother,
> Devotedly yours in Our Lord,
> DE LA SALLE

———— ✦ ————

The original of this letter, extant in 1835 at the time of the process of beatification of John Baptist de La Salle, has since been lost, but a copy made at that time has been preserved.

This Letter provides a good example of the critical work of Brother Félix-Paul in his research for internal evidence to determine the name of the recipient and to estimate the date of the letter when there is no explicit evidence. To establish the approximate date, Brother Félix-Paul used the reference in paragraph 12 to Brother Joseph as being Director of the community. It is known that Brother Joseph was Director of the schools of Rouen, which would have included Darnétal, between 1706 and 1710, as indicated in Letters 40 and 42 to Brother Robert. To determine the recipient of the letter, Brother Félix-Paul used the evidence that Brother Robert had received similar counsels in other letters from De La Salle. The allusion to trienniel vows in paragraph 19 eliminates Brother Denis as the Brother to whom the letter is written, even though he also lived in the community of Darnétal, since Denis had made perpetual profession in 1697. Furthermore, vows were to be made in May of 1709, and decisions regarding them made a few months earlier. Since Letter 44 was written to Robert on April 26, and with fair certainty in 1709, Brother Félix-Paul suggests the date for this letter to be March 1709 (EC, 311–312).

LETTER 44
To Brother Robert

AM; AMG; EC 58; BL I.50

April 26, [1709]

1 There is no doubt, my very dear Brother, that you made a big mistake getting into a quarrel at Saint Yon. That sort of thing must never happen. It is disgraceful among the Brothers. I am very glad that you have done some penance for it.

2   When you have requests to make at Saint Yon, speak in a low voice and politely.

3   Make all your spiritual exercises faithfully and leave whatever you are doing at the first sound of the bell.

4   Get into the habit of always speaking in a low voice and from near at hand, not from a distance. Be prompt in answering the door, and be exact in ringing the bell the prescribed number of strokes.

5   Apply yourself fully to recollection. Recognize how much you need this.

6   Be careful never to strike the children; it is a serious fault.

7   I am very pleased that your community is very faithful to the Rule.

8   Be faithful in your obedience and do nothing without permission. This is what will draw God's blessing down on you.

9   Don't let people enter into your house and, out of love for God, put up with the trouble that people give you outside the community.

10   Did you really need to write to your sister?

11   Be prompt to leave everything for the spiritual exercises.

12   There is no need for Brother to work in the garden. If there is something to be done, it should be you or a gardener who does it.

13   See that spiritual reading is made regularly.

14   I am glad Brother does not go out; see that he keeps this practice.

15   Make sure that you keep an even disposition in class, and don't give way to impatience. It is not good to throw the ferule at the students in class, but it is disgraceful to slap them, especially in church.

16   It is good to know that you have a large number of students. Be sure to see that they make good progress.

17   Brother Thomas must give you what you need without so much fuss. It is not true that he has instructions to humble you, but you must act respectfully.

18   It is not our practice to weigh out the bread for the Brothers to eat. They eat what they need. You are to get what salt you need.

19   You do well to adapt yourself to the present conditions and to put up with difficulties willingly.

20   I am pleased that your school is progressing well and that you have plenty of students. Be sure to teach them well.

21 Who is the Brother who gave money to one of the children to get him some snuff? And which boy was it?

22 When you learn of something that is contrary to the rules, you must let me know.

23 I don't understand what you mean when you say the Brother makes the purchase of books an excuse to go to Rouen.

24 Tell Brother Thomas that the Brothers do not have to produce a written order to get what they need and that he must supply them with what is wanted.

> I am, my very dear Brother,
> Devotedly yours in Our Lord,
> DE LA SALLE

————— ◆ —————

The translation of the word *monde* in paragraph 9, rendered as "people," is subject to debate. Battersby translates it "worldliness." Brother Félix-Paul considers that De La Salle is referring to people begging for food or alms during the famine of 1709 and insulting the Brothers when they were outside the house.

The Brother mentioned in paragraph 12 who should not work in the garden may have been Brother Jean Chrysostome, a young man 19 years old at the time, whom De La Salle knew to be in poor health and did not want fatigued by such work. His family name was Pierre Blin. He entered the Institute on October 23, 1707, so this may have been his first year in community. He died in Calais on October 20, 1719, at the age of 29. Blain says that between 1681 and 1719, 42 of the 60 Brothers who died were under 30 years old (CL 7: 250).

The "ferule" (*férule*) mentioned in paragraph 15 was made of padded leather about ten inches long and two inches wide. It was used as a punishment for misdemeanors, the Brother striking the palm of a student no more than twice (CL 24: 169).

The word translated in paragraph 21 as "snuff" is unclear in the original manuscript and has been variously interpreted as the French *cerises,* meaning "cherries;" or *devises,* a term limited to heraldry in the seventeenth and eighteenth centuries. The interpretation "cherries" would obviously be incorrect because of the time of the year; and *devises* would make little sense in the context. Consequently, the French word *prises* is the most probable reading. This can be translated as "a pinch of tobacco" or "snuff." De La Salle was opposed to the use of tobacco and, further, giving money to one of the children to make a purchase would have violated the point of Rule that states that the Brothers must not ask their students to run errands for them or deliver messages. From the fact that De La Salle reminds Robert in paragraph 22 that he should report irregularities that he comes to know about, we can assume that the Brother in question was not his young companion in Darnétal but a member of the Rouen community. De La Salle wanted to know whether the boy who got the snuff for the Brother was one of the students, which would be a greater fault, or someone else.

From previous letters we have learned that Brother Robert was a rough-and-ready man, given to impatience both in and out of class, shouting angrily at the woman living next door to the school, and chasing students in the streets. Paragraph 17 indicates that Robert had no patience with Brother Thomas, one of whose duties as procurator was to provide the Brothers with their needs; nor did he hesitate to accuse De La Salle of instructing Thomas to humble him by seeming to refuse his requests. In spite of all these very human failings, Robert persevered in the Institute until his death in Meaux in 1734.

LETTER 45
To Brother Robert

Ms. 22, 4; AMG; EC 59; BL III.4

[1709]

1   It seems to me, my very dear Brother, that you ought to be more obedient and submissive than you are.

2   We didn't enter the religious life to bargain with anyone. We are not to make conditions at all; obedience should be our guiding rule.

3   Be assured that God will bless you only insofar as you live by this rule.

4   For the love of God, do not make statements like those you made in your last letter. They are certainly not becoming in a man of obedience.

5   It is true that we must put our trust in God's grace, but in a religious community we receive graces only to the extent that we are obedient.

6   So ask God for an unquestioning obedience; there is nothing you need more.

7   Listen to the inspirations of the Holy Spirit and not so much to your dislikes and difficulties. It is not when you feel no repugnance that you show that you are obedient, for everyone can easily obey under those circumstances, but only when you overcome it.

8   I am delighted that you feel motivated toward virtue. The main one you should practice is obedience.

   I am, my very dear Brother,
   Devotedly yours in Our Lord,
   DE LA SALLE

LETTER 46
To Brother Robert

Ms. 22, 3; AMG; EC 60; BL III.3; CL 8: 369 and 444

[1709]

1   I am delighted, my very dear Brother, that you have recovered from the wretched state that you were in for so long and that you acknowledge the change God has brought about in you.

2   I assure you that I feel no greater joy than when I know that those whom I direct walk courageously in the path of virtue.

3   I pray that God may continue what he has begun in you, my very dear Brother, and I thank him for having given you a love for the holy virtue of mortification.

4   And now that you recognize your faults, for example, your failure to be obedient and to observe your rules and so on, I beg you, think before God how you are going to correct them.

5   Since you realize that your lack of mortification and obedience was the cause of this, take steps to become more mortified and more submissive.

6   I am really pleased with your self-renunciation, which leads you to do whatever is required of you.

7   Since you are prepared to obey in all things, never say "I want," for that does not bear the stamp of obedience.

8   I find no difficulty in believing that you have a dislike for obedience. All that is required is that you overcome this dislike. Remember that it is obedience that sanctifies the actions of a member of a religious community. . . .

———— ◆ ————

This letter does not have the signature of De La Salle. It is therefore considered by Brother Félix-Paul in the *Edition Critique* as an incomplete letter reconstituted from Ms. 22 and from two separate quotations from Blain.

LETTER 47
To Brother Robert

Ms. 22, 2; AMG; EC 61; BL III.2; CL 8: 443

[1709]

1   I am not at all upset by the trouble that you think you have caused me, my very dear Brother. The only thing that causes me concern is that you don't know what is good for you.

2   Be assured that what is best for you is what obedience brings you.

3   That is why you should pay attention to your behavior in what concerns not only yourself but others also. For it is impossible to please God if you do not live amicably with others, nor will you have peace of soul unless you show consideration for those for whom you ought to be a source of edification.

4   Pray to God, I beg you, that he may touch your heart and make you docile to his will.

5   Take pains to please him in all you do. For my part, I will also pray for this intention for you.

6   Please do not let the troubles you experience prevent you from making your retreat and learning from them to be completely obedient. Make your retreat because I ask it of you.

> I am, my very dear Brother,
> Devotedly yours in Our Lord,
> DE LA SALLE

———— ◆ ————

A comparison of the sources of Letters 45, 46, and 47 helps us to see in them a unity. Ms. 22 gives them as fourth, third, and second in a series, while Blain records them in a single chapter of his biography. Three out of four of Blain's extracts appear consecutively on pages 443 and 444 of volume 2 of his biography (CL 8). Since Letter 46 bears the date 1709 (though only on the copy in Ms. 22 and so is listed as conjectural) and since all three seem to have succeeded each other at short intervals, they are all dated that year.

LETTER 48
To Brother Robert

AM; AMG; EC 62; BL I.48

November 3, [1710]

1   Please be prudent, my very dear Brother, and don't do anything rash.

2   We shall take the best measures we can for your community.

3   Please go to Rouen and tell the Director that he is to give you Brother Louis to live in community with you.

4   He is a good Brother and I know you will be satisfied with him.

> I am, my very dear Brother,
> Devotedly yours in Our Lord,
> DE LA SALLE

I will shortly write to you more fully. I am in a hurry to catch the post.

———— ◆ ————

From the tone of this short letter, it would seem that some crisis had arisen in the community. Perhaps trouble developed between the young Brother and Brother Robert. Knowing Robert's hasty temper, De La Salle warns him against imprudent action and replaces the second member of the community with Brother Louis from Rouen.

Brother Louis, Jean Robin, was born on March 18, 1688, in the Diocese of Dijon and entered the novitiate at Saint Yon on March 17, 1709, but he completed his novitiate in Paris when the novices moved there during the famine. He began his teaching career in Rouen in October 1710. Later he was in Rethel as Director and signed the record of Brother Barthélemy's visit there in 1717. He assisted at the General Chapter of that year, and also at the Chapters of 1720 and 1725. He made perpetual vows on August 15, 1725, in accordance with the Bull of Approbation. Brother Louis died a saintly death in 1728 after many years of ill health. Blain included a short life of Brother Louis among those whom he considered most closely followed De La Salle as his exemplary disciples (CL 8: supplement, 80–84).

LETTER 49
To Brother Ponce

Brother Ponce, Poncelet Thiseux, is not listed in the *Catalogue* of 1714, but in the *Livret des premiers voeux,* which listed Brothers who took vows between 1694 and 1705; he is named as having made perpetual vows on September 26, 1696.

Blain speaks of Brother Ponce's harsh treatment of the young Brothers when in 1702 he was Director in Paris. This resulted in the enmity of De La Chétardie toward De La Salle. (See commentary on Letter 19.) We learn from the opening lines of Letter 49, that Brother Ponce still had a problem dealing kindly with others.

In Letter 19, dated September 4, 1705, De La Salle mentions to Gabriel Drolin that Brother Ponce is in charge of the schools in Rouen. Later in September, 1706, Ponce was sent to Avignon, then to Mende in 1707, and back to Avignon in 1708. He exercised the role of representative of De La Salle in the south probably as early as 1707. In 1711 he organized the school in Vans which opened in November. That is the last reference to him and it is probable that he left the Institute around that time, which was a period of considerable trouble for De La Salle in Marseilles. (See the commentary on Letter 19 for the suspicion surrounding Brother Ponce's departure. See also Letters 64 and 64(A) for further references to Brother Ponce.)

Letter 49: To Brother Ponce
Ms. 22, 16; AMG; EC 70; BL III.16; CL 8: 481

[January, 1706]

1   You should be most careful, my very dear Brother, not to speak so haughtily, as you tell me you sometimes do. The Spirit of God does not allow that sort of talk.

2   So let humility and gentleness be always evident in what you say. "A soft answer," says the Wise Man, "breaks down the hardest nature." Nothing will make you more pleasing to God and men than these two virtues.

3   But if you ought to speak to your Brothers with humility and gentleness, you ought to be no less careful to act in the same way toward people outside the community. Saint Paul requires this of all Christians.

4   So never rebuff anyone; that gives very bad example. On the contrary, speak politely, which is altogether in keeping with the Spirit of God.

5   You must be on your guard against speaking too freely with your students, for this takes away all respect.

6   In class you must avoid levity, for it does a lot of harm.

7   It is against our rules to teach catechism in church.

8   Women are not to be admitted.

9   Students are not to be given anything to drink.

10   You are not just to ask for a Mass on the feast of Saint
      Nicolas, but offer a stipend for one to be said.
            I am, my very dear Brother,
            Devotedly yours in Our Lord,
            DE LA SALLE

--------- ✦ ---------

Although some of the letters included in Ms. 22 bear the complete date
on which they were written, Letter 49 bears simply "1706. R." This has
led to the assumption that it was addressed to a Brother in Reims, Rethel,
or Rouen. Of these, the schools in Reims and Rethel date back to the first
years of De La Salle's founding of the Institute of the Brothers. In both
places the methods and practices he had established for teaching were well-
known and accepted. The schools in Rouen, however, were founded more
recently in 1705. The Brothers there were already having problems with
the administration of the Hospice for the Poor, to which they were at first
attached. They had to put up with opposition to De La Salle's concept
of the Christian school and to teaching catechism in the school. The supposition that this letter had been sent to Rouen would make understand-
able De La Salle's insistence in paragraph 7 that the Brothers teach
catechism, not in the church, but in the school. Catechism was to be an
essential part of the Christian schools of the Brothers. We see this same
emphasis in his remarks to Brother Gabriel Drolin in Letter 18, August
28, 1705.

The prohibition against teaching catechism in church is probably an
interpretation of the Rule of 1705, chapter 1, article 2: "They [the Brothers]
cannot be priests, nor aspire to the clerical state, nor even sing or wear
a surplice, nor carry out any other function in church."

The prohibition of women (*personne d'autre sexe*), mentioned in
paragraph 8, is not completely clear. If it refers to girls, the word would
be *filles*, as in the Rule of 1706 (chapter IX, article 20). If it refers to women
attending the catechism lesson, such a practice would be contrary to the
principle described in the *Conduite des Ecoles chrétiennes* of 1706: "Concerning the externs who assist at catechism on Sundays and feasts" (CL
24: 232–233). It is not known whether this practice was authorized before
1706, but if so, it certainly would have been followed on an experimental
basis before being so precisely authorized in 1706. The lessons were evidently a tribute to the reputation of the Brothers as catechists at that time.

The *Conduite des Ecoles chrétiennes* spells out the custom alluded to in paragraph 9 to be observed while the students are eating breakfast and lunch in school (CL 24: 9). In the *Conduite* there is no mention of any kind of drink being given to the students.

The feast of Saint Nicolas, patron of children, was a full holiday instead of Thursday. The students, however, were required to attend Mass on that feast. De La Salle specifies in paragraph 10 that the Director maintain an independence of the parish clergy by having a Mass offered (i.e., paying the stipend), not just asking that a Mass be said.

LETTER 50
To Brother Clément

Brother Clément, Jacques Gatelet, was born on September 28, 1684, at Romagne in the Diocese of Reims. He entered the novitiate on April 20, 1700, and made his novitiate in Paris. He made his perpetual vows in accordance with the Bull of Approbation in the year 1725. In 1745, he was a member of the community of Meaux as Director. He died at the age of 69 at Meaux in 1753.

Letter 50: To Brother Clément
Copy; AMG; EC 9; BL II.3

June 26, 1706

1   I am greatly consoled, my very dear Brother, that your rheumatism is cured. Take care, I beg you, to be very prudent and also to conform yourself in all things to God's will, with a submission that is not only external but from the heart too.

2   Take care not to slap your students; you know that is forbidden by the rules.

3   I am very glad that you have a good confessor and that he gives you such good advice. Try to take advantage of this as long as you have him.

4   If you wish to become interior, it is a matter of great importance for you to control your mind and your eyes. Without this kind of mortification, it is almost impossible to make much progress in virtue.

5   Make sure that you are indifferent as to what you are ordered under obedience. This is one of the things which most of all will draw upon you the grace of God.

6   It is a good practice to read the rules often in order to be quite faithful to them. As you know, it will be their observance that will ensure your sanctification.

7   Having God in view in all your spiritual exercises will contribute most to your making them well. God not only requires the outward appearance of your actions; he wishes them to be carried out with interior dispositions.

8   Take only one defect at a time in your daily examination of conscience, and keep at it for several days consecutively.

9   If you know what I should do to save the Brothers' schools from ruin, please let me know, for we must take the means to keep them going.

10   I think we must dismiss the students who are not regular in their attendance or who come late, for to tolerate either the one or the other brings about disorder in the school.

11   During the holidays we shall see what can be done regarding a Director for you. In matters of conscience do the best you can until then.

12   You don't have to conform to the other Brothers in matters of food unless you feel completely well.

I am, my very dear Brother,
Devotedly yours in Our Lord,
DE LA SALLE

———— ✦ ————

This letter is preserved only in a copy, which was probably made in 1784 or 1785. At the time that it was written to Brother Clément, he was a member of the community of Laon, under the Directorship of Brother Hubert (Letters 7 to 12). From the recommendations in paragraph 10 concerning school policy, it appears that Clément was in charge of one of the schools attached to the community. De La Salle shows himself solicitous for Brother Clément's health and welfare, urging him, in paragraph 12, to excuse himself from the regulations concerning the type and quantity of food to be served to the Brothers. Brother Clément is also mentioned in Letter 64(A).

LETTER 51
To Brother Séverin

Nothing at all is known of Brother Séverin except what can be learned from this letter. The manuscript of this letter bears the heading "Paris,

July 13, 1706," and on the reverse is written, also in the Founder's hand-writing, "Brother Séverin, Saint Yon." This manuscript was found together with manuscripts of letters to Brother Mathias and to Brother Paulin in Pernes, near Avignon.

Letter 51: To Brother Séverin
AM; AMG; EC 63; BL I.18

Paris
July 13, 1706

1   There is no reason, my very dear Brother, for you to upset your conscience for having, as you say, slandered a woman who has died.

2   It is neither necessary nor advisable for you to go to the place where you uttered it in order to repair the calumny.

3   For that you have only to follow the advice of your confessor, that is, to write to the pastor of the parish and ask him to tell the woman's husband that what was said of his dead wife is untrue and that the person who made the statement retracts it as being a falsehood.

4   Once you have done this, I absolve you of all guilt before God. So you are not to worry yourself any more about it.
    I am, my very dear Brother,
    Devotedly yours in Our Lord,
    DE LA SALLE

———— ✦ ————

This letter is probably in answer to a plea for advice from a young man who recently entered the novitiate and whose conscience was assailed by guilt for an earlier fault which has been grossly exaggerated by the novice's sensitivity. De La Salle, out of his vast experience as confessor and director of souls, suggests a solution to the young man's problem and reduces his fears to appropriate proportions.

Letters 52 to 54
To Brother Joseph

Brother Joseph, Jean Leroux, was born on February 18, 1678, and entered the novitiate of the Brothers at Vaugirard, Paris, in 1697. Brother Joseph began teaching in Paris; but after De La Salle and the Brothers lost the court cases brought against them by the Writing Masters in 1704 and 1706, which forced the closing of the Brothers' schools there, he moved to Rouen. There he was in charge of the community and the schools attached to it, with authority that extended to the Brothers at Darnétal also. Joseph was later appointed the representative of De La Salle to the communities and schools in the neighborhood of Reims in 1708, and subsequently to the communities further afield in the northern part of France. (See Letters 52 (a, b, and c).)

At the Chapter of 1717, Joseph was elected one of the Assistants to Brother Barthélemy. In August 1725, he was the Director-General of the communities at Saint Yon, where he died on February 18, 1729.

Blain eulogizes Brother Joseph briefly in his biographical sketch of Brother Barthélemy, which is at the end of his biography of De La Salle (CL 8: supplement, 28).

LETTER 52
To Brother Joseph

Ms. 22, 28; AMG; EC 75; BL III.28

[December, 1706]

1   You can readily see, my very dear Brother, that you should not get upset so easily about transfers from one community to another.

2   Surely you can see that the position you are in now suits you better than your former one.

3   I find it quite inconvenient to make changes.

4   I am convinced that you could put an end to the disorder brought about by Brother's students in church and to their lack of discipline in class. That is why I ask you to see that things are done in our traditional way.

5   As you can see, if I were to give in easily in this matter of transfers, it would be imprudent and people could well be annoyed.

6   I am sorry, my very dear Brother, that I left without say-
    ing good-bye. I sent for you several times but, as you did
    not come, I thought you were not in the house.

7   Please see that there is good order in the community. If
    things do not go well, I will be pleased if you let me
    know.

8   Take care that the classes run well. I will do my best to
    support your efforts.

9   My good wishes to Brother M.
        I am, my very dear Brother,
        Devotedly yours in Our Lord,
        DE LA SALLE

———— ✦ ————

While there is no direct evidence to indicate the recipient of this letter
or the time it was written, "Brother M" suggests the name of Brother Martinien, who was a member of the community at Rouen at the same time
as Brother Paulin, that is, from October 1705. Brother Joseph was named
Director of the four schools at Rouen in October 1706; responsibility for
these several schools might explain his absence from the community house,
referred to in paragraph 6. It is probable that De La Salle visited the
community in November 1706, and wrote this letter to Brother Joseph,
as Director, in December. For this reason it is included here with the others
addressed to him, although the *Edition Critique* classifies it among the
anonymous letters.

LETTER 52(a)
To Brother Joseph

AM; AMG; EC 41(a); BL IV.4

July 15, 1708

I, the undersigned, Priest, Doctor of Theology, Superior of
the Brothers of the Christian Schools, send our Brother
Joseph to make the visitation of the communities of
Rethel, Guise, Laon, and Reims. For this reason I enjoin
the Directors of these communities to receive this Brother
in this capacity and inform him of all that takes place in
their community.
    Given at Paris, this fifteenth day of July 1708.
    DE LA SALLE

LETTER 52(b)
To Brother Joseph

AM; AMG; EC 41(b); BL IV.4

July 30, 1709

I, the undersigned, Priest, Doctor of Theology, Superior of the Brothers of the Christian Schools, send our very dear Brother Joseph to the communities of Guise, Laon, Reims, Rethel, and Troyes in order to carry out the visitation of these communities.

In testimony of this I have signed this document.
Given at Paris, this thirtieth day of July 1709.
DE LA SALLE

LETTER 52(c)
To Brother Joseph

AM; AMG; EC 41(c); BL IV.4

November 16, 1711

I, the undersigned, Priest, Doctor of Theology, Superior of the Brothers of the Christian Schools, declare to all whom it may concern that I send our very dear Brother Joseph of the aforesaid Society to carry out the visitation of the communities of Moulins, Dijon, Troyes, Reims, Rethel, Laon, Guise, Calais, Boulogne, Rouen, Saint Yon, Darnétal, Chartres, Versailles, and Saint Denis which are dependent on the Society of the Christian Schools.

In testimony of this, I have signed this document.
Given at Paris, this sixteenth day of November 1711.
DE LA SALLE

———— ♦ ————

The above three documents, given in legal form called "obediences," delegated to Brother Joseph the power of the Superior. They indicate the growth of administration in the expanding Institute of the Brothers. Brother Ponce held a similar position in regard to the communities of the south of France.

LETTER 53
To Brother Joseph

AM; AMG; EC 40; BL I.35

December 23, [1710]

1 I received your letter at midday today, my very dear Brother.

2 On Saturday I will set out for Troyes. Don't leave; wait for me there. I will be there on Monday and we will discuss all the business concerning that town and your proposals about those properties at Reims.

3 Don't tell anyone, not even Brother Albert, that I have to go there.

4 I will do my best to bring things to a successful conclusion and to everyone's satisfaction.

> I am, my very dear Brother,
> Devotedly yours in Our Lord,
> DE LA SALLE

5 See that no action is taken with regard to the closing of the school before I arrive.

6 Please pay the postage of this letter to M. Bourgoing.

———— ◆ ————

Mention of Troyes in paragraph 2 determines the date of this letter as 1710. The Brothers in that town had been given the use of the presbytery for their living accommodations by the parish priest, who was also the superior of the Seminary and lived there. On his death, the new parish priest, not being the superior of the Seminary, requested that the Brothers' use of the presbytery be terminated. By December 1710 the situation had become delicate and threatened the closure of the school. Brother Joseph was present on visitation in the community of Troyes at that time, but evidently De La Salle thought that his own presence was warranted. His intervention was successful and the school continued, for Troyes is mentioned as one of the communities listed in the deed of conveyance drawn up by De La Salle on November 14, 1718 (CL 26: 313).

De La Salle had refused to establish the first schools of the Brothers with his personal fortune. Rather, he distributed his fortune to the poor during the famine of 1683–1684, preferring, as he said, to found his schools on Providence. Still, this attitude of dependence on Divine Providence did not prevent him from doing his utmost to see that the Institute that he had founded was able to continue its work unhindered by problems of finance. Therefore he formed a group of trustworthy men, which included his brother, Canon Jean-Louis, to purchase properties that would provide revenue to supplement the meagre income of the Brothers in charge of the schools and to help support the novitiate. In paragraph 2 of this letter, we learn that Brother Joseph, Assistant, had some ideas regarding the use of this revenue which he wished to discuss with De La Salle.

Brother Albert, mentioned in paragraph 3, was Director of the community and school at Troyes. He was the Brother often spoken of to Gabriel Drolin as the one who would be able to put things right in a matter of six months or so. Drolin was not keen to have him with him in Rome. In paragraph 20 of Letter 31, dated December 16, 1712, and addressed to Drolin, De La Salle refers to the remark made by Father Ricordeau about the dissension in the community of Troyes.

On the back of this Letter 53, written in Brother Joseph's hand, is a prayer that illustrates his religious spirit: "My God, I promise you to keep my resolutions with the help of your grace. I desire always to do everything I can to be obedient in all my actions with a view to please you. I will endeavor to speak softly and not allow myself to be carried away by natural impulse but to have great kindness toward our dear Brothers on occasions that arise and to keep careful watch over my tongue when I am obliged to speak with people outside the community, to be completely guided by you on all occasions. It is, O my God, under the protection of the Most Blessed Virgin, of Saint Joseph, and my guardian angel that I place my resolutions, O my lovable Savior."

On the back of Letter 54 Brother Joseph wrote again, this time his uncomplimentary description of Brother Bernard, the early biographer of De La Salle (CL 4: XIII, n. 1).

LETTER 54
To Brother Joseph

AM; AMG; EC 41; BL I.40

February 6, [1711]

1   I received your three letters all at the same time, my very dear Brother, and am answering the most urgent of them.

2   It seems advisable that Brother Placide go to Guise.

3   I am having Brother Fabien set out with the young Brother from Mende who is to take Brother Placide's place. In two or three years he will be better able to profit from the novitiate than he is at present, and he will become a capable teacher.

4   Let Brother Fabien have the horse to come back here; he will be at Reims on Tuesday evening.

5   Brother Dosithée would not have written to you if you had not first written to him, nor would the Brothers from Guise.

6   I don't know why you write like this to the Brothers just according to whim. It is not a wise thing to do. There should be no correspondence like that from one community to another; it is unbecoming among Brothers like us. If you wish to prevent it, you must not do it yourself.

7   It is to be hoped that M. Bourgeois has learned how to sew and how to cut hair well. This is important.

8   I don't know if a young man, a stonemason, has called to see you since I left. If he still seeks admission, you must put him off until after Easter. But they must not both enter at the same time.

9   Please see that Brother Rémi is given what he needs. He mentioned to Brother Thomas that he required wool for a pair of stockings, for he had none, and for an undershirt.

    I am, my very dear Brother,
    Devotedly yours in Our Lord,
    DE LA SALLE

———— ✦ ————

The autograph manuscript of this letter does not tell us the year in which it was written, but the internal evidence indicates that it should be dated 1711.

Brother Placide, Thomas Gayot, mentioned in paragraph 2, was born on July 25, 1691, in the Diocese of Laon and entered the novitiate in Paris on April 29, 1710. He died on December 20, 1714, at the age of 23, in Rethel, where he was in charge of the school.

The young Brother from Mende mentioned in paragaph 3 is no doubt the first vocation to come from the recently founded school in that town. The town of Mende in the district of the Cévennes was considered as a stronghold of the Camisards, the White Shirts, and of Protestantism. In spite of the violent civil war which was waged against the Camisards from 1702 to 1705, the Protestant Church of the region was far from vanquished. The bishop, as part of his campaign to win over the Protestants, asked the Brothers to take charge of the free school in the town. As with other young aspirants, two of whom are mentioned in Letter 3, as well as the Brother Irénée addressed in Letter 119, the young Brother from Mende was given a probationary period of some years in class before he entered the novitiate proper.

The young Brother's name was Brother Benedict, Robert Esbrayat. He was born on October 21, 1694, in Mende and has been characterized as the first vocation for the Institute from mission territory, in that the region of Cévennes was mostly Protestant at this time. He entered the Institute on September 15, 1711, apparently having made such a favorable impression on De La Salle that he did not have to wait the two or three years of probation mentioned in paragraph 3. He signed the record of Brother Barthélemy's visit to the community of Laon on March 4, 1717. He made perpetual vows at Saint Yon in 1728, participated in the General Chapter of 1734 as a professed Brother, and was Director of the school in Dieppe in 1744. He died there in 1750.

Though Brother Joseph was De La Salle's representative in the northern region, in paragraph 6 he is clearly reprimanded for his unnecessary correspondence. As with useless talk, De La Salle was very strict with regard to useless correspondence. There are numerous references to this stricture in his letters to Gabriel Drolin. It was also mentioned specifically in the Common Rules of 1705. "The Brothers will not write any letters simply for reasons of friendship or kindness or to their relatives, nor shall they write any without evident necessity or without permission" (CL 25: 91).

Brother Dosithée, Joseph's correspondent mentioned in paragraph 5, was a mature man of 37 when he entered the novitiate at Saint Yon. He had been a well-to-do owner of a vineyard and had followed an extensive course of classical studies. He successively became the Director of Rouen, prefect of the young men committed to the house of detention of Saint Yon, procurator of the Institute in Paris, and in 1729, Assistant to the Superior General, Brother Timothée, as a replacement for Brother Joseph. He died in 1737, surrounded by the attentive care of his associate in the Assistancy, Brother Irénée. The obituary notices of the eighteenth century record that his death took place "in the perfect love of God and detachment from all things."

M. Bourgeois, mentioned in paragraph 7, was born in 1696 in the Diocese of Laon, and applied to the Institute as a serving Brother, intending to be a tailor and a barber. He entered the novitiate at the age of 15 on May 13, 1711, and took the name of Brother Pascal. According to *Edition Critique,* he died in the Institute prior to 1716, and in March of that year another Brother took the name of Pascal.

Of Brother Rémi, mentioned in paragraph 9, little is known. He apparently was in the community of Rethel in 1706 and in Reims in 1711. He may have died before 1716 because another Brother Rémi is listed that year in the record of names.

Letters 55 to 64
To Brother Mathias

No definite information has come to light about the identity of Brother Mathias. His name does not appear in the *Catalogue* of 1714. It is probable that he left the Institute some time before July 1, 1710, since another Mathias, a certain Laurent de Douay, received the habit on that day. Battersby attributes these letters to this second Brother Mathias. However, this attribution is not possible, since the latter entered after these letters had been written.

The ten letters addressed to Brother Mathias were found in the attic of a house in Pernes, near Avignon, about 1850, and were deposited in the Institute Archives in 1864. They were all written within a span of a year and a half, from December 3, 1706, to May 16, 1708, while Mathias was first in a Reims community, then transferred to Paris at his request early in 1707, then transferred again at his request to Mende in June of 1707. At Mende he was eager to be sent back to Paris. In Letter 64(A) written by Brother Ponce, Brother Mathias was being transferred again, this time to Avignon in June of 1708. He probably left the Institute from Avignon to reside in nearby Pernes where the letters were found.

De La Salle's letters to him reveal Mathias as a man of changeable temperament and of irascible disposition, but a capable teacher in spite of his deplorable handwriting and spelling and his apparent inability to compose a readable letter.

LETTER 55
To Brother Mathias

AM; AMG; EC 42; BL I.20

December 3, [1706]

1   You are the first one to whom I am writing this month, my very dear Brother.

2   I want nothing more than to be able to comfort you in your troubles, but you must see that I cannot do so unless I know what they are. I am not at all sure what worries you.

3   You simply tell me that you are not well. I do not know if this is your only reason for asking to come back to Paris or to be sent elsewhere. Let me know what the cause of it all is.

4   You tell me hardly anything in your letters. A thing that needs saying only once, you repeat over and over again.

5   Let me know all your problems. If they come from the fact that I don't write to you, from now on I will write to you every time that I write to the Brothers. But, please, make sure that your letters are written in a better hand and with better spelling, for I can hardly read them.

6   In your prayer, continue to occupy yourself with the preparatory acts. You are doing well to apply yourself to become interiorly recollected and to avoid distractions.

7   The only reason you give me for transferring you is that you do not fit in with the community in Reims. Surely you realize that in our Society we must adapt ourselves to wherever we may be sent by our Superiors, since obedience is the principal rule and the source of the greatest contentment among the Brothers.

8   I do not understand what you mean by saying that you are disgusted with the way you are treated. Explain this to me, and I will try to remedy what troubles you.

9   Be assured, my very dear Brother, that I want only your welfare and peace of mind, and that I am
       Devotedly yours in Our Lord,
       DE LA SALLE

———— ✦ ————

The line in paragraph 5, "from now on I will write to you every time that I write to the Brothers," was originally written by De La Salle as "from now on I will write to you every time that the Brothers write to me." The original line was then crossed out and the present wording written between the lines. This change made by De La Salle himself would seem to indicate that he would answer only those letters from the Brothers that required an answer, that he did not answer all letters, but for Mathias he would not fail to answer all his letters. If it is true that De La Salle did not answer all of the letters from the Brothers, this would be one reason why there are fewer letters of De La Salle extant than would be expected. (See also Letter 4, paragraph 1, where De La Salle says that he was unable to answer two letters because he did not have time.)

LETTER 56
To Brother Mathias

AM; AMG; EC 43; BL I.23

Paris
November 18, 1707

1   I received your first letter, my very dear Brother, the day
     before yesterday, and today the second one, which was for-
     warded to me from Rouen. You must always address your
     letters to Paris, no matter where I may be. I am writing
     you a reply on the day you say you are expecting an
     answer to your first one.

2   Who has been telling you that God does not want you to
     be doing what you are presently doing?

3   You are content, you are at peace, you are undisturbed,
     when you are supported by someone. I am well aware, my
     very dear Brother, that you need such support, and that
     once you have it, you will do well.

4   I know how you were while in Paris.

5   I think that your suffering is more mental than physical.

6   So long as you are obedient, God will support you.

7   I am sorry that you are distressed, and I will do all I can
     to remove the cause of your distress.

8   You ask me to let you come to Paris; surely you can see
     that winter is no time for that.

9   It is a good idea of yours to make a novena to ask God to
     grant that you may do his holy will. Give yourself com-
     pletely to his will; get on well with Brother and God will
     bless you.

10   I do not know in what way or by whom you are treated in
     such an inhuman manner.

11   I fail to see what Brother Ponce has done to you that is as
     annoying as you claim it to be. You allow yourself to get
     too upset and that does you a lot of harm.

12   Be assured that I will do all I possibly can for you and
     that I am, my very dear Brother,
         Devotedly yours in Our Lord,
         DE LA SALLE

———— ◆ ————

A letter dated March 22, 1707, written by Father Boulet from Paris, was
discovered in the departmental archives of Lozère, the department where
Mende is situated. The letter brings to light the aims the Archbishop of
Mende, François de Piencourt, hoped to achieve as the result of the

establishment of the Brothers in his diocese. He envisaged a cluster of small schools in the area, those for girls to be managed by the Sisters of the Infant Jesus, founded by Father Barré, and those for the boys to be managed by teachers trained by the Brothers in a kind of teacher-training program similar to the one established by De La Sale in Reims in 1687 and in Paris in 1699. Brothers Mathias and Sébastien arrived from Paris to form the new community under the direction of Brother Ponce. That De La Salle chose Mathias to be a member of the community that would open such a school attests to the Brother's capability as a teacher. In fact, the municipal council wrote a letter of thanks to the archbishop assuring him that "the three Brothers of Father De La Salle's Society have begun their classes with wonderful success." But Mathias did not get along with Brother Ponce and requested an early transfer back to Paris.

Unfortunately Bishop Piencourt had not long to live, and even though he provided generously for the Brothers in his will, the plan to have a teacher-training program for his diocese was never realized by the Brothers.

Brother Sébastien, Jean-Baptiste Terrion, was born on March 5, 1682, in the Diocese of Reims and entered the Institute on May 22, 1701. He was in Paris in 1706 when the Brothers were indicted there. He was Mathias' companion in Mende until 1708, when he participated in the foundation in Grenoble. He was in Chartres when Brother Barthélemy visited there in 1716 and made his perpetual profession at Saint Yon in 1725. Later he was Director of the community in Calais, attended the Chapter of 1734 as former Director of Calais, and died in Guise on June 20, 1745.

Brother Ponce is undoubtedly the same Brother mentioned in Letters 19, 49, and 64(A). (See the commentaries on these letters.)

LETTER 57
To Brother Mathias

AM; AMG; EC 44; BL I.24

December 30, [1707]

1   I don't know why, my very dear Brother, you write so impolitely to me and say things so contrary to the truth.

2   Up to the present I have given you no cause for this, since I have done nothing that was not for your own good and sent you where you are now only after you had insistently requested it over a very long period of time.

3   Instead of telling your problems to people outside the community, tell them to Brother Ponce or write to him if he is not at Mende.

4   I have delegated him to attend to all that needs to be
    done for the welfare of the Brothers in that area.

5   You should not have been so insistent that I send you so
    far away and then want to return so soon afterwards. Sure-
    ly you can see that we cannot have the Brothers come back
    from such a distance before Easter and that journeys are
    not to be undertaken to avoid the Lenten fast.

6   You may be sure, my very dear Brother, that, acting on
    what Brother Ponce tells me, I will do all that is best
    for you. So, let him know all your difficulties and your
    thoughts. In doing so you will find that God will give you
    his blessing.

    I am, my very dear Brother,
    Devotedly yours in Our Lord,
    DE LA SALLE

---------------◆---------------

This letter gives the earliest direct indication from De La Salle that Brother
Ponce had been commissioned by him not only as Director of the community of Mende but also as the representative of De La Salle for the communities of Avignon, Marseilles, and Alès.

LETTER 58
To Brother Mathias

AM; AMG; EC 45; BL 1.25

January 13, [1708]

1   I think, my very dear Brother, that you bring very little
    attention and very little affection to carrying out your
    spiritual exercises. However, you will draw God's blessings
    on yourself only by performing them out of love and as
    best you can.

2   You write to me in a very angry manner, and that is not
    good at all, for I have not given you any reason for doing
    so.

3   If I have sent you where you are now, it was only after
    you had begged me for three months to send you a long
    way off.

4   As for your problems, as long as you write to me in con-
    fidence, I shall try to solve them.

5   I will see that you are led to God through kindness and
     not through harshness. There is nothing that I will not do
     for your welfare and salvation. But, on your part, you
     must act more graciously and not through whim or pas-
     sion.

6   Do you take time for prayer? Do you receive Communion?
     It is very difficult to do so in the dispositions you have.

7   Take time for prayer, my very dear Brother, and ask God
     to let his holy will be done in you. I will often ask this of
     him too.

8   You must turn to God, my very dear Brother, and work
     hard at your salvation. Do not misuse the means God
     gives you for this purpose.

9   Two of your brothers came here on Sunday and asked me
     to write and tell you to remain peacefully in your voca-
     tion, saying that you could not be better off.

10   Those people you have been to see don't know you very
     well.

11   I will often pray to God for you. I wish you a happy and
     holy New Year, and I am, my very dear Brother,

         Devotedly yours in Our Lord,
         [*The signature of this letter has been cut off.*]

12   You ask permission to write to your relatives and you have
     already done so. That is not the right thing to do.

LETTER 59
To Brother Mathias

AM; AMG; EC 46; BL I.27

February 8, [1708]

1   I am very sorry, my very dear Brother, that my letters an-
     noy you. I write nothing to you, however, that could cause
     you annoyance. I write as cordially as I can and write
     nothing but for your good. So I think you should take it
     in good part.

2   I am happy that you faithfully carry out your respon-
     sibilities, as you say you do. I do not know this, although
     you say that I do.

3   I would have been careful not to have given you permis-
     sion to write to your relatives, seeing that, before I

Letter 60, to Brother Mathias

answered your letter, your two brothers came to tell me
that you had written twice to your mother who had died,
and that your letter had been sent on to them. Surely you
can see that to write before asking to do so is very wrong.

4 I am quite distressed that you are not well. Be careful,
however, that your illness is not merely imaginary, for you
seemed better in Paris than you said you were.

5 I have not been at all inclined to bring you back to Paris.
I did not agree to your making such a long journey only
to have you come back so soon.

6 Please, do not make a great fuss over such trifles as you
do.

7 I think I mentioned that your brothers asked me to tell
you to stay where you are, that it is for your own good
and is the best thing you can do. I am delighted that you
feel the same way and wish to remain where you are.

8 Please don't give way to your whims or follow the first
idea that comes into your head.

9 I will see to it that you are satisfied with those you live
with.

10 After Easter I will try to send you to some place other
than Mende, since that is your wish.

    I am, my very dear Brother,
    Devotedly yours in Our Lord,
    DE LA SALLE

———— ✦ ————

This letter, sent almost a month after the previous one, seems for the most
part to repeat the earlier letter.

The original of the letter was kept by Brother Léandris, Assistant,
until his death in 1915 and was then placed in the archives of the
Generalate of the Brothers in Rome.

LETTER 60
To Brother Mathias

AM; AMG; EC 47; BL I.22

March 23, [1708]

1 I think you are as well off as you could be, my very dear
Brother, and that you ought to be satisfied with the
Brother who is charged with directing you now.

6.

Letter 61, to Brother Mathias

2 So, try to carry out your duties well and apply yourself to your spiritual exercises, for it is these that will sanctify you and lead you to God.

3 Resolve to become very recollected and to take all possible means to do so.

4 Act in such a way as to increase the number of your students as much as you can.

5 I am quite convinced that the Brother who is with you is not at all annoying and that you are satisfied with him.

6 Aren't you ashamed of saying, "Imagine such a handsome young man as I in such a vocation as this"?

7 You are very fortunate to be in your vocation, which is holy and leads to holiness and which does you honor both in this life and for your salvation.

8 What a wonderfully handsome young man you are! How can you talk about yourself like that! Is this the way a religious should speak?

9 If I am not satisfied with the letters you write, it is because you sometimes write offensively. Be careful to write more discreetly and more courteously.

10 Surely you see that it is very wrong to get angry and to harbor resentment.

11 You also see that it is very bad to lose your temper and follow your feelings; that is to act more like an animal than a reasonable being.

12 Take care not to let yourself be carried away by impatience in class, for that is not the way to establish order or silence.

13 Answering back is detrimental to the obedience you should practice.

14 It is very wrong to let yourself be carried away by every idea that comes into your head, for many such thoughts are wrong.

15 Let yourself be guided by obedience and you will see that God will bless you.

16 I beg him to pour out his graces on you, and I am, my very dear Brother,

>Devotedly yours in Our Lord,
>DE LA SALLE

◆

We learn from paragraph 1 that Brother Mathias is now under a new Director. We learn from other documents that it is Brother Antoine who has been appointed as Director of the community at Mende. Brother Ponce has been transferred to direct the house at Avignon, while Brother Albert, of whose organizing ability De La Salle speaks so highly, has moved on from Avignon to take over the direction of the schools in Rouen. Brother Antoine's handwriting is to be found on the majority of the vow formulas from 1694 to 1705; possibly he acted as secretary to De La Salle during that period.

Brother Antoine, Jean Partois, was born on October 20, 1666, in Reims. He was one of the earliest followers of De La Salle, having entered the Institute in September 1686. He is listed second in the *Catalogue* of 1714 after Gabriel Drolin. He was one of the 12 who pronounced the first perpetual vows in 1694. He was Director of the community in Laon, 1701–1702, founded the school in Dijon in 1705, and after two years as Director in Mende went to Paris with a document authorizing safe-conduct written by the bishop. He was in Dijon again in 1717 and Director there in 1725, when he made his profession in accordance with the Bull of Approbation. He was Sub-Director at Saint Yon in 1734 and died there on April 1, 1743.

LETTER 61
To Brother Mathias

AM; AMG; EC 48; BL I.28

April 4, [1708]

1   I am delighted, my very dear Brother, that you now have such good intentions and that you are prepared to remain faithful to your vocation, which will surely lead you to holiness and to the fulfillment of your responsibilities.

2   I don't think that I will place you with Brother Cyprien. Brother Albert is not the type for you. You often don't realize what you are asking.

3   I would very much like to know if there is anything at the moment that prevents you from staying in your present community.

4   You have reason, I think, to be satisfied with the Brother who is your Director, and so I think that God wants you to remain at peace and stay with him. Since you ask me to do all that is needed for your welfare, that seems to me to be best.

5   Why will it be better for you that I change you as soon as possible? I don't think it is. You are with a fine Brother who will give you good example.

6   You are right in asking pardon of me for your letters, for they have sometimes been not only very tactless but also very offensive, and I don't know how anyone can write in such a fashion.

7   I have tried, however, not to take offense and, for my part, not to get annoyed.

8   You ask me to let you be with good Brothers, and so you are. What are you complaining about? Please be more consistent, steady and obedient; otherwise God will not bless you.

9   I recommend myself to your prayers during this holy season and I am, my very dear Brother,

> Devotedly yours in Our Lord,
> DE LA SALLE

———— ✦ ————

Little is known of the Brother Cyprien mentioned in paragraph 2. He is on none of the lists of names kept for this period, except in the history of the community of Rethel. There he is listed as having been Director and having died there in 1713. Another Brother taking the name Cyprien is listed as entering the Institute on May 12, 1713, which confirms the death of the first Cyprien before that date.

Brother Albert mentioned in paragraph 2 is also named in Letter 16. He was evidently a good administrator, having founded the schools in Avignon, Marseilles, and Valréas. De La Salle speaks favorably of this ability in Letter 19. Brother Félix-Paul in the *Edition Critique* suggests that Brother Albert had a natural inclination to deal with the public and a lack of deep religious spirit. It was for these reasons that De La Salle did not think he was the right Director for Mathias.

LETTER 62
To Brother Mathias

AM; AMG; EC 49; BL I.29

April 13, [1708]

1   I am very pleased, my very dear Brother, that you are now disposed to remain willingly in the Community. I will try to help you as much as I can with your problems.

2   I will take steps to see that you do not stay much longer in your present community, but you must be patient a little longer.

3   You will not be put to inconvenience, I assure you, but you must follow your rules and the same rules as everywhere else. You are well aware that there cannot be variations from one community to another.

4   I am told that your community is very lax. Perhaps you are given too much freedom. You must get back on the same footing as regards fidelity to the Rule as you were in Paris.

5   I am told that you take meals out of the house. You know that that is quite contrary to the rules and that you are never to visit anyone at all.

6   You must carry out not only your class duties, but also the other exercises, for classwork without the spiritual exercises will not do.

7   When you have made your spiritual exercises faithfully for a while, you will have no more difficulty with them. You have to be hard on yourself for some time out of love for God.

8   Let me know if Brother Antoine follows a different routine from the one usual in the Society and in what way his differs from that followed by Brother Ponce. But write to me only at the time Brother Antoine does.

9   I am told that Brother Sébastien's shoes were too small for him, but that they fit you. Take them for yourself and don't wait to be told twice.

10 We will have to get a pair of breeches made for you, if you need them. I will see that you are given what you need.

11 So be faithful in carrying out your rules and God will bless you and shower his graces on you.

12 Ask him in prayer to keep you always in the dispositions you are now in to go wherever he pleases.

13 I also beg you to be always very obedient to your Director.
        I am, my very dear Brother,
        Devotedly yours in Our Lord,
        DE LA SALLE

———— ✦ ————

According to the *Edition Critique*, De La Salle uses the word "Community" in the first sentence of this letter to refer to the Institute, not the local community. This supposition is based on Mathias' earlier indications of uncertainty about persevering as a Brother. That De La Salle uses the word in this way reflects his earlier use of it to speak of his project of the

Christian Schools, as in the *Mémoire sur l'habit*. It was also a general term used to speak of religious congregations. The use of the word *Société* appears in the formula of vows in 1694. The word *Institut* is used in the preface to the *Recueil* written in De La Salle's own hand (but not signed). The *Recueil* was first printed in 1711, and the preface also uses the word *communauté*, but in the general sense applicable to all congregations.

LETTER 63
To Brother Mathias

AM; AMG; EC 50; BL I.30

[1708]

1   I don't know why you write so many letters to me at the same time, my very dear Brother. We can't afford so much postage. Include your letters with those of your Director; that will be enough, and never write without permission. You know well that things must be done in an orderly manner.

2   I will see that you are transferred soon.

3   So, be faithful to the Rule, circumspect and very obedient, for God will bless you only insofar as you are.

4   Why do you want breakfast on Sundays and feast days?

5   In your letters you often sound like one who is far from being obedient. For the love of God, make an effort to become very obedient, for this is most necessary for you.

6   I can see that you are fond of having your own freedom but, believe me, it will do you a great deal of harm.

7   You must be faithful to the Rule and ready to obey. Does Brother Antoine ask anything different of you from what would be required of you if you were here? If this is the case, let me know and I will put things right.

8   Brother Antoine is right in not allowing all this running about town. Surely you see that such behavior is unbecoming for Brothers. Perhaps you had too much freedom in the past. You can see that you need to correct yourself in this matter.

9   I pray that God may give you his Spirit and I am, my very dear Brother,

Devotedly yours in Our Lord,
DE LA SALLE

There is no date on the manuscript of this letter, but it fits in naturally between Letters 62 and 64, and in this way, can be dated late April or early May 1708. In paragraph 1 De La Salle points out one of the practical objections to frequent letter writing. The person to whom the letter was addressed had to pay the postage. So it was the custom for all the monthly letters from the community to be collected and sent off in one packet. De La Salle suffered from a chronic shortage of ready cash so that every sou counted. He mentioned in paragraph 15 of Letter 19 to Drolin that he had to make up his accounts every day in order to determine where he stood.

The manuscript Rule of 1705 mentions that the Brothers will take breakfast in the refectory at 7:15 A.M. on ordinary days, but there is no mention of this meal for Sundays and feast days. Paragraph 4 of this letter refers to this custom. The Rule simply states that on Sundays and feasts, "This [Mass] will be followed by reading in common of the New Testament. . . . At 8:00 A.M. the Brothers will gather in the oratory . . ." (CL 25). This oversight was corrected in the Rule of 1718.

LETTER 64
To Brother Mathias

AM; AMG; EC 51; BL I.31

May 16, [1708]

1   In reply to your two letters, my very dear Brother, I have to tell you that I have written to Brother Ponce asking him to go to Mende and put things in order. I think that he will be able to transfer you and put you in his community.

2   I am very happy to see that you are ready to go where I wish to place you. I am not prepared just now to bring you closer to Paris or to place you there.

3   I am very pleased that you are happy in the district you are now in and that, in the future, you wish to give me as much satisfaction as you have caused me displeasure.

4   Since you ask it, I will see that you have plenty of students. Be keen on carrying out your school duties, but please be as keen about your spiritual exercises as you are about class.

5   I am very glad that you will try to be ready for anything and that, when you write, it will be to give me an account of your conscience. Please be exact in doing this.

6   I shall not fail to pray to God that he may grant you perseverance to the end of your days, as you ask me.

7   Brother Ponce will provide for your needs. Show the breeches to Brother Antoine. You must do all he tells you.

8   Be assured that God will bless you inasmuch as you are obedient.

9   It is quite shameful to harbor those feelings of resistance against the Brother who guides you and to lose your temper with him.

10   Be on your guard that your distractions at vocal prayers and during your own prayer do not come from your acting thoughtlessly and being given over to external things.

11   Try to practice recollection and obedience, as you tell me you are doing, because, as you say, this is very necessary for you. These are the main virtues you must endeavor to acquire.

12   You know quite well that you must make your spiritual exercises in the community and not go running about town. There is a walk on free days.

13   I am convinced that in the future you will be exact and faithful in doing nothing without permission and that you are anxious to keep the rules since you really want to carry out your duty, which consists in such fidelity.

I am, my very dear Brother,
Devotedly yours in Our Lord,
DE LA SALLE

14   Your family has asked me to tell you to keep calm and not to write letters to them without necessity, as you have been doing.

LETTER 64(A)
From Brother Ponce to Brother Mathias

The following is a letter written by Brother Ponce, who, at this time, was Director of Avignon and representative of De La Salle in the south. He was Mathias' former Director at Mende and wrote to Mathias giving him detailed instructions about his journey to join the community in Avignon.

Letter 64(A): From Brother Ponce to Brother Mathias
AM; AMG; EC 51(a)

Avignon
June 4, 1708

My very dear Brother,

1   Perhaps you are thinking I have forgotten you. No, I have not done that, but I was waiting for the providential moment.

2   This letter is to notify you that you are to set out on Saturday, June 9, early in the morning to reach Villefort that same day. Go to the "White Horse"; it is at the edge of the town of Villefort. There you will find a Brother who is to join you.

3   You must leave Mende at daybreak. It is seven leagues to your destination. You will cover them quite easily since the days are long.

4   Bring the little packet that contains all my letters and other documents of our Society that I left with Brother Antoine.

5   Bring with you also the copy of the rule for school, the one in very small handwriting, for there are two of them. The one I want you to bring is in the form of a letter written in very small hand by Brother Clément. Brother Antoine will know just which one it is.

6   Also ask Father Martineau for the plan of the bishop's residence and of the Cathedral, which I drew; there are two or three sheets—in fact, all the papers that I gave him. Add them to the packet that I left with Brother Antoine but do not undo it.

7   Add these papers which Father Martineau has to this packet and bring it with you.

8   Mme De La Farge will, as she always does, kindly lend you some old pieces of linen to wrap the parcel in.

9   The Brothers will arrive on the feast of Corpus Christi, I think. So have everything ready on Friday.

10 If you get the chance, give my good wishes to M. Durant and Mme De Pouillac. As I mentioned above, you will be expected on Saturday, June 9, without fail.

11 Also, if you have the opportunity, give my regards to M. and Mme Laurent, and assure them of my best wishes.

12 Don't show this letter to anyone but the parish priest, if you consider it advisable. There is no need even to say that you are going away.

13 You are to travel from Mende to the hamlet, Crematte; from there to Cubières; from Cubières to Laprade. It is only a league from there to Villefort. It is a rather long journey. Brother Antoine is to give you enough money for your journey.

14 I close, assuring you, my very dear Brother, as I wait for your arrival, that I am

> Your very humble and very obedient servant,
> Brother Ponce

15 Leave your mantle for Brother Irénée. I am letting Brother Antoine know that we would appreciate it if he can give you 10 or 12 pounds of bacon. It costs five francs a pound here. You will easily be able to carry it as far as Villefort, and the Brother waiting for you will have a horse.

16 If it happens that the Brother is not at Villefort on Saturday evening, try to assist at Mass on Sunday and then set out for Les Vans, then from Les Vans go to Barjac, from Barjac to Bagnols and from Bagnols to Avignon. You will perhaps meet him on the way.

———— ◆ ————

Since one *lieue* equals four kilometers, or about 2.5 miles, the seven leagues noted in paragraph 3 from Mende to Villefort was approximately 17.5 miles. The journey altogether from Mende to Avignon was over 75 miles as the crow flies, but it was up and down hill for Mathias.

The Brother Irénée mentioned in paragraph 15 is a predecessor of Brother Irénée of Letter 118.

Mme De La Farge, the sister of Father Martineau mentioned in paragraph 8, was one of those charitable women who kept an eye on the needs of the Brothers' communities.

"The Brothers" in paragraph 9 is a tentative translation of a difficult reading of the manuscript. If correct, they are probably Brothers Irénée and Joachim, who were in Mende in 1709.

Brother Clément, mentioned in paragraph 5, is the one to whom Letter 50 is addressed; he is also mentioned in Letter 8.

M. Durand and Mme De Pouillac, mentioned in paragraph 10, are otherwise unknown. It is possible that these were among the people Brothers Mathias and Ponce visited contrary to the Brothers' Rule. In paragraph 5 of Letter 62, paragraph 8 of Letter 63, and paragraph 12 of Letter 64, De La Salle addresses the issue of visiting.

This letter is the last direct contact we have with Brother Ponce. He is, however, mentioned in the minutes of a meeting of the municipal council of Les Vans as representing De La Salle when he went to that town to organize the school there in 1711.

In Letter 32, dated December 5, 1716, paragraph 4, De La Salle explains to Gabriel Drolin that the letters sent through Avignon would be safe, saying, "I have confidence that the Brother who is now in charge at Avignon will faithfully forward your letters to me. He is a very discreet man." This man was Brother Timothée, future Superior General, who succeeded Brother Ponce as Director of Avignon. De La Salle hinted to Gabriel Drolin on other occasions that his letters and those of Drolin were being intercepted, and the blame seemed to fall on Ponce. Blain, certainly, had not a good word to say of him.

Letters 65 to 70
To Various Unnamed Brothers

The recipients of these letters, all Brothers, are not known. Letters 65 to 70 are grouped together because various indications date all of these letters in 1709. Letters 66 and 67 most probably were addressed to Directors, and one of them may have been addressed to Brother Hubert. Since the evidence, however, is not conclusive, both are included here.

LETTER 65
To a Brother

Ms. 22, 8; AMG; EC 92; BL III.8

[Reims]
[September 14, 1709]

1   A little humility would certainly do you a lot of good, my very dear Brother. You are too proud; it is a serious failing of yours.

2   Unless you continue to mortify your mind and your senses, you will fall from the practice of virtue without noticing it.

3   You may be sure that the less obedient you are, the less love you will have for what concerns your vocation.

4   I am not surprised when you tell me that you rarely think of God. How could this be otherwise? You abhor all the virtues and practice none of them.

5   We think of God only insofar as we love him. It seems that your love for him is very weak. If you don't remedy this state of affairs, you are going to lose yourself.

6   You greatly need some humiliations. Consider this seriously and welcome humiliations graciously and with gratitude.

7   You will gain many graces and will surmount your natural inclinations when you overcome the repugnance you feel for humiliations.

8   I pray that God will give you this grace.
    I am, my very dear Brother,
    Devotedly yours in Our Lord,
    DE LA SALLE

LETTER 66
To a Brother [Director]

Ms. 22, 14; AMG; EC 71; BL III.14; CL 8: 389
[September 14, 1709]

1 You are well aware, my very dear Brother, that we must have great love for one another and for that purpose we must bear with one another in the mistakes into which we often fall through human weakness.

2 It is in this way especially that we carry out the precept of charity, which we should all hold in great honor.

3 We must love our Brothers in order to correct them with gentleness and affection, for otherwise a reprimand will not normally bear fruit.

4 The Brothers have to overcome themselves to correct their faults. You too must do the same to correct yours and to give them good example.

5 You will usually correct them more effectively in that way than by all the harsh reprimands that you can give.

6 You must not be alarmed over those who fall into faults, but you have to draw attention to them with winning cordiality, and particularly by doing so in a few words. This is very important.

7 Do, please, try to have an engaging manner, and make it one of your chief occupations to bring about union among your Brothers.

8 I pray that God will grant you yourself this union.
> I am, my very dear Brother,
> Devotedly yours in Our Lord,
> DE LA SALLE

───────── ✦ ─────────

This letter can be regarded as a rather complete summary of the ideals of De La Salle for the Director's relationship with the Brothers of his community, particularly in regard to the Director's role in spiritual direction.

LETTER 67
To a Brother [Director]

Ms. 22, 20; AMG; EC 72; BL III.20; CL 8: 328

Reims
[September 15, 1709]

1   Be careful, my very dear Brother, not to make your spiritual reading out of curiosity, for that is a serious fault.

2   I am happy that your reading gives you encouragement. Bring to it as much attention as you can.

3   It will be of great help in your prayer, to which you must endeavor to devote yourself wholeheartedly.

4   Your spiritual reading will even help you considerably to become interior and make progress in virtue.

5   I am delighted that you take pleasure in observing the rules. The great love you show for their observance is a sure sign of your vocation.

6   You are right in being concerned that the rules are not observed. However, it will not be the concern which you feel that will remedy the situation. It will rather be the good example that you yourself give, for you have to be, as it were, the prime mover and bring about their observance by your prudent action.

7   Come now, does that look so difficult? I would like you to let me know if it does.

8   So now, make every effort to be devout, modest, and devoted to the observance of the rules. In doing so you will give good example to your Brothers.

9   I pray that God will give you the grace to do this.
     I am, my very dear Brother,
     Devotedly yours in Our Lord,
     DE LA SALLE

LETTER 68
To a Brother

Ms. 22, 23; AMG; EC 88; BL III.23; CL 8: 292 and 297

[September, 1709]

1   Whenever you have something to do, remember, my very dear Brother, that we are not happy in this life except when we do things with God in view, for the love of him and only to please him.

2   It would appear that your love for him is very weak and
     I'm not surprised, since you say that you rarely think of
     God. Well then, what chance have you of making progress
     in the virtue of holy love, if you never think of him who
     should be the sole object of your thoughts?

3   You must know that as long as you are in this frame
     of mind, you will continue to feel dislike for all the
     virtues.

4   You see that you are not practicing even one in the apathy
     you are presently experiencing.

5   Humble yourself often, then, before God. Tell him that
     you are as content as if you were enjoying consolations,
     and that it is he whom you seek, not consolation.

6   When you find yourself distressed by apathy during
     prayer, have recourse to God and tell him that, since he is
     your refuge, he must also be your consolation.

7   Apply yourself to your spiritual exercises in such a way
     that you will not have to say that, though you began
     under the inspiration of the Spirit, you finish under the
     impulse of the flesh, that is, in a purely natural manner.

8   We must practice mortification if we are to have God in
     view in all that we do.
            I am, my very dear Brother,
            Devotedly yours in his love,
            DE LA SALLE

LETTER 69
To a Brother

Ms. 22, 6; AMG; EC 91; BL III.6

[Paris]
1709

1   The thought of abandoning you did not enter my head,
     my very dear Brother. I was waiting for the answer from
     M. . . . regarding your needs. You must be patient a little
     longer.

2   Brothers everywhere must be helped, especially when the
     cost of living is as high as it is this year.

3   As you can see, Providence comes to your aid. Rest assured
     that it will not fail you so long as you serve God well.

4   People are against you; it seems that everything fails you,
     all at the same time. Then God raises up someone else to

speak on your behalf and to see that you get what you need.

5   I don't think that you will have to cut out breakfast. You can do without it if you wish. Here we eat brown bread. It is put on the table. Similarly in Reims, the portion is a half pound at each of the main meals and four ounces at breakfast.

6   I hear from Avignon that the inhabitants are reduced to one pound of bread a day, and a 14-ounce pound at that. The Brothers get four ounces for breakfast and five ounces for dinner.

7   I can't send you any picture cards. I haven't enough to buy bread for the 40 people we have here.

I am, my very dear Brother,
Devotedly yours in Our Lord,
DE LA SALLE

———————— ◆ ————————

The information contained in this letter indicates that it was probably written from Paris in 1709, in the time of famine, when the novices had to be moved from Saint Yon to the capital city. They lived in the Brothers' house, "which was big enough for the Brothers of Paris but proved too small on the arrival of the newcomers. The occupants, about 40 in number, were living on top of one another, so to speak" (CL 8: 59).

LETTER 70
To a Brother

Ms. 22, 36; AMG; EC 101; BL III.36

[Reims]
[September 21, 1709]

1   It is consoling to hear of your goodwill, my very dear Brother. I pray that God will give it to you in even greater abundance.

2   You must not be surprised if you experience difficulties. The devil has no desire to see you at peace.

3   You will find that the remedy for this is to turn to God in prayer and to make your troubles known to your Director and to me in all simplicity. In doing this you will find that God will enable you to bear them.

4   Be very faithful to the Rule and obedient, and rest assured that, when you act in this way, God will give you many graces.

5   You must not be upset or anxious over the temptations you experience. When they come, place yourself in God's hands as you would with a good father. Beg him to help you, being convinced that you cannot help yourself.

6   Approach the sacraments eagerly; it is in them that you will find the strength to overcome your difficulties.

7   Surmount all the thoughts that come to you during your prayers.

8   It seems to me from the way God has guided you and from the desires you have had for so long, that he is calling you to the vocation you have embraced.

9   All that you ought to do now is not to question, but to correspond faithfully with your vocation.

10   You should have entered your present state only if you were ready to endure hardships. In this way, when you experience them, you will not feel that you have been deceived.

11   Offer yourself every day to God with all your sufferings, so that he may accomplish by them whatever he wishes.

12   I pray God to bless you and not let you fall into inconstancy, wanting now one thing, now another.

13   When we give ourselves to God, we must be more steadfast and seek him alone. Inconstancy is a sign that we often pay a great deal of attention to our own wishes.

14   I pray that God will give you the spirit of your vocation.

> I am, my very dear Brother,
> Devotedly yours in Our Lord,
> DE LA SALLE

LETTER 71
To Brother Charles

Rethel, mentioned in Ms. 22 at the head of this letter, no doubt refers to the community of the Brother Director to whom it was addressed. This reference would then indicate that the letter was addressed to Brother Charles, whom the community chronicle of Rethel for those years described as "a very simple Brother," and listed as head of the community. This is apparently the same Brother Charles mentioned as the topic of gossip in

Letter 8 to Brother Hubert, June 1, 1706. The mention in paragraph 7 of Brother Joseph, who was again in Paris, suggests that the letter was written about 1710 or 1711. During that time, Brother Joseph used his community in Paris as the base from which he made visitations to the communities of northern and western France.

Letter 71: To Brother Charles
Ms. 22, 18; AMG; EC 73; BL III.18

[1710–1711]

1   I am at a loss to know why there is so little order in your community, my very dear Brother.

2   Is it not because you do not keep silence? Examine yourself on this point. Complaints are made that you speak too loudly.

3   Be careful, then, to keep silence strictly. You know very well that silence and recollection are two means of becoming interior.

4   Take care not to talk in the streets.

5   See that you walk in a dignified manner. Say the rosary devoutly. This is the way to guard your eyes and control your thoughts and particularly to win from God the grace to carry out your school work well.

6   As you know, there have always been complaints that you walk much too fast.

7   It would have been much wiser not to have replied further to the priest who spoke to you in the street after you had told him that Brother Joseph was back in Paris again.

8   Take care never to get into arguments with anybody, for in doing so you can offend against charity, which should be outstanding among you.

I am, my very dear Brother,
Devotedly yours in Our Lord,
DE LA SALLE

———— ◆ ————

The reference in paragraph 7 to the priest who asked for the whereabouts of Brother Joseph recalls the point laid down in the Rule of 1705, that the Brothers were not to tell people outside the community where the Brothers were stationed, even if asked (CL 25: 58). No doubt De La Salle wanted to preserve the autonomy of the Institute (and his own administration) from any interference by outsiders, especially from the clergy who often tried to take it over and replace De La Salle.

LETTER 72
To Brother Anastase

Brother Anastase, Antoine Paradis, was born in the Diocese of Laon on February 28, 1689, and entered the novitiate at Paris on July 23, 1709. He was 22 years old and in his second year in the Institute when he received this letter. He was later in Boulogne when Brother Barthélemy made his visit there in 1717, and in Paris on November 11 of that year to sign his acceptance of the new Superior General. He participated in the General Chapter of 1720 as Director of Calais and made his perpetual profession according to the Bull of Approbation at the Chapter of 1725, being then the Sub-Director of the community in Paris. He was the Director of Grenoble in 1730 and took part in the Chapter of 1734. He was the first Director of the community of Maréville in 1749 and remained there until his death at the age of 85 on April 8, 1774. He had been the oldest Brother in the Institute since 1767.

Letter 72: To Brother Anastase
AM; AMG; EC 1; BL I.36

January 28, 1711

1   Apply yourself above all, my very dear Brother, to be motivated by faith so that your actions may be well done.

2   I am very glad that your whole aim and intention is to do God's will.

3   In order to succeed in this, you should strive particularly to be entirely submissive and to observe your rules well, for it is in this that you will carry out God's will.

4   Take great care about prayer and try to do all your actions in a prayerful spirit. The more faithful you are in these matters, the more God will bless you.

5   Often recollect yourself in order to renew and strengthen in your mind the remembrance of the presence of God. The more you try to achieve this, the easier you will find it to perform your actions and carry out your duties well.

6   I am very pleased with the frame of mind that you say you have, to do all I want of you.

7   I ask God to give you in abundance the spirit of your state, and I am, my very dear Brother,

Devotedly yours in Our Lord,

DE LA SALLE

Letters 73 to 79
To Various Unnamed Brother Directors

The following seven letters are grouped together because all are addressed to Directors. Neither the names of these Brothers nor the dates of the letters are known. The first three are found in both Ms. 22 and Blain's biography of De La Salle. In quoting them, Blain says that these particular letters were addressed to the same Brother but quotes Letter 74 before Letter 73. In this series of letters and elsewhere, Ms. 22 and Blain differ slightly from one another because each uses the letters to illustrate different points and the slight changes accommodate their individual purposes. An example of how they differ in a particular letter is given in the commentary on Letter 80.

LETTER 73
To a Brother Director

Ms. 22, 1; AMG; EC 66; BL III.1; CL 8: 368

1   I am very pleased, my very dear Brother, with your intentions to work hard to remedy your faults and overcome yourself.

2   When the chance of giving way to impatience occurs, have frequent recourse to God. For your part, in order to overcome the temptation, remain silent and take no action until the occasion has passed.

3   Humble yourself at the sight of your weaknesses when you fall into faults.

4   Faithfully admit them and be assured that the shame you feel in doing this, together with the penance you are given, will be of great help to you in correcting your faults.

5   You are right in saying that the thoughts you indulge in from time to time about the difficulties of your vocation are nothing but a deception of the devil, who seeks only to discourage you and to prevent you from lovingly bearing the hardships that are part of it.

6   Be convinced that your happiness as a Christian consists in overcoming yourself and bearing all the difficulties God sends you.

7   I pray that he will give you the grace to do this.
        I am, my very dear Brother,
        Devotedly yours in Our Lord,
        DE LA SALLE

LETTER 74
To the Same Brother Director

Ms. 22, 11; AMG; EC 67; BL III.11; CL 8: 368

1   I am delighted to know of your good dispositions, my very dear Brother.

2   I am very happy that you have a high esteem for your vocation.

3   Try to preserve this grace and take the means to see that there is among you a great love for seeking the salvation of your neighbor, and that all is done with kindness and propriety, as among Brothers who should have a mutual love for each other and bear with each other's faults.

4   This is what will draw down on you the graces and blessings of God. For that to happen, you must bear with one another.

5   Often ask God for this peace and union.

6   As you say, it is true that you have a great need for charity in order to keep yourself in peace, but be assured that you have no less a need for the excellent virtue of obedience, that noble achievement of charity. Moreover, God will always bless your community to the extent that it possesses the spirit of obedience.

7   I am as desirous as you are that peace be preserved. Try to do so, and the God of peace will be with you.

8   I can easily see, as you point out, that there is not much order in your community. You must try to remedy this.

9   The fact that you dislike being in a position of authority pleases me very much. Remain always in these dispositions. In this way God will bless you.
        I am, my very dear Brother,
        Devotedly yours in Our Lord,
        DE LA SALLE

LETTER 75
To the Same Brother Director

Ms. 22, 15; AMG; EC 68; BL III.15; CL 8: 369 and 472

1   I cannot understand why, my very dear Brother, you did not tell me earlier of the temptation you experienced. Don't you know that an illness is already half cured when you tell the doctor about it?

2   So you see how weak you are even after renewing your protestation that you belong completely to God.

3   It is not true that in your vocation suffering goes unrewarded. Every state of life has its own difficulties. You must not be surprised at having to suffer. This is part of the plan of God, who wishes us to gain merit in this way.

4   Now, my very dear Brother, if you had patiently borne the pain that Brother had caused you, how many of God's graces you would have merited! Make sure, then, that in the future you bear your sufferings with patience.

5   If you wish to be pleasing to God, offer him your sufferings in union with those of Our Lord Jesus Christ.

6   The anxiety you have concerning your faults cannot do you any good. The only thing to do is to consider before God what means you can use to overcome them.

7   A little patience, and God will take care of everything.

8   You worry too much.

9   Take care that you don't let others see that you are in a state of anxiety.

    I am, my very dear Brother,
    Devotedly yours in Our Lord,
    DE LA SALLE

LETTER 76
To a Brother Director

Ms. 22, 25; AMG; EC 74; BL III.25

1   Endeavor to be very attentive during Holy Mass, my very dear Brother.

2   If we dwell on distractions, it means that we do not hear Mass.

3   Bring your attention to the Mass by following the method that is prescribed in our Society, that is to say, in an interior manner. That is the best way for you. Follow it humbly.

4   Do not forget to thank God for all the blessings he bestows on you, for ingratitude for favors is most displeasing to him.

5   It is true that in the Diocese of Reims the feast of the Visitation is kept only on the 8th of the month. As regards the date, we follow the diocese, but we use the Roman Office. If you haven't the books for this, but you have those of the diocesan rite, do the best you can.

6   You are quite right to say you are disturbed over the altars in the classrooms.

7   You must be very careful not to busy yourself so much about externals.

8   You know that I don't tolerate all these altars in school. That is why I ask you to give the students all the things Brother left behind in the class.

9   But you can keep the little chalice in order to teach them how to serve Mass.

       I am, my very dear Brother,
       Devotedly yours in Our Lord,
       DE LA SALLE

———— ✦ ————

In 1698 De La Salle prepared for publication *Instructions et Prières pour la Sainte Messe.* Permission was given for its publication for a period of five years. A copy of this edition, dating from 1734 but with the indication that it was given approbation in January 1703, is kept in the archives of the Generalate in Rome. There also exist copies of *Recueil,* compiled by De La Salle, dated 1711, which contain a *Méthode pour bien entendre la Sainte Messe,* referred to in paragraph 3 (CL 15: 70).

    The word "altars" in paragraph 8 is given as the translation of the French *chapelles.* De La Salle was not referring here to the pious shrines, popular during the nineteenth and early twentieth centuries and often erected in classrooms during, for example, May and June. In paragraph 9 he refers to the collection of articles used in the sacrifice of the Mass and placed in the classroom as aids in teaching the children how to assist at and serve Mass. De La Salle was against too elaborate a preparation for this aspect of the catechism lesson.

LETTER 77
To a Brother Director

Ms. 22, 29; AMG; EC 76; BL III.29

1   It is indeed a very serious fault, my very dear Brother, to eat and drink outside the community.

2   I bless God that he has brought you to realize this and to the determination not to commit this fault again.

3   As you well know, this sort of thing gives scandal and is the result of gluttony or weak will.

4   In order to make up for this fault through love for God, try to be very faithful to the rules.

5   The fact that you are a little more detached and a little more prudent in Reims than you were in Paris is a great consolation to me.

6   I thank God also that your eyes are not as bad as they used to be. I will see that this ailment of yours is attended to.

7   You do not tell me who has been sick.

8   Watch over yourself a little more in order to restrain your impetuosity, and try not to be so concerned with externals.

9   I pray that God will give you the grace to do this and to be less impulsive in your actions, for impulsiveness is unbecoming.

>   I am, my very dear Brother,
>   Devotedly yours in Our Lord,
>   DE LA SALLE

LETTER 78
To a Brother Director

Ms. 22, 31; AMG; EC 77; BL III.31

1   You are well aware, my very dear Brother, that one of the most important things in community is to ring the bell at exactly the right time, especially for the morning rising.

2   Be exact to leave what you are doing at the first sign and as soon as you hear the bell. You know that this is important in a community.

3   You must leave everything at the first sound of the bell, so that you can begin the next exercise as soon as it stops

ringing. It is to this sort of fidelity that God ordinarily attaches many graces.

4   The times for prayer and for spiritual reading are not to be spent doing anything else. For the love of God, be exact in this and see that all the exercises are carried out right on time.

5   Everything must also be done through a spirit of fidelity to rule. God will bless what you do only insofar as you practice this fidelity. Where there is little fidelity, we deprive ourselves of many graces.

6   Often ask God, then, for this fidelity. I will also ask it of God for you.

> I am, my very dear Brother,
> Devotedly yours in Our Lord and in his holy love,
> DE LA SALLE

LETTER 79
To a Brother Director

Ms. 22, 35; AMG; EC 78; BL III.35

[R. August 23]

1   I am most displeased, my very dear Brother, with the annoyance these two Brothers have caused you. They must be very insubordinate indeed.

2   I realize that as long as the Brothers are not submissive, there will be no order at all in your community.

3   When Brothers refuse to eat their meals one day, they are not to be allowed to have them the following day.

4   The first day it will be through their capriciousness; the next day it will be as a penance for this capriciousness. By no means are you to beg them to eat.

5   You did quite right to tell him to come to dinner with the others.

6   You did quite right, too, in not letting him have anything at all to eat that evening. That is what you must do every time they won't obey.

7   And so I command you to say to Brother that every time he follows his own will and refuses to obey, I have instructed you to let him have nothing to eat.

8   You must never resort to force in a community; that wouldn't be right. But when there is no other course left, you must cut out the meals.

9   So you drink water; we do, too. You should not have
    bought beer.

10 Take care not to let those two Brothers do as they wish,
    nor let them avoid carrying out their penance.

11 I do not know why it is said that nobody gives an account
    of his conscience.

12 Do not let the Brothers make their spiritual reading in
    books other than books of devotion. That is not wise nor
    is it to be permitted.

13 Please make every effort to see that the community is
    faithful to the Rule.

14 On the octave day of Corpus Christi, the program in the
    morning is the same as that of the weekly holiday, except
    that there is no community outing.

15 Be very careful not to fall into negligence, for God gives
    few graces to those who are negligent. They have little suc-
    cess in what they do.

16 I pray that God may shower his graces on you.

    I am, my very dear Brother,
    Devotedly yours in Our Lord,
    DE LA SALLE

———— ✦ ————

In Ms. 22 the text of this letter is introduced by the words, "Penances to
be imposed on those who suffer from epilepsy." The idea that penances
should be given to those who are epileptic was considered normal in the
eighteenth century, when this illness was looked on as a special punishment from God. This letter makes no reference to epilepsy, however.
Paragraphs 2 to 8 deal with the obstinate refusal of Brothers to take their
meals with the rest of the community, and a misreading of the text probably led the compiler of Ms. 22 to believe that this reference had to do
with epilepsy. In any case, the Founder's severity comes as something of
a shock. There seems to be confusion in the French text as to whether there
were two or only one of the Brothers guilty of the fault.

The years 1709 and 1710 were years of famine in the northern part
of France, hence the restriction mentioned in paragraph 9 on the use of
beer at meals.

The Rule of 1705 made no reference to special practices for the feast
of Corpus Christi and its octave. The Daily Schedule of 1713 and the Rule
of 1718, however, made provision for a quarter of an hour's adoration
before the Blessed Sacrament on that feast day and during the octave. The

Rule of 1718 also required the Brothers to assist at Benediction of the Blessed Sacrament during these days (CL 25: 133). Evidently, the octave day of Corpus Christi was a special feast day in some dioceses, and so in paragraph 14 De La Salle gives a directive to the Director to cover this circumstance.

Letters 80 to 104
To Various Unnamed Brothers

De La Salle wrote Letters 80 to 104 over a number of years to various Brothers. The exact dates of these letters are not known, nor are the names of the recipients. Letters 80 to 87 have been preserved in both Ms. 22 and in Blain, and for that reason they are grouped together here. Both of these sources used the letters to illustrate various teachings or virtues of De La Salle. Letters 88 to 94 have been preserved in Ms. 22 only, and Letters 95 to 104 have been preserved by Blain only.

It is of interest to compare the different ways in which Blain and Ms. 22 present the letters. In *Cahiers lasalliens* 10: 138 we read: "Neither Blain nor Ms. 22 gives adequate proof of authenticity. The texts are clearly adapted and sometimes excerpted. No doubt the Brothers for their edification made collections of De La Salle's letters, going so far as to compose some of them from excerpts of different documents. Several of these collections were passed around; Blain could have used one; Ms. 22 another."

It is notable also that not one of the autographed letters quoted in Blain's biography or in the other early biographies of De La Salle has been preserved in the original, while in turn these same biographies contain no quotations from the preserved autographed letters.

In *Edition Critique,* Brother Félix-Paul takes Blain's version of a letter as the primary source, but the final version is a reconstruction which includes or adapts elements that are also in the Ms. 22 version of the letter. The commentary following Letter 80 presents an illustration of this method of reconstruction.

LETTER 80
To a Brother

Ms. 22, 7; AMG; EC 82; BL III.7; CL 8: 420

1   I am sure, my very dear Brother, that you have no doubt that the one virtue most necessary for you is humility.

2   As you can see, you are not entirely submissive in your mind. Come, my dear Brother, make an effort to acquire this virtue, I beg you, and realize that you can be happy in this world only insofar as you practice humility, obedience, and patience. These three are inseparable, and you have equal need of all three.

3   So do your best to acquire them, and you will see that you will experience peace of mind and contentment in your vocation to the degree that you possess them.

4   There is nothing I will leave undone to relieve your anxiety, my very dear Brother; but, believe me, the best way to overcome it is to make an effort to acquire the virtues I have just proposed to you.

5   However, it seems to me from reading your last letter that you don't try hard enough to acquire them. Take good care to do this, I implore you, for without them you will never do anything that is good and agreeable in God's sight. Moreover, you will never do much of anything, either exteriorly or interiorly, without them.

6   You surely realize that it is a lack of this virtue that prevented you from receiving Holy Communion on the feast of the Epiphany.

7   For the love of God, my very dear Brother, change your ways.

> I am, my very dear Brother,
> Devotedly yours in Our Lord,
> DE LA SALLE

———— ◆ ————

Although the name of the recipient of this letter is not known, according to Blain this letter and Letters 81 and 82 were written to the same Brother.

It is possible that the Brother addressed here was forbidden by his Brother Director to receive Communion for some considerable failing against one of the virtues mentioned by De La Salle. The Rule of 1705 advises that "The Brother Director may deprive them [the Brothers] of Communion for some serious exterior fault."

To illustrate the differences between the reconstituted Letter 80 of the *Edition Critique* (which is used in this volume also) and the versions of Blain and Ms. 22, the following translation is given. The parts common to both Blain and Ms. 22 are in regular type, the parts found only in Ms. 22 are in *italics,* and the parts found only in Blain are in CAPITALS.

1   I am sure, *my very dear Brother,* that you have no doubt that the one virtue most necessary for you is humility.

2   As you can see, you are not entirely submissive in your mind; *nevertheless you must* COME, MY DEAR BROTHER, make an effort to acquire this virtue, I BEG YOU, AND REALIZE THAT you can be happy in this

world only insofar as you practice humility, obedience, and patience. THESE THREE ARE INSEPARABLE AND YOU HAVE EQUAL NEED OF ALL THREE.

3   So, do your best to *have these three virtues.* ACQUIRE THEM AND you will see that you will experience peace of mind and contentment in your vocation to the degree that you *do* POSSESS them.

4   There is nothing I will leave undone to relieve your anxiety, my very dear Brother, but believe me the best way TO OVERCOME IT is to make an effort to acquire *these* THE virtues I have JUST proposed to you.

5   However, it seems to me from reading your last letter that you don't *practice* TRY HARD enough to acquire them. TAKE GOOD CARE TO DO THIS, I IMPLORE YOU, FOR WITHOUT THEM YOU WILL NEVER DO ANYTHING THAT IS GOOD AND AGREEABLE IN GOD'S SIGHT. *Moreover, you will never do much of anything, either exteriorly or interiorly, without them.*

6   *You surely realize that it is a lack of this virtue that prevented you from receiving Holy Communion on the feast of the Epiphany.*

7   *For the love of God, my very dear Brother, change your ways.*

> I am, my very dear Brother,
> Devotedly yours in Our Lord,
> DE LA SALLE

LETTER 81
To the Same Brother

Ms. 22, 12; AMG; EC 83; BL III.12; CL 8: 421

1   Instead of being upset when your long-standing faults are pointed out to you, my very dear Brother, you ought on the contrary to thank God constantly for it. Try once again to turn this to your advantage.

2   Take in good part all that is said to you at the advertisement of defects. This exercise will be very useful to you if you know how to profit from it.

3   Indeed, what sort of humility have you if you cannot bear something that causes you a little confusion?

4   Now I see quite clearly what you want, my very dear
Brother. You very much like to profess that you are a
great lover of humility and that you have great esteem for
it, just as long as you can avoid humiliations as much as
possible. What good will it be for you to love the virtue
and to refuse to practice it?

5   What! You complain that others haven't enough charity,
but you don't complain that you haven't enough humility.
What good is that great desire you have for this virtue if it
does not help you to be more aware that you are culpable
before God?

6   Don't give way, then, to any more complaints about the
advertisements you are given, and don't think that your
Director is in any way annoyed with you.

7   If he is strict in reproving you and in giving you penances,
though he doesn't treat others in the same way, it is
because he sees that you are well-disposed and because he
is more interested in your progress in virtue.

8   Show by your attitude that this is true, and let your only
wish in the future be to welcome joyfully the reproofs and
the penances you get and to correct your faults.

9   It is on such occasions that the means to do so are found.
So watch over yourself and do not get upset about something that can be only for your own good.

10   I pray God to give you this grace, and I am, my very dear
Brother,

    Devotedly yours in Our Lord,
    DE LA SALLE

———— ✦ ————

Blain suggests that Letter 81 was written to the same Brother as Letter 82
but was written after Letter 82.

LETTER 82
To the Same Brother

Ms. 22, 13; EC 84; BL III.13; CL 8: 420

1   Take great care, my very dear Brother, not to take offense
when your defects are pointed out to you.

2   No matter how you are told them, Our Lord had worse said to him, and you claim to be his disciple.

3   If you really are, you will be glad to be treated like your master, who patiently bore all the insults that were offered him. So did the saints, his servants.

4   So when your faults are pointed out to you in a way that shocks you and seems to show contempt for you, remember to adore God's justice in the one who does this.

5   My dear Brother, you must have great love for this exercise and look on it as a means given you by God to rid yourself of your defects. Even if there were no other good in it but humiliation, you ought still to cherish and love it.

6   Be especially on your guard not to be upset by your faults on account of the penances you may be given to make up for them. This would be a sign that you are seeking your own peace of mind and the satisfaction of your senses rather than God, and that you are serving him like a slave.

7   One of the things most likely to draw God's graces down on you is your willingness to carry out the penances imposed on you. Do this with love, I beg you.

  I am, my very dear Brother,
  Devotedly yours in Our Lord,
  DE LA SALLE

LETTER 83
To a Brother

Ms. 22, 5; AMG; EC 85; BL III.5: CL 8: 268

1   If God through his divine and adorable Providence wishes you to remain in your present state, my very dear Brother, you ought to will what he wills and give yourself up entirely to his guidance.

2   We are committed to this by our religious profession, and we ought continually to adore the plans that Providence has for us.

3   If you wish to leave this state you are in to seek consolations, it is to be feared that you are seeking your own consolation rather than the God of consolations.

4   Surely you know that the essential virtue of a religious is obedience.

5   So even if you were to have more difficulty still, you ought to submit out of love for God.

6   As you can clearly see, my very dear Brother, the difficulties you experience arise from your lack of submission.

7   What you must do in such circumstances, if you wish to overcome these difficulties, is to accept blindly and say to yourself, "I will do this through obedience no matter what may be my arguments to the contrary or what dislike I have."

8   If you act in this way, you will soon be free of your problems.

9   I am really delighted that you write to me in such a straightforward way.

10 I will try to help you as much as I can, but it is not enough to tell me in a general way that you are not keeping the rules; you have to give me details so that I can apply the necessary remedies.

11 I want you to work out a plan for doing this.
       I am, my very dear Brother,
       Devotedly yours in Our Lord,
       DE LA SALLE

LETTER 84
To a Brother

Ms. 22, 21; AMG; EC 86; BL III.21; CL 8: 287–288

1   My very dear Brother, I do not know why you say that you have an hour and a quarter of prayer instead of one hour. I think that prayer is carried out in the same way everywhere and ends at the same time.

2   You are disturbed that the time for prayer is too long. That is a sign that you do not have much love for it.

3   Ah, my very dear Brother, it is the mainstay of our spiritual life; would you want to neglect it?

4   If you cannot keep your attention on one act, move on to another. In times of apathy, occupy your mind with reflections.

5   At the thought of your faults, remain humbly before God.

6   Your thoughtless behavior is the cause of the difficulty you experience in applying yourself to prayer and is both the sign and the result of the unsettled state of your soul. This

is the reason why you must take strong measures to overcome this fault.

7 Above all, make sure that you have a thorough knowledge of the method of prayer as it is practiced in the Society and follow it. I am not surprised that, since you do not follow it, you have difficulty in applying yourself to prayer.

8 At the present time, you have the opportunity to think of God and often to enter into yourself. Do this, I beg of you.

> I am, my very dear Brother,
> Devotedly yours in Our Lord,
> DE LA SALLE

LETTER 85
To a Brother

Ms. 22, 17; AMG; EC 87; BL III.17; CL 8: 276

1 It is a great consolation to me, my very dear Brother, to know that you are wholeheartedly in love with your vocation. I bless God for this.

2 You ask me to treat you as if you were the least of your Brothers. We shall see later on if we can grant you this request.

3 You say that often you don't know how to keep from speaking. You must try to learn this. It is great wisdom to know how to keep silence when the occasion requires it.

4 You say, too, that you fear that you do not have enough patience to bear all you have to suffer. You must make this your daily study. Silence and self-control will earn this for you.

5 Be very exact with regard to silence. It is one of the principal points of fidelity to the Rule, and without it a community soon falls into disorder.

6 You will tell me perhaps that you very much want to observe it, but that the situation in which you continually find yourself of having to answer those who ask you questions does not allow you to do so.

7 What a trifling excuse! Don't you know the occasions when you should reply and those when you should remain silent?

8   It is only for the sake of charity that you should reply; on all other occasions you should remain silent.

9   If someone else speaks to you, be silent

10 Always speak respectfully to your Director, looking on him as taking the place of God as far as you are concerned.

11 Be careful not to contradict others during recreation. You must never show that you oppose the opinions of your Brothers.

12 Let this always be your frame of mind.

> I am, my very dear Brother,
> Devotedly yours in Our Lord,
> DE LA SALLE

LETTER 86
To a Brother

Ms. 22, 19; AMG; EC 89; BL III.19; CL 8: 296

1   You realize, my very dear Brother, how important it is to follow the inspirations that come to you from God.

2   They are precious and it is to them that God ordinarily attaches his graces. He does not mean them to be given to you for no purpose. He knows how to punish those who are not faithful to them.

3   So those inspirations that God gives us are to be valued, and he grants his graces only insofar as we are faithful in following them.

4   This is a special grace that God has given you, a sign that God wishes you to be steadfast in your vocation.

5   The sure means you must use to avoid the evil you have been considering is obedience, together with the daily accusation of faults.

6   Rest assured that these two practices will prevent you from succumbing to the temptation.

7   Make a great effort to reject all thoughts contrary to your vocation.

8   Listen to the voice of the Holy Spirit speaking to you in the depths of your heart.

9   I pray God to give you the grace to do this.

> I am, my very dear Brother,
> Devotedly yours in Our Lord,
> DE LA SALLE

LETTER 87
To a Brother

Ms. 22, 22; AMG; EC 90; BL III.22; CL 8: 314

1   Apply yourself often to remember the presence of God, my very dear Brother. Look upon this practice as your greatest happiness.

2   Your recollection and self-control should be great enough for you to achieve this.

3   They will be for you a means of overcoming yourself in times of temptation and will prevent you from acting from natural motives by inspiring you to have continually in mind the will of God, for this should be your sole aim.

4   You are certainly right in saying that you are too thought-less, my very dear Brother, for that is just what you are, since you so rarely think of God's presence even during the holiest of your exercises.

5   Try, please, to perform all your actions with the thought of God's presence in mind and through sentiments of faith, for that is the spirit of your state.

6   I am very sorry for you in the situation in which you find yourself and sympathize with you for the distress you feel, endlessly having to reject the useless thoughts that assail you.

7   But, let me tell you this: they overwhelm you like this only because you do not make your spiritual exercises with sufficient fervor and because you occupy your time with a host of trivialities.

8   I beg you then, in the name of Jesus Christ, make an ef-fort to overcome this negligence of yours, for there is nothing that can do you so much harm in God's service as that.

I am, my very dear Brother,
Devotedly yours in Our Lord,
DE LA SALLE

LETTER 88
To a Brother

Ms. 22, 10; EC 94; BL III.10

1 The mortifications that others make you practice are wonderful opportunities for you to advance in virtue, my very dear Brother.

2 That is why out of love for God you must conceive a liking for them, especially since they concern the mind only and cause you no bodily discomfort.

3 On such occasions say within yourself, "You must mortify yourself in your mind and senses frequently." And afterwards add, "My God, give me the grace to love all that helps to mortify my mind." In each separate occasion say, "I love this opportunity and find it good because it helps me to mortify myself."

4 I am very pleased that in your last letter you faithfully told me all the faults you had committed.

5 For your penance you are to give yourself 20 strokes of the discipline on two occasions, and from now until the feast of the Assumption, every time you pass by the Brother, you are to kiss his feet and ask his pardon, provided it is not during one of the Community exercises.

    I am, my very dear Brother,
    Devotedly yours in Our Lord,
    DE LA SALLE

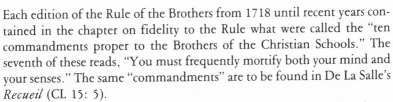

Each edition of the Rule of the Brothers from 1718 until recent years contained in the chapter on fidelity to the Rule what were called the "ten commandments proper to the Brothers of the Christian Schools." The seventh of these reads, "You must frequently mortify both your mind and your senses." The same "commandments" are to be found in De La Salle's *Recueil* (CL 15: 5).

The penances imposed by De La Salle in this letter seem to be at variance with the direction of the Rule quoted in the commentary following Letter 6.

LETTER 89
To a Brother

Ms. 22, 14; EC 95; BL III.24

1   You know that to receive the sacraments with all the requisite dispositions, my very dear Brother, you must have deep faith and fervor.

2   Before you confess your sins, be sure to make acts of contrition.

3   Be very careful not to miss the sacrament of penance.

4   It is this sacrament and the reception of the Eucharist that will support you in your difficulties, and you should regard it as a great happiness to receive the Eucharist frequently.

5   You should take steps to correct yourself of your faults, but it would be an even greater fault not to receive Communion.

6   You are not to receive Communion after refusing to obey.

7   But you must not stay away if you fail in obedience through weakness.

8   During the night, it often happens that the devil brings about natural emissions in order to keep you from receiving Communion. So I believe that you should not dispense yourself from receiving the Eucharist for this reason, nor should you fast because of it.

9   If you received Communion daily, you might do so; but since the day for Communion is for the community, I don't think it should be changed.

     I am, my very dear Brother,
     Devotedly yours in Our Lord,
     De La Salle

LETTER 90
To a Brother

Ms. 22, 27; EC 96; BL III.27

1   You must take care not to be disheartened by the trials you experience, my very dear Brother. On the contrary, you should humble yourself at the sight of your weakness and have recourse to God, in whom and through whose help you can do all things.

2   Firm courage and a little generosity will enable you to overcome all your difficulties. Take advantage of your times of fervor to buoy yourself up. The more you conquer your dislikes by mortification, the more God will bless you.

3   For the love of God, do not let yourself fall into despondency. That would be a sign that you are still very weak.

4   Take care not to get upset over trivialities. It is neither wise nor sensible to allow your mind to be disturbed over mere trifles.

5   I have just received your last letter and from it I gather that you are not at all now in the same frame of mind. You allow yourself to fall into despondency at the first difficulty you meet.

6   Don't give in so easily to your hasty temper. A little patience and God will take care of everything. He wishes you to gain merit through your trials.

7   Don't do anything without permission.

8   See to it that you curb your impetuosity.

> I am, my very dear Brother,
> Devotedly yours in Our Lord,
> DE LA SALLE

LETTER 91
To a Brother

Ms. 22, 30; AMG; EC 97; BL III.30

1   I do not fail, nor shall I fail, to pray to God for you, my very dear Brother, that he may keep you faithful to your vocation. Indeed, you need him to sustain you in it.

2   You will give me great pleasure if you also pray for me. The affection with which you write to me, my very dear Brother, touches me very much.

3   I am very grateful for the concern you have for my health. Please God he will give you the best of health and make you truly holy.

4   For that you must consistently practice mortification.

5   Be faithful in giving an account of your conscience. It is this that will keep you in peace and true to the spirit of your state.

6   Be careful not to talk too familiarly with your Brother Director, and adore God in his person.

7   You know that it is very wrong to go out alone and to do anything without permission.

8   Above all else, make sure that you are prudent and very faithful to the rules. In this way you will give your Brothers good example.

9   I pray God to give you this grace.

     I am, my very dear Brother,
     Devotedly yours in Our Lord,
     DE LA SALLE

LETTER 92
To a Brother

Ms. 22, 32; AMG; EC 98; BL III.32

1   Be careful, my very dear Brother, not to give way to impatience in school. This is very important, for it could bring the disfavor of God on your school.

2   It is a fault that we often have the occasion to commit. We have to keep careful watch over ourselves so that we do not lose control of ourselves.

3   For the love of God, do not slap your students. It is not by dint of blows that people are drawn to good or to God.

4   And don't use a pointer, either. As for the rod, use it only when necessity demands it. Return it to its place as soon as you have used it, so that there will be no chance of using it when you are moved to impatience.

5   Therefore, watch yourself very closely in class in order not to give way to impatience.

6   You must be exact in performing all the exercises on time in class, for to have order everything has to be well-regulated.

7   You must take fidelity to the Rule as the mainspring in all you do; God will bless all your actions if you are faithful to this. Frequently ask God for this fidelity. I, too, will ask it for you.

     I am, my very dear Brother,
     Devotedly yours in Our Lord,
     DE LA SALLE

LETTER 93
To a Brother

Ms. 22, 33; AMG; EC 99; BL III.33

1   You are well aware how harmful levity is in the classroom, my very dear Brother. That is why you must not only avoid this fault but be faithful in accusing yourself of it.

2   Since you fall into it so often, you have more reason to accuse yourself of it.

3   Avoid all such frivolity in class and be prompt in correcting it, for it will bring about disorder.

4   Make sure that you teach your students well.

5   I am glad that the rules are better observed in the school and in the community than they formerly were.

6   Do nothing in class without permission.

7   Be very careful not to accept anything from the students. That would certainly be a very serious fault.

8   Don't allow any shouting in the school and don't give the students or their mothers any cause for complaint.

9   You must be prudent in the means you take for this. If you dismiss students because they shout, others will do the same thing so that they will be dismissed too.

10   You know what happened to you before and the harmful consequences it had.

      I am, my very dear Brother,
      Devotedly yours in Our Lord,
      DE LA SALLE

LETTER 94
To a Brother

Ms. 22, 34; AMG; EC 100; BL III.34

1   You will do well to work hard at your lessons in religious instruction, my very dear Brother. To give them well, you must begin courageously, even giving them poorly, for no one does anything well the first time.

2   I think that you trouble yourself too much over what is merely external and not the principal purpose of your state, but simply a means. This is the concern of your

superiors rather than yours. You must leave yourself in their hands.

3   As long as you teach your students to the best of your ability, you can have a clear conscience in the matter.

4   Why are you not as keen about teaching catechism well, which is the main purpose of your vocation, as you are about writing, which is merely a means to this end?

5   You know how necessary it is for the Brothers to study religion, and yet this is one of the things most neglected.

6   Writing is necessary, but religious studies are surely more in keeping with your profession.

7   It must be the first of your daily occupations, since your first care is to instill a Christian spirit into your students.

8   Don't spend so much time and effort on writing and arithmetic; the four rules are all you need. It doesn't take so much time to learn them.

I am, my very dear Brother,
Devotedly yours in Our Lord,
DE LA SALLE

LETTER 95
To a Brother [Director]

EC 79; CL 8: 472–473

. . . A Director should be a man of such great patience and such proven virtue that he should look upon himself as a receptacle for all the rubbish of the community. By this I mean, he must be ready to put up with everything without showing any annoyance or displeasure. . . .

———— ◆ ————

This passage, preserved as an indirect quotation from De La Salle, was apparently reconstructed by Blain. There is no evidence that it formed part of a letter. Blain may have based it simply on a remembrance of a Brother.

LETTER 96
To a Brother [Director]

EC 80; CL 8: 312

. . . It is your fault. Why don't you take the trouble to acquire that evenness of temper that is so necessary for you?
Your Brothers complain that they never see you in a
good mood, and they all say that you look like a prison
door. . . .

———— ✦ ————

As with the previous passage, this is probably a remembrance of a Brother,
preserved by Blain. It is a remark which Blain attributes to De La Salle
when a Director complained that his Brothers did not have confidence
in him as a Director. There is no evidence, however, that the quotation
was taken from a letter.

LETTER 97
To a Brother

EC 81; CL 8: 410

. . . Well then, my very dear Brother, so you still want me
to be your spiritual guide. I will be glad to act in this
capacity on one condition, however: that you tell me my
faults without any flattery. It is fitting that you should do
so, since you are the oldest of our Brothers. . . .

———— ✦ ————

Brother Gabriel Drolin, born in 1664, was probably the oldest Brother
at the time, so De La Salle was perhaps thinking only of the Brothers in
France, among whom Brother Antoine, born in 1666, was the oldest.

LETTER 98
To a Brother

EC 103; CL 8: 313–314

1   . . . Thoughtless behavior and curiosity are grave imped-
iments to the service of God. So, my very dear Brother,
you must make an effort to become interiorly recollected

once more. As you are well aware, recollection is fundamental and will lead you surely to God.

2   Your eyes are your two worst enemies. That is why you must keep continual guard over them and let them see only what is necessary.

3   The greatest good you can procure for yourself is recollection, and when you have achieved it you can say what Solomon said of Wisdom, that all good things have come to you with it.

4   Curiosity is one of the greatest obstacles to growth in piety. Therefore, you must be on your guard against it; and above all else try to be recollected and aware of the presence of God, for in this we have the surest means of becoming interior. Come now, for the love of God, make the effort.

5   You know the harm thoughtless behavior does you. So, control your eyes and your tongue for this reason. There is nothing so important for you as this.

6   In this way you will make your spiritual exercises with God in mind and will learn to make them well both interiorly and exteriorly. God, you see, not only wants your actions done well outwardly; he wants them also to be carried out with the right interior dispositions. . . .

7   You complain that you have to fight against a whole host of useless thoughts. If you really try to keep your attention fixed on God, you will not find it so easy to keep useless thoughts in your mind.

LETTER 99
To a Brother

EC 104; CL 8: 472

1   . . . Take great care not to give way to impatience in carrying out your ministry, otherwise it will be quite unproductive.

2   When you feel moved to impatience, control yourself and wait until the impulse has passed before you act. When you allow yourself to be carried away by impatience, as you say in your last letter you have done, ask your Director to reprimand you and give you a good penance. This will be an effective way of bringing you to correct yourself of this serious failing.

LETTER 100
To a Brother

EC 105; CL 8: 232

. . . The spirit of faith is a sharing in the Spirit of God who dwells in us, which leads us to regulate our conduct in all things by the sentiments and truths that faith teaches us. You should, therefore, be wholly occupied in acquiring it, so that it may be for you a shield against the fiery darts of the devil. . . .

LETTER 101
To a Brother

EC 106; CL 8: 268

. . . Do not have any anxiety about the future. Leave everything in God's hands for he will take care of you. . . .

LETTER 102
To the Same Brother

EC 107; CL 8: 268

1   . . . Make sure, I beg you, that in spite of your illness, you leave yourself entirely in God's hands, for it is his right to dispose of you as he wishes. . . .

2   Take care not to let yourself be discouraged by anxieties and ailments; life is full of them.

3   While you are young, you should prepare yourself to accept them courageously and, as you have already been doing, make use of the maxims of the Gospel to welcome them and draw profit from them. . . .

LETTER 103
To a Brother

EC 108; CL 8: 329

1   . . . Have a great love for the observance of your rules, I
beg you, for Our Lord will bless you only insofar as you
make an effort to observe them exactly.

2   But if you ask me for an easy way to observe them as you
should, I would say that you should look on them as the
expression of God's will for you, and then you will find no
difficulty in them at all.

3   Of all the rules, the one you should observe most carefully
is to be exact in doing nothing without permission. This is
of utmost importance. . . .

LETTER 104
To a Brother

EC 109; CL 8: 247

1   . . . You ask me, my very dear Brother, to settle a difficult question for you.

2   In this matter, the only answer I can give is that, since the
bishops are our leaders and I am only a simple priest, I
cannot be the judge. It is to the Pope and the bishops
that such questions should be addressed, to find out their
opinion and decision on what you ask me. . . .

Letters 105 to 114
To Members of Religious
Communities

These ten letters are written to members of religious communities seeking spiritual direction from De La Salle. The first is written to a man, the others to women. They appear in Canon Blain's biography, and Brother Bernard has quoted sections of two of them. It is possible that Blain adapted the actual wording of these letters for his own purposes, possibly combining parts of various letters which deal with the same topic into what he presents as a single letter. He may also have combined and grouped verbal testimony to form some of these passages. However, from material available to him, Brother Félix-Paul made a study of Blain's use of documents and found that Blain's quotations were faithful to his source (Circular No. 335, p. 195).

There is good evidence that De La Salle was much esteemed as a spiritual director, though Blain says that De La Salle considered that this ministry took too much time from his work as Superior and confessor for the Brothers. This conclusion may be only Blain's projection of what a *saint* and *founder* should do. It is of interest to note the differences in both substance and tone in De La Salle's letters to these religious in comparison with his letters to the Brothers, even when he is dealing with the same basic principles of the spiritual life.

LETTER 105
To a Member of a Religious Community of Men

EC 119; CL 8: 390

1 . . . Dislike for our neighbor and resentment for wrongs done to us prevent our prayers from reaching God. If our hearts are torn by anger or hatred, it is impossible for us to maintain union with Jesus Christ; so, ceasing to be members of his mystical body, we cannot expect the Father to hear our prayers since he does not recognize the Spirit of his Son in us. . . .

2 Adapt yourself with gracious and charitable compliance to all your neighbor's weaknesses and, in particular, make it a

rule to hide your feelings in many matters of an indifferent nature.*

3 Give up all bitterness toward your neighbor, no matter what, and be convinced that your neighbor is in everything better than you are. This will not be difficult for you if you keep even a little aware of yourself, and it will give you the ability to overcome your feelings of resentment.

4 Each day look for every possible opportunity of doing a kindness for those for whom you feel dislike. After examining yourself on this matter every morning, form your resolutions and be faithful in keeping them with kindness and humility.

5 Be especially careful to anticipate the needs of those who are weak, in spite of the natural aversion you may feel. However, all must be kept within the limits of good order and the regular observances practiced in your community. If you have to refuse some request, make sure that your refusal does not cause unhappiness.

6 Be sure to be warmly affable toward everyone, to speak to and to answer everyone with a very great gentleness and deference, keeping in mind the way Our Lord spoke and replied to others, even when he was most harshly treated.

7 Never comment on the faults or the behavior of your confreres. When others speak of them, put a good interpretation on their actions, and if you cannot, say nothing at all.

8 Never let another take the blame in order to conceal your own guilt. Even if it was he who did the wrong and you were in no way guilty, through a spirit of charity and humility you should be quite content to let others believe it was you. Make it a habit never to defend yourself, much less conceal your guilt at the expense of others.

9 Unless necessity obliges you, don't ever complain about others in any matter at all, and should you be obliged to do so, do not make it a formal complaint.

10 However unreasonable the opinions and wishes of others may seem, if you cannot yield to them and at the same time keep your rules, try to satisfy them with words spoken with gentleness and humility.

---

*EC numbers this paragraph 3, and thus differs with the numbering of this and all the following paragraphs of this letter.

11 Should you happen to contradict someone or openly disagree with another's opinion, as soon as you realize what you are doing, if you are still speaking, stop; and if asked why, say that you had no right to speak like that. You commit plenty of more serious faults which you will have to account for, without putting a wrong interpretation on what others do.

12 You are full of zeal but it is not well-regulated, because you want others to be reprimanded for their faults but do not wish to be reproved for your own. Put up with the faults of others and be generous in the interpretation you put on them.

13 In short, take as your rule never to speak of the failings of others nor to reprimand them no matter how serious they seem to you. Whenever you see someone fall into some fault, call to mind what is said in the Gospel, "You can see the splinter in your brother's eye, but you cannot see the beam in your own. . . ."

LETTER 106
To a Member of a Religious Community of Women

EC 121; CL 8: 331; BR 77

1 . . . You should be guided in what you do by your rules, not by the example of those who transgress them. If you have read thoroughly the work of the Abbot of La Trappe, you surely have realized that it is not singularity to observe your rules in a community in which several others do not do so. Let people think what they wish of you, and do not be troubled, provided that you are doing what you ought.

2 Be zealous against your faults and for your own advancement, and if you wish to show zeal for others, let it be simply by giving them good example.

3 Look upon yourself as a novice and act as a fervent novice in the matter of faithful observance of the Rule. How carefully and with what loving ardor she follows the rules in the smallest detail and watches over herself so as not to omit even one of them. This is what you should be like and perhaps you are not. Think about this, I beg you.

4 Slackness and rationalizing will lead you into many faults. From now on, look on your rules as an explanation and an application of what is contained in the Gospels. Observe them as such. The spirit of faith will lead you to give practical application to this frame of mind.

5 Just as you must not easily follow all your impulses to do something good nor lightly take them to be inspirations from God, so you must have a great aversion for those that lead to laxity. For those you should even have a holy abhorrence, and with regard to impulses of both kinds you must take advice before coming to any decision. But if you do not have the time or the opportunity for this, and it is a question of something to be done or not done on the spur of the moment, you must ask God's help. Then with resolution, courage, and singleness of heart, do what you think would be in accordance with the advice you would get under similar circumstances. Natural repugnance for a course of action should induce you to follow it, rather than abandon it.

6 In all matters concerning the observance of your rules, I advise you to act as being in the presence of God and not to please others, because you know that to take pains that others have nothing to reproach you with and not to be concerned about God is to act as a Pharisee, a hypocrite, and not as a Christian.

7 In a word, dear Sister, keep to your rules and your daily regulations. Look upon both as being of primary importance for you. That will be better for you than working miracles. Above all, out of love for God, be all the more exact in carrying out what is most opposed to human nature and causes you the most pain rather than what pleases you most.

8 I am glad that your health permits you to follow the community exercises. That is what you must cling to and what I most want of you because it is an excellent means of making yourself pleasing to God, in whose love I am. . . .

———— ✦ ————

In his short biography of De La Salle, Brother Bernard informs us that this letter and Letter 107 were written to the same person.

Abbé Armand-Jean Le Bouthiller de Rancé, the Abbot of La Trappe mentioned in paragraph 1, was the reformer of that monastery and in 1689 composed a book bearing the title *The Rule of Saint Benedict, Newly Translated and Explained in Accordance with His True Spirit*. His reform seems to have influenced De La Salle very much, especially with regard to the strict observance of the Rule of the community, particularly the rule of silence.

LETTER 107
To the Same Member of a Religious Community of Women

EC 124; CL 8: 444; BR 76

1   . . . It is only through obedience and total submission for the love of God that you will draw down on yourself the graces of Our Lord. . . .

2   In order to seek God's will, practice obedience with interior submission to the Spirit of Our Lord, who dwells in those who take his place. Often adore the Spirit, by whose inspiration you must allow yourself to be led in all you do.

3   Be faithful to ask permission for the slightest exemptions without listening to the arguments of self-will. Human nature craves nothing more insistently than to shake off the yoke of obedience. Be faithful to this practice, I beg you.

4   It is natural to find no difficulty in doing what we like to do; but doing only what agrees with our inclinations is not obedience. To carry out commands indiscriminately, no matter how opposed they are to our feelings and inclinations, that is the sort of obedience God wants of us.

5   For our obedience to be pure, we must act through the spirit of faith. We must not examine the reasons or the purposes behind the commands we are given, but surmount all questioning and all objections. Simply follow out the commands you are given; that is how you must act from now on.

6   You are to carry out all the instructions you are given and always with unquestioning obedience. Whatever difficulty you find in doing what you are told, let nothing appear in your attitude that could call for an order contrary to the first one, unless you are convinced that it is a question of the glory of God. In this case you may express your opinion without, however, requiring that it be followed.

7   Never come to decisions on your own, for such a course of action is contrary to the obedience and dependence that members of a religious community should have. In all you

have to do you must follow the orders of your superiors. When they give you any instructions, directions or orders, accept them and carry them out without reply. Do this no matter how foolish what you are told to do or what is said to you may seem. Be assured that once you take reason as the basis for your compliance, you are no longer acting through obedience. A fine sort of religious perfection that would be, to be ready to do only what pleases you! Do not act like that, I beg you. Let there be no argument about what you are told to do nor about who gives you the orders. In the sight of God, everything is good when seasoned by obedience.

8 I pray that God will bring you to this frame of mind. . . .

LETTER 108
To a Member of a Religious Community of Women

EC 122; CL 8: 473-474

1 . . . Throw yourself into the arms of God and of his Holy Mother and you will be supported in your great weakness, not by means of sensible consolations, but as God wills it and you yourself merit it. The violence that you have to do to yourself will not always be so great nor will it last so long, for on his part God will bring you relief, and on your part you will not have so long to live. But even if it should go on and on, do not your sins deserve it, and does not the example of Jesus Christ demand it, and are not the love of God and the possession of eternal happiness worth it?

2 Confide all your failings to Jesus Christ and trust in his goodness. He will not let you be overcome by your distress if you do not give him cause through your infidelity. So be patient and wait; consolation will come in good time.

3 All the trouble and anxiety you experience afford you good opportunities for making satisfaction to God for your past life. Be faithful in this and remember that you will give an exact account of the use you have made of these opportunities. Always cling, I beg you, to the Cross of Jesus Christ and never separate yourself from it. In the face of all the threats of the devil, boldly say that you will

never leave it, nor will anything separate you from it. If you make this generous resolve, Our Lord will at once come to your help and support you in his hands.

4   Let us accept our wretchedness joyfully, since our God is always in his eternal happiness. That should calm our anxieties. Let us live through our wretched life as long as it pleases God, without complaining to anyone, not even to him who can free us from it. Let us seek only his will. I admit that the continual violence you have to do to yourself is most disagreeable to human nature, but ought we not suffer in order to win back the paradise we have lost and to avoid the hell we deserve? Everything must be seen in relation to these two great eternal truths. Let God be your sole recourse in your struggles against human nature and your dejection, and let your visits to the Blessed Sacrament be your only remedy for your distress.

5   If your present state of mind is a martyrdom, it is the best thing you could wish for, because it is most profitable for your sanctification. Even if your submission to God's will in your sufferings is only minimal, it is enough. What you must avoid is revealing your feelings to others, except those who direct you. Be careful of that.

6   I realize, my dear Sister, that you are in great suffering and I deeply share in your difficulties; but you should not, it seems to me, grieve so much. Your feelings of abandonment touch only the exterior. The profound darkness which you experience is the means that God gives to draw you more surely to himself. You know quite well that the more darkness and doubt you experience in your life, the more you will live by faith; and you know that it is faith alone which should motivate the lives and actions of those who belong to God. Often say to yourself from the depths of your desolation, "Even if I become a reprobate, I will do all that I can for God." And if out of 20 actions, there is only one that is good or even only partly good, still it will be so much done for love of God. Humble thoughts are sometimes good in your present state, but courage and confidence in God will serve you better. Once again I say, turn to God in prayer. Could doing this annoy him? Cast such a thought from your mind, dear Sister. I assure you that prayer always draws down some grace from God, even on the most hardened sinners. It is almost their only

resort. And were you simply to remain in God's presence, that would still be a great help to you, supporting you in your troubles and helping you to bear them patiently. As often as possible make your prayer in the presence of the Most Blessed Sacrament. This will help very much to bring peace of mind and tranquility to the depths of your soul.

7   Never let yourself be wrongly persuaded that God has abandoned you. On the contrary, be sure that God is more ready than ever to welcome you into his arms, and that as your distress increases so does his mercy towards you increase and abound. He knows just how weak you are and how needed his grace is to establish and strengthen in you what your weakness and laxity put you in danger of losing at every moment. . . .

LETTER 109
To a Member of a Religious Community of Women

EC 123; CL 8: 421

1   . . . You must be convinced that your vocation demands of you quite a different degree of humility and quite a different renunciation of the world and its spirit, and even of yourself, so that what would be tolerated in another person should not seem tolerable in you at all.

2   Looking on yourself as the lowest of creatures, you should place yourself beneath everyone else and be astounded that anyone can put up with you and that the earth is willing to bear you on it.

3   See how far you are from having such sentiments and be ashamed that you know yourself so little. Ask Our Lord to engrave this humility deep in your heart.

4   You cannot go too far in humbling yourself, in self-contempt and self-abasement, for this is the only way to salvation that is left to you.

5   If you wish to make great progress in the practice of this virtue, carry out the following directions:

6   No matter what the source of the humiliation, accept it as what you deserve.

7   Wait for humiliations to come, unless God gives you a special inclination to seek them out and the occasion presents itself naturally.

8 Dear Sister, look on everything that happens as good, especially when it humbles you and is most opposed to your natural inclinations. There is no better way of destroying your deep-seated pride than the acceptance each day of humiliations. If you want them and love them because you wish to be completely united with Our Lord, he will provide you with ample opportunity in addition to those already furnished by your self-will and your poor disposition. If you have such a hunger for humiliations and separation from the world, with the grace of Our Lord, you will succeed.

9 Your opinion of yourself should always be a lowly one. Humble yourself in everything and in regard to everyone. Humble yourself when you cause suffering to others, considering that this is all you are capable of; and when you find others criticizing what you do, be convinced that they are right.

10 It is good for you to be discredited in the eyes of others so that you may become more withdrawn from the world, opposed to its ways, and more closely united to God.

11 When reproved for some fault you have not committed or when rebuffed, thank those who do this with the same gentleness and humility as if they were doing you a favor. At the same time show that you are willing to correct yourself. You are well aware that you deserve no respect, no deference, not even any approval at all. You do not deserve that anyone should even listen to you. Let that be your frame of mind.

12 Always take the lowest and most inconvenient place, in spite of any repugnance you may feel, for this repugnance springs from your pride. It will always be much to your profit to be treated as the servant of the others and you should eagerly desire this: 1. to destroy your pride; 2. to overcome your laxity; and 3. to acknowledge that your sins are so many and so great, and should place you at the feet of everyone, especially of your Sisters. When you come to realize that you deserve nothing but contempt in the eyes of God and look on all created things as the instruments that in his mercy and justice he uses now to raise you up, now to humble you, and that Divine Providence makes use of them only for your salvation and his glory, you will be little affected by the harsh treatment that may be dealt you.

13 Keep yourself always in your proper place, that is to say, beneath the feet of the demons themselves, for that is where you have so often deserved to be and where perhaps you could still be forever. In this frame of mind, take your place beneath your Sisters without expecting others to show you any consideration or to treat you with any respect. You must be convinced that there is none who is not more virtuous and more spiritual than you. They could hardly be less so without putting at risk their eternal salvation as you have so often done. If, my dear Sister, you can engrave these sentiments on your heart and live by them, loving abjection, contempt, and the rebuffs of others, seeking them and embracing them as being what you deserve, I think that you will have found an efficacious means, perhaps the only means, of drawing down God's mercy on yourself. . . .

LETTER 110
To a Member of a Religious Community of Women

EC 125; CL 8: 353

1 . . . Always remember that all you have to do is try to save your soul, since you are in this world only for that purpose. Remember, too, that the Savior, who knew all your weaknesses beforehand, died only to win for you the graces and the means to help you work effectively at your salvation.

2 You must then overcome this wretched human respect, for a sinner like you should no longer be concerned about her good name and reputation. They have been lost in the sight of God and of the saints, so she ought to have no other desire than to be known for what she is—that is, an object of disgust to heaven and earth.

3 It is most important that you learn to know yourself better than you do, because, I tell you honestly, you have not the slightest understanding of the sinfulness of your life. As long as you persist in this blindness, you will be living a lie and therefore alienated from God who is truth. . . .

4 I pray that God will make you humble, chaste, and penitent. You have equal need of all three. With tears and moans ask him for these virtues every day. Above all else distrust yourself and put all your hope in him who can lift

the poor man from squalor and, as the Prophet says, seat him with the princes of his kingdom.

5   Although you have little natural liking for virtue, yet God wishes to imbue you with it through the power of his love.

6   You will not find it very difficult to give yourself to God if you have a little generosity. I hope he will give it to you. Take courage, my dear Sister; just begin to want suffering and all will be smooth and easy for you.

7   Realize that your vocation comes from God, and it would therefore be acting against his will to grow weary of it. Bless him daily for having called you to share in the various aspects of his passion, and be really ashamed that through your infidelity you have not done so.

8   Is it not an honor, a very great honor, for you to give yourself entirely to God? This, I think, is the one thought that should occupy your mind.

9   If you seek God and not consolation, you will find peace of mind.

10   Sometimes it seems that Our Lord is asleep, but then he awakens and sets us on our way. We must not go faster or at a different pace from what he wants of us, and we must rest when he wishes it.

11   My dear Sister, do you have to experience consolations to remain in God's service? Are you not prepared to be his simply out of love for him? Throw yourself into his arms; he is your Father and he will carry you when the road is rough, that is, in time of temptation.

12   It is not from men that you must expect your salvation when you ask for their help; it comes from God alone. Perhaps it is because of the lack of this spirit of faith that God does not give you the help you need.

13   In short, I pray that God will open your eyes more and more so that you will realize on the one hand the depth of the abyss from which you have been saved and, on the other, the infinite love that has lifted you from it. May this twofold realization lead you to repay him with a love and fidelity that are in proportion to your sinfulness and his mercy. Amen.

———— ✦ ————

Blain introduces this letter by saying quaintly that it was written to a Sister "whose life, considering her religious calling, was as sinful as it should have been saintly."

LETTER 111
To a Member of a Religious Community of Women

EC 126; CL 8: 289

1   . . . Frequently spend time in prayer, and during periods of aridity try to find your consolation in it, for it is there that you will find God most surely. In periods of dryness and darkness when you feel no attraction, remain constantly faithful to prayer. This is a good frame of mind to be in and a very sanctifying one.

2   Prayer, made the way I have taught you to make it, will lead you in a short time and effortlessly to live mindful of the presence of God.

3   Prayer is to be preferred to everything. After the Divine Office you should consider it an essential point of Rule.

4   Prayer of suffering is best of all, and when God lets you experience it, you must look upon it as most fortunate for you. Do not use a book during such times; you do not need one.

5   Do not be surprised if God seems to withdraw from you and if you experience aridity during prayer; you alone are the cause of this. Renounce your self-will, do violence to yourself, be faithful to whatever demands grace makes of you. Then, however unworthy you may otherwise be of the caresses and favors of the Spouse of souls, he will overwhelm you with them.

6   Be all the more faithful to prayer when you feel, on the one hand, God deep in your heart drawing you to it and, on the other, the devil making every effort to dissuade you from it. . . .

7   Prayer should be your main support; therefore, you must never miss it except when you are ill. It is prayer that will dispel the darkness of ignorance from your soul. Live by the spirit of faith. You are in God's presence; that is more than enough for you. Do not give way to self-pity, but rather fear that and distrust it.

8   Your prayer is good just as you are making it; continue to make it that way. God is in your prayer, making it for you. All you have to do is from time to time disown with peace and tranquility of heart all the repugnance and the distractions that you experience, and put yourself completely in the hands of Our Lord, so that he may come

and live in you and himself master your inclination to evil.

9   You ought to welcome the state in which you find yourself during prayer as a penance God wants you to do for your sins. It will be quite some time before you recover from it. You must bear it patiently, even joyfully. Is it not enough for a wretched soul to know that she is in God's presence? That is the reflection you should make from time to time during the day and also during your prayer in order to win for yourself some degree of interior and exterior recollection.

10   Your present state of prayer, as you describe it to me, is not the dangerous form of idleness that you think. Provided you hold on to the thought of God and make progress toward him, why should you be upset? He has no need of all your efforts. Idleness is to be avoided, but at the same time you must not hamper yourself with a great number of acts in prayer. All you need and all God wants of you is that you remain in his presence.

11   In a word, turn once again to prayer for help and remain in an attitude of abasement before God, divesting yourself of all that is not God. In simplicity of heart ask him to help you out of your present wretchedness. If you cannot pray, tell God that you cannot and then remain at peace. He will not ask you to do the impossible. Or, say to him as the Apostles did, "Lord, teach me to pray." Then remain humbly before him as one who is incapable of doing anything, and that will be your prayer. . . .

LETTER 112
To a Member of a Religious Community of Women

EC 127; CL 8: 276

1   . . . It is this sort of silence that ought to be the portion of every soul that really loves solitude and has withdrawn herself from the love of the world.

2   She ought to remain composed and silent because in this way she will always be able to rise above herself. There is nothing more dangerous for her than to allow herself to be torn away from conversation with God to stoop toward conversation with men. . . .

LETTER 113
To a Member of a Religious Community of Women

EC 128; CL 8: 276

1 . . . Now is the time for little speech and much action. Let your aim be to become very silent and very humble and to apply yourself very much to prayer, for this is what God wants of you.

2 To do this you need little thinking, little desiring, and little understanding, yet it is the way to live at peace.

3 You will find silence a very useful, even a very necessary virtue, if you are to adore God, serve him in spirit and in truth, resist temptations, and save yourself from falling into sin. . . .

4 You must learn how to be silent, to conceal your feelings, and to speak only when necessary. So that you may not fall into the habit of excessive talking, try to observe strictly the following rules:

5 Do not speak at all outside recreation time unless the need is urgent, and even during recreation speak but little. The present state of your soul demands that you be faithful to this. And you must not make even a single comment about what goes on, remembering, however, that your silence is not to spring from pride.

6 Take care never to justify yourself, but, on the contrary, admit that you were wrong, without of course telling an untruth. If you cannot speak without justifying yourself, remain completely silent. I do not see that you ever have any reason to justify yourself.

7 You are not to talk of what happens in the community or of the disorders that you think exist in it. Under such circumstances be satisfied with offering a prayer to God. When matters of importance, and even unimportant ones, are spoken of, never offer your opinion, being convinced that you have little understanding or sense of judgment.

8 Always remain silent when others annoy you, and let God alone be the witness of your innocence.

9 Lastly, if after you have held yourself in check, you do in the end speak of what you have with difficulty concealed, and even of the graces that God has granted you, you will lose what your silence has won for you, and you must set yourself a penance for your failure. . . .

LETTER 114
To a Member of a Religious Community of Women

EC 129; CL 8: 296

1   . . . You may be sure that you will not make progress in
the way of love except insofar as you are faithful not to
harden your heart to the inspirations of grace. You know
what the Holy Spirit says by the mouth of the Prophet, "If
today you hear his voice, take care not to harden your
heart," for this could bring about his withdrawal from
you, perhaps forever. . . .

Letters 115 to 118
To a Laywoman Requesting Spiritual Direction

The following extracts are taken from letters of spiritual direction written to a laywoman of some social standing. They are found only in Blain. It is of interest to compare De La Salle's remarks to this woman about the spirit of faith with his instructions to the Brothers on the same topic.

LETTER 115
To a Laywoman

EC 130; CL 8: 232

1   . . . Faith is the way by which God wishes to lead you to himself and by following this way you will please him most. Perhaps human nature will feel repugnance, but what does that matter? Is it not enough for you to know God alone? Surely this is of more value than all the other knowledge of the most learned men. . . .

2   Not only is the way of faith which God wants you to follow most advantageous for you, it is also very necessary, for you are well aware that other ways almost led you astray and caused you to lose God, once you abandoned the way of faith. . . .

LETTER 116
To the Same Laywoman

EC 131; CL 8: 233

1   . . . The Most Blessed Virgin lived her whole life by the spirit of faith, and it is this spirit that God wants you to have. This is why you would derive much benefit from asking her in prayer to lead you to Our Lord along this way which is the one most pleasing to him. . . .

LETTER 117
To the Same Laywoman

EC 132; CL 8: 233

1   . . . Look on everything with the eyes of faith. You must never fail to do this, no matter what the reason.

2   Viewing things with the eyes of faith will earn for you in one day more good, more interior application, closer union with God, and greater vigilance over yourself than a month of those penances and austerities to which you are attracted.

3   Believe me, you will see its effect, though perhaps for the present you will not understand it.

4   Let me repeat, the more uncomplicated your view of faith, the more surely you will be disposed to simplicity of action and conduct which is the disposition God wants of you. . . .

LETTER 118
To the Same Laywoman

EC 133; CL 8: 233

1   . . . I am very pleased to know, Madame, that your life is more peaceful now and more in keeping with the spirit of faith.

2   You are right in saying that, in the light of faith, you see things quite differently from when they are looked at in themselves without going beyond the natural view. . . .

LETTER 119
To Brother Irénée

Brother Irénée, Claude François Dulac de Montisambert, was born in Tigney in the Diocese of Orléans, on October 30, 1691. He became an officer in the French army at the age of 14, and at the battle of Malplaquet in 1709 was wounded. In 1713 he left the army and for some years led a life of penance while trying to discern what God wanted of him. He tried to join the Capuchins and then the Carthusians but was not accepted by either order. After a pilgrimage to Rome and to Loretto, he returned to France and spent some time in retreat at Parmenie near Grenoble. There he met De La Salle who, after the trying times he had experienced at Marseilles, was also at Parmenie on retreat to consult Sister Louise, a hermitess. In June 1714, shortly before he returned to Paris, De La Salle received the young man as a novice. Claude de Montisambert made his novitiate under the guidance of the Director of the community of Grenoble. While still a novice, he taught class at Avignon and was then sent to Paris to complete his novitiate under the care of De La Salle himself and later under Brother Barthélemy. Initially, Brother Irénée was not a success as a teacher. It was probably Irénée whom De La Salle promised to send to Gabriel Drolin in Rome, identifying him as the Brother who was somewhat knowledgeable of Italian. Instead, Irénée became the Director of novices and was referred to by De La Salle when he wrote in Letter 126, "The new master of novices, having received no training for his work, scarcely knows what he should do himself or what the novices should do."

Eventually Irénée became a very capable Director of novices, retaining the position until the General Chapter of 1725. At that Chapter, which also received the Bull of Approbation, he was elected Assistant to the Superior General, Brother Timothée, remaining in that post until his death in 1747.

In 1733 Brother Timothée, Superior General, sent Irénée, as Assistant, to visit the communities of the Institute, directing him also to stop in at his own family castle to visit his mother and younger brother. Some time after the death of Irénée's mother, his young brother was in an accident which caused a temporary mental breakdown, and the young man was cared for by the Brothers in their boarding school at Saint Yon.

The following letter is an extract taken from the *Vie du Frère Irénée,* by Abbé De Latour, published in Avignon in 1774. De Latour claims that De La Salle wrote this letter in response to one of the monthly letters in which Irénée gave his usual account of conscience and conduct. De Latour states that, like all beginners in the religious life, Irénée was violently tempted to give up his vocation because of the prohibition against main-taining family ties, because of the wealth he had renounced, and because of the lowliness of the state he had embraced. In a particular way he was tempted to abandon his vocation because of his limited success in class, and because one of his students, better looking than the rest, reminded him continually of someone he had loved prior to his entry into religious life. This daily reminder increased his feelings of regret at having given up his freedom for the life of a Brother. In the biography, De Latour uses this extract to demonstrate the importance of a frank manifestation of con-science in giving an account of one's conduct to one's superiors.

Letter 119: To Brother Irénée
  EC 39

[1716]

1   . . . When you are beset with impure thoughts, if you are in class, try to occupy yourself with the work you have on hand.

2   Such thoughts as these are the most subtle temptations of the devil, and you must keep your mind on the present and not worry about the future. This idea of returning to the world to devote yourself to good works has been the downfall of many religious.

3   You will find penance a great help in correcting your defects and advancing in virtue.

4   Whatever your dispositions, you must strive to bring your will to accept reprimands and corrections. If you have dif-ficulty in accepting them in your heart, at least say that you accept them.

5   Do not upset yourself trying to make acts of penance fre-quently; that could injure your health. It is enough simply to direct your thoughts to God from time to time.

6   Why are you afraid of the days set aside for confession? Instead, you should look forward to them.

7   Don't talk a great deal in class. Get in the habit of using the usual signals as is our custom.

8   When you feel tempted to give way to impatience, hold yourself in check and do nothing until the impulse has passed.

9   I am devotedly yours in Our Lord. . . .

LETTER 120
To His Nephew, Jean-François Maillefer

On June 17, 1715, the Archbishop of Reims excommunicated and placed under interdict three canons and three parish priests of Reims for refusing his official instruction that the Bull *Unigenitus* be accepted by all within the archdiocese. The Bull had been proclaimed by the Holy See in September 1713 and had been acknowledged and accepted by the assembly of the hierarchy of France on January 23, 1714. One of these recalcitrant canons was a nephew of De La Salle, and it is to him, Jean-François Maillefer, that De La Salle writes this letter.

Only Blain preserves this letter and presents it to demonstrate De La Salle's respect for ecclesiastical superiors. De La Salle, Blain says, addressed in this letter a close personal friend who was a priest to express his shock that he was not submissive but had appealed to civil magistrates against the suspension imposed by the ecclesiastical superior. Blain may not have known that this priest was De La Salle's own nephew, or he may have avoided naming him in order not to offend the priest's brother, François-Elie Maillefer, whose biography of De La Salle he used for his own work.

Letter 120: To His Nephew, Jean-François Maillefer
EC 118; CL 8: 247

[Early 1717]

1   . . . This is the third time that I have taken up my pen to do myself the honor of writing to you since the beginning of the year. I hope that it will be a good and happy one for you.

2   May I mention the sorrow you cause me by what you are doing. It arises from the fact that you have involved yourself in the suspension imposed on your colleagues and that you have taken the case before civil magistrates. By implication, you consider these magistrates your superiors in ecclesiastical matters.

3   I am surprised that you have not arranged that the chalice and the surplice be restored to you with appropriate ceremony by some officer of the court, as if recognizing in him as much right to restore to you your priestly faculties as your bishop had in bestowing them in the first place.

4   How can you recognize laymen as your judges in a matter that is as surely the province of the Church as ever there was? Indeed, how could you, who have a deep understanding of your vocation and are not indifferent to what

concerns it, how could you have recourse to a purely lay and secular jurisdiction?

5   Perhaps you will reply that many others have followed the same course. Are you then acting through human respect?

6   And then you will add, I suppose, that you did it because your colleagues laid this responsibility on you. But surely you realize that they have no right to require you to betray the rights of the Church and submit to the judgment of a secular court in a matter outside its competence.

7   I know that Saint Peter and Saint Paul require us to submit to temporal authorities, but they never claimed that this should extend to spiritual matters. Furthermore, when an appeal is made to higher authority and jurisdiction, it must be a case *in eodem genere,* that is, solely for matters that fall within the province of that higher jurisdiction and not outside it. In this case the right to the chalice and surplice is outside secular jurisdiction. . . .

8   You could apply to this situation, though not in quite the same sense, what Saint Paul says in the sixth chapter of his first Letter to the Corinthians: "Dare any of you, having a quarrel with a fellow Christian, bring your case to be judged by the unjust, that is, the Gentiles, and not by the saints, that is, by Christians?"

9   As for me, I am quite prepared to say of any cleric who brings legal proceedings against his ecclesiastical superior, "Does he dare to submit himself to civil rather than to ecclesiastical judges, who are his rightful judges in such matters?" "Do you not know," adds the holy Apostle, "that the saints will be appointed judges of this world?" And you, are you not aware, that the bishops of the Church have been appointed as the judges you must turn to in such matters as these?

———— ✦ ————

The six clerics under suspension appealed to the court of Paris against the archbishop. The case opened on April 29, 1716, and the decision was given in favor of the six clerics, the action of the archbishop of Paris being declared contrary to the laws of France and therefore invalid. Such a decision was not surprising since France was then under the regency of Philippe of Orléans, who favored Gallicanism and the Jansenists. The magistrates of the Paris Court followed the course set by their ruler.

Among the six who rebelled against the archbishop's instruction was Jean-François Maillefer, Canon of the collegial church of Saint Symphorien,

Reims, and nephew of De La Salle. He was one of the three sons of Marie, De La Salle's sister, and her husband, Jean Maillefer, to reach adulthood.

In a marginal note to his *Mémoire et Journal,* Jean Maillefer wrote, "My good wife would have died a thousand deaths if she had been alive when her beloved son was persecuted for the Constitution [*Unigenitus*], as I have described in another place" (*De La Salle: Saint and Spiritual Writer,* by W. J. Battersby, p. 93, n. 1).

The appeal to a General Council against the Bull *Unigenitus* was later suppressed in action taken by the Chapter of Saint Symphorien. Canon Maillefer, however, maintained his agreement with the appeal and his original opposition against the Bull, and further opposed this new action by his own Chapter. He was excommunicated in August 1721. He died in October 1723.

The other two sons of Jean Maillefer and Marie de La Salle were Simon-Louis and François-Elie. Both were Benedictines of Saint Maur, and it was François-Elie who wrote the biography of his uncle, John Baptist.

LETTER 121
To M. Gense of Calais

This extract is found only in Blain, where he devotes three pages to his eulogy of Gense. Gense was a layman of Calais, praised by Blain for his steadfast attachment to the Church, his strong opposition to the appellants in the Jansenist controversy, and for having "remained a devout layman" when Church benefits were much sought after and so easily acquired (CL 7: 386–388).

Letter 121: To M. Gense
EC 115; CL 8: 228

[After April 1717]

1   . . . It gives me great pleasure to hear of the zeal you show for the defense of the Catholic religion which is at present a prey to so many disorders in this country.

2   You would like me to join you in this issue to which, with the aid of God's grace, I have up to now been devoting my attention.

3   I will not fail to pray earnestly that God may bless your zeal with success which will counteract all the efforts of the devil to destroy the peace of the Church at this present time. . . .

———————— ✦ ————————

According to Blain it was to Gense and his friend, De La Cocherie of Boulogne, that De La Salle opened his heart to tell them of the difficulties he had experienced in the establishment of the Institute of the Brothers: "Let me tell you, Gentlemen, if God in showing me the good that this Institute could effect had also let me see the difficulties and the crosses that would come with it, my courage would have failed, and I would not have dared to touch it with the tips of my fingers . . ." (CL 8: 358).

The allusion in Blain's biography to "appellants" indicates that the letter was written after April 1717.

Letters 122 and 123
To Laymen
Who Knew the Brothers

Both of these letters were written after the General Chapter of 1717 and, therefore, after Brother Barthélemy had replaced De La Salle as Superior.

LETTER 122
To a Layman, Benefactor of the Brothers

EC 116; CL 8: 413–414

[After the 1717 Chapter]

1   Though I am but a poor priest of Saint Yon, Sir, may I be so bold as to enclose this note in the letter from Brother Barthélemy, Superior of the Brothers, and beg you in your kindness to do on their behalf what he takes the liberty of proposing to you.

2   I am so convinced of your zeal and affection for the Brothers that I am sure my poor request is unnecessary; his own letter would be sufficient, for I know your generosity so well.

3   However, it does give me the opportunity of reassuring you that I always have for you the highest esteem and regard. This is so important to me that I beg you to let my note at least serve to tell you of my sentiments and to assure you that I am, Sir, with the greatest respect,
   Your very humble and obedient servant,
   DE LA SALLE, a poor Priest

———— ◆ ————

This letter was written after the General Chapter of 1717, when De La Salle officially laid aside the position of Superior of the Brothers. The ceremonious style, reminiscent of that used in Letter 1, suggests that the recipient was a person of some social standing. This letter was enclosed with a letter from Brother Barthélemy, and there is no indication of the name of the person to whom it was addressed.

LETTER 123
To a Layman

EC 117; CL 8: 413

[After the 1717 Chapter]

1   May I say, Sir, that you were apparently misinformed when you were told that I am doing so much good in the Church and that I send school teachers to towns and villages to teach the young.

2   It is true that I began training Brothers to conduct schools gratuitously, but I was relieved of their direction a long time ago.

3   It is one of the Brothers, Brother Barthélemy by name, who is now in charge. He lives in this house and the Brothers, even those of Saint Denis, acknowledge him as their superior. . . .

Letters 124 to 130
To Brother Barthélemy

Brother Barthélemy, Joseph Truffet, was born on February 11, 1678, in the Diocese of Cambrai, and entered the Institute at Paris on February 10, 1703. After a very short novitiate, he was sent to teach at Chartres. However, he fell ill there and from then on was attached to the novitiate. In August 1705 he took charge of the novitiate. He was elected first Superior General of the Institute on May 18, 1717. He died shortly after De La Salle, on June 8, 1720.

LETTER 124
To Brother Barthélemy

EC 2; CL 8: 313

[Between August, 1705, and July, 1709]

1   . . . At Saint Yon, I noticed you swinging your arms carelessly when you walked. This is a disgraceful habit in a master of novices who ought in all things to be a model for those whom he instructs.

2   You must walk in a dignified manner, keeping your arms folded, and you must not let your novices do otherwise. . . .

———— ✦ ————

This extract was addressed to Brother Barthélemy when he was the Director of novices.

The chapter on modesty in the 1718 Rule of the Brothers insists on rather stringent regulations regarding posture, gestures, and manner of walking.

LETTER 125
To Brother Barthélemy, Superior General

AM; AMG; EC 3; BL I.42

Seminary of Saint Nicolas du Chardonnet
January 17, 1718

1   Brother Thomas told me that he was setting out today, my very dear Brother.

2   He had me write a receipt for your dividends and state that these dividends now go to the heirs of Madame De Louvois; and he had me write an ordinary receipt a few days earlier.

3   Do not attach any worth to either one or the other of these receipts, I beg you, except insofar as it suits you. I made a statement, as you required of me at the time of your last journey, about the time of the feast of the Conception of the Blessed Virgin, declaring on December 11 last year that your four certificates of dividends on the town dues of the city of Rouen do not belong to me. I stated that I had simply allowed my name to be used on them; that they are the property of the Brothers of the Christian Schools of the house of Saint Yon, in the suburb of Saint Sever in that city; and that the money was provided by Charles Frappet, also called Brother Thomas, at that time bursar of the same house. I then put the declaration signed by me in the hands of Father Berton, procurator of this seminary, who has taken the responsibility for it.

4   As regards the house of Saint Yon, whether you buy it or not and how you go about it, concerning which matters you ask my advice, pay no regard to what Brother Thomas may tell you or give you to understand from me or about me. Pay heed only to what I set down in this letter. I can give no advice in this matter; you will have to consult persons who are more enlightened than I, since it is a matter of some importance.

5   As the business has not been finalized, give it serious thought.

6   I do not advise you to borrow money to purchase it. However, I do not say absolutely not to do so; you may consult others on the matter.

7   I think that what you do in this will always be well done. It is not fitting that I should take any part in these matters, since I am of no importance, and you, being the Superior, are the one responsible.

8   Concerning the persons whom you tell me in your letter to call on, I will go to see them if you so wish. If that is the case, please send me word that you, as my Superior and that of the Brothers, so instruct me, and I will go at once, or on the first free day, and tell them that you directed me to visit them.

9   I wish you and all the Brothers, to whom I send my greetings, a successful and happy New Year.

10   I am, my very dear Brother, respectfully,
         Your very humble and obedient servant,
         DE LA SALLE

———————— ◆ ————————

De La Salle had rented the property of Saint Yon from the Marchioness of Louvois in 1705. The lease had been renewed for a further nine years in 1711. By 1718 the heirs of the Marchioness informed the Brothers that they wished to sell the property and that the Brothers should either buy it or vacate it.

The above letter is De La Salle's answer to Barthélemy's request for clarification regarding some financial transactions made in the past.

After De La Salle handed over his superiorship to Brother Barthélemy, he lived at the Seminary of Saint Nicolas du Chardonnet for some months in order not to make it awkward for the new Superior.

Brother Thomas, the Institute's bursar or procurator, had been directed by Brother Barthélemy to gather together the financial resources of the young Institute in view of the purchase of Saint Yon.

LETTER 126
To Brother Barthélemy, Superior General

EC 4; CL 8: 328

[March 1718]

1   I am writing to you, my very dear Brother, because I am astounded to see the sorry state of your novitiate: the two or three novices are receiving no formation at all and observe the rules no better than they did when they first entered the house.

2   Moreover, there are five aspirants who are full of defects and who see almost no good example.

3   The new master of novices, having received no training for his work, scarcely knows what he should do or what the novices should do. He says he has no rule to follow and neither do the novices.

4   I do not think that I have seen, at least for a good many years, a novitiate like this in the Community, and yet, with such a situation, you hope to establish new foundations!

5   . . . There are even complaints that the novices at Rouen do not show much evidence of the spirit of their state and pay no attention to detail.

6   I beg you, take steps to remedy this situation as soon as
      possible, for you know that the strength of the Institute
      depends on the formation of the novices in fidelity to the
      Rule. . . .

7   I am now well enough to take part in the principal exer-
      cises with the other Brothers, to sleep in the common
      dormitory, and to take my meals like the others in the
      refectory. Please do not raise any objections to this.

8   We look forward to your return, for your presence is
      needed in this house.

9   I am, my very dear Brother, in Our Lord,
            Your very humble and obedient servant,
            DE LA SALLE

It has already been mentioned how Brother Irénée was at first unskilled
as Director of novices. In this letter to his Superior General, De La Salle
shows what forthright zeal he had for the welfare of the Institute, despite
the fact that he was no longer in full charge. He felt that the future of
the Institute was in serious jeopardy. He may have been mindful of the
vow he had taken with Gabriel Drolin and Nicolas Vuyart to uphold the
Society and may have felt that he was obliged to make representation to
his Superior in the strongest possible terms.

Five postulants entered the novitiate at Saint Yon in 1717 and are
named in the *Catalogue*: Brother Félicien, 13 years old, is listed as "sent
away;" Brother Gérard, 28 years old, entered a second time in August and
is listed as "left;" Brothers Marcel and Sixte, each 23 years old, and Brother
Stanislas, 19 years old, benefited from De La Salle's complaints and
persevered (CL 3). Marcel died at Saint Yon (no date listed), Stanislas died
in 1731, and Sixte lived until 1788, the last Brother to survive who had
lived as a Brother during the lifetime of De La Salle.

Only three Brothers took the habit in 1718: Brother Victor, 29 years
old; Brother Eusèbe, 21 years old; and Brother Albert, whose age is not
recorded. The first two persevered and died in the Institute in 1759 and
1782, respectively.

The "novices at Rouen," mentioned in paragraph 5, are the young
Brothers in their first year of teaching. No doubt they made their novitiate
in 1716 and were losing their first fervor amid all the activities of school.
Thirteen novices took the habit in 1716, only six of whom persevered:
Brothers Spiridion, Maurice, Joachim, Denis, Quentin, and Pascal.

De La Salle's request mentioned in paragraph 7, to sleep in the common dormitory, was not honored. His room, however, was not exactly the
best in the house. The property plan of Saint Yon indicates that his was

actually one of two rooms on the ground floor at the corner of the barn-yard where the chickens were kept; the other room was that of a serving Brother. De La Salle was later moved to the infirmary, "in a room which is near the chapel," as he wrote in his last will.

LETTER 127
To Brother Barthélemy, Superior General

EC 5; CL 8: 275

[1717–1718]

1 . . . I seriously think that, since I have given but little time to prayer for so long, it is right that I should now spend more time in prayer in order to learn what God wishes of me.

2 To my mind, what I must ask of God in prayer is that he tell me what he wants me to do and that he inspire me with the disposition he wants me to have. . . .

LETTER 128
To Brother Barthélemy, Superior General

EC 6; CL 8: 203

[After 1717]

. . . It is hardly right to have dealings with persons of this sort, much less to be dependent on them. . . .

——— ♦ ———

De La Salle is no doubt referring to a situation such as that which arose in Calais. Brother Barthélemy indicated to the Brother Director of the community at Calais that he must defend the orthodox position of the Brothers who would not receive the sacrament of reconciliation from clergy who had aligned themselves with the Jansenists. Later, just a few months before his death, De La Salle wrote Letter 132 to the Director of Calais refuting the allegation made by the Dean of Calais that De La Salle was one of the appellants against the Bull *Unigenitus*.

LETTER 129
To Brother Barthélemy, Superior General

EC 7; CL 8: 450

[After May 1717]

. . . You know that I am always ready to obey you in everything since I am now subject to your authority, and I did not vow obedience to do what I like. . . .

LETTER 130
To Brother Barthélemy, Superior General

EC 8; CL 8: 450

[After May 1717]

. . . If I am to be considered a member of the Brothers of the Christian Schools, it seems to me that my present position ought to be one of simple submission and that I should make no move in what concerns them except through obedience. . . .

———— ✦ ————

In Letters 129 and 130 De La Salle recalls the vows of obedience and association he had pronounced in 1691 and 1694. He renewed these vows in 1718 on the feast of the Holy Trinity, the traditional day for the renewal of vows in the Institute of the Brothers. It is only under obedience, De La Salle says, that he should concern himself with matters that affect the Institute.

LETTER 131
To His Niece, Jeanne-Remiette de La Salle

Jeanne-Remiette de La Salle, whose religious name was Sister Françoise of Saint Agnes, was the daughter of Pierre, De La Salle's brother. After being a boarding student with the Sisters of the Congregation of Notre Dame, founded by Saint Peter Fourier, Jeanne-Remiette entered their novitiate at the age of 17 in May 1716, and made her religious profession on June 13, 1718. One of her own sisters was also with Jeanne in the same congregation. At this time a total of seven relatives of the Founder were members of the Sisters of Notre Dame, a congregation devoted to teaching the poor.

Letter 131: To His Niece, Jeanne-Remiette de La Salle
EC 120; CL 8: 275

[1718]

My very dear Niece,

1   On Ascension Thursday I answered the letter that you kindly sent me but, as it may not have reached you, I am writing a second time.

2   I am very grateful to you for letting me know the date of your religious profession and share with you your joy and your ardent desire to consecrate yourself entirely to God. It will win for you in this life a foretaste of life eternal.

3   How fortunate I think you are in separating yourself from the cares and anxieties of the world!

4   I will not fail to unite myself with you in prayer to ask God to give you the grace to make this sacrifice wholeheartedly.

5   I would very much like to be present at your profession, but I am prevented for two reasons. The first is that I am the only priest here to hear the confessions of 50 people, and it is difficult to get another for this community which is far from the town. So, I can't abandon them just now. The second is that, since I have a Superior, I am not my own master.

6   So, I ask you, please be satisfied that I join with you in this holy action in the same dispositions as those with which, by God's grace, you will make your profession.

7   With my best regards and all my affection. . . .

———— ♦ ————

This letter was written between Ascension Day, May 26, 1718, and June 13, 1718, the day of the profession. Since 1716 De La Salle had delegated his authority as Superior to Brother Barthélemy in order to prepare the Brothers and others for the time when the Superior General of the Institute of the Brothers would not be a priest but one of the Brothers themselves. Thus when Barthélemy was formally elected in 1717, he had already been exercising this authority for some time.

When De La Salle says in paragraph 5 that he is the only priest at Saint Yon, it may be that he had arranged it that way in order to avoid a precedent that could create some difficulty for the new Superior General, a lay religious. During his lifetime, however, there were always priests staying in communities of Reims, Vaugirard, and Paris, who helped out while spending time in retreat.

The 50 persons at Saint Yon included the different types of boarders as well as the Brothers.

LETTER 132
To Brother Director of the Community at Calais

There are two sources for this letter: one is a copy of the original letter made during the superiorship of Brother Agathon, 1777–1798, and kept at the Generalate of the Brothers in Rome; the other is from Blain. Neither source mentions the name of the Brother to whom the letter was addressed. Blain even suppresses the name "Calais," but a little later states that ["the Dean"] had not been able to forget the gentle and polite reprimand that he had received from the Saint on the subject of the Assumption of the Most Blessed Virgin." On the occasion of a visit of De La Salle to Calais, the Dean had asked him to celebrate the Mass in honor of the Assumption. To De La Salle's surprise, the Dean did not mention the day's feast in his homily.

The Director of the community of Calais is thought to have been the Brother Norbert referred to in Letter 12. He was the Director in 1717 at Calais, but shortly thereafter he was transferred to Saint Yon. His successor was Brother Anastase, addressed in Letter 72; he, together with his community, felt the brunt of the Dean's anger in 1720.

Letter 132: To the Brother Director at Calais
Copy; AMG; EC 65; BL IV.Ap.1; CL 8: 224

Rouen
January 28, 1719

1   I do not think, my very dear Brother, that I have given the Very Reverend Dean of Calais any reason for saying that I am one of the appellants.

2   It has never been my intention to appeal any more than it has been to embrace the doctrines of those who appeal to a future council.

3   I have too much respect for our Holy Father the Pope and too great a submission to the decisions of the Holy See not to give my assent to them.

4   In this matter I wish to follow the example of Saint Jerome, who was in the difficult situation brought about in the Church by the Arians. When they insisted that he acknowledge three hypostases in God, he considered it his duty to consult the chair of Saint Peter, on which, he said, he knew the Church was founded. Addressing Pope Damasus, he declared that, if His Holiness ordered him to admit three hypostases in God, notwithstanding the difficulty he would find in so doing, he would have no fear in acknowledging three hypostases. That is why he closed his letter by urgently begging His Holiness in the name of Jesus Christ, the Savior of the World, and in that of the Holy Trinity of divine persons in one same nature, to be pleased to write to him, authorizing him either to affirm or to deny that there are three hypostases in God.

5   Neither the Dean nor anyone else ought to be surprised if, following the example of this great saint who was so enlightened in matters of religion, I consider it sufficient for myself that he who is today seated in the chair of Saint Peter has declared by a Bull, which is accepted by almost all the bishops of the world, his condemnation of the 101 propositions taken from Father Quesnel's book. After such an authentic decision by the Church, I say with Saint Augustine that the case is closed.

6   Such are my sentiments and such are my dispositions, which have never been different and which I will never change.

7   I am, my very dear Brother,
        Your very humble and obedient servant,
        DE LA SALLE, Priest

[*Added as a postscript to his letter, De La Salle wrote the following:*]

1   Mihi cathedram Petri censui consulendam. . . . Super illam petram aedificatam Ecclesiam scio.
    [I have decided that I must consult the chair of Peter. . . .
    I know that the Church has been built on that rock.]

2 Discernite, si placet, obsecro, non timebo dicere tres
  hypostases, si jubetis.
  [Make a decision, please, I beg you, and I will not fear to
  say that there are three hypostases, if you order it.]

3 Obtestor beatitudinem tuam per crucifixum mundi salu-
  tem, per homousion trinitatem, ut mihi epistolis tuis sive
  tacendarum sive dicendarum hypotaseôn detur auctoritas.
  [I beg your Holiness in the name of the crucified Savior of
  the world and in the name of the Holy Trinity of divine
  persons to authorize me by letter either to deny or to affirm the hypostases in God.]

---------- ✦ ----------

The declaration that De La Salle presents as a unified argument in this letter is to be found in various parts of a letter attributed to Saint Jerome. The text of that letter is in volume IV of Jerome's writings, published between 1693 and 1705 in Paris, possibly the edition from which De La Salle took his argument. The three propositions from Saint Jerome's letter in Latin after De La Salle's signature, together with the formal ending of the letter, so different from his usual manner of closing letters to the Brothers, indicate that he was not writing for the Director of Calais alone, but rather so that the letter might be used as his public refutation of any association with the appeal against the Pope to a General Council. By it he also gave his assent to the condemnation of the propositions drawn from Quesnel's *Réflexions Morales.*

On March 5, 1717, four bishops of France among whom was Pierre de Langle, Bishop of Boulogne, the Diocese of which Calais was a part, appealed against the Bull *Unigenitus* to a future General Council. They declared the Bull contrary to Catholic doctrine. Their appeal was supported by the Sorbonne and 12 other bishops, one of whom was the Archbishop of Paris, De Noailles. From this date the name *appellants* was given to these bishops and to members of the clergy who gave their signatures to the appeal. The appellants were condemned by a decree from the Holy Office and also by a further Bull *Pastoralis Officii.* The appellants were finally excommunicated.

Among the appellants was Jean-Louis, Canon of the cathedral chapter of Reims and brother of John Baptist de La Salle. His name is shown on the copy of the baptismal entry as Jean-Louis, while in the copy of his epitaph, inscribed by his nephew, his name is given as Jean-Baptiste Louis de La Salle (CL 27: 65 and 73). It seems that Jean-Louis also called himself Jean-Baptiste Louis. The Dean of Calais easily confused the Founder of the Institute of the Brothers, a former canon of Reims, with his brother, a canon at that time.

De La Salle, however, left no doubt whatever in the Dean's mind. His letter states unequivocally his attitude toward the papacy and the decisions of the Holy See. He disassociates himself completely from the appellants who claimed the *Augustinus* of Jansenius as the authority for their doctrinal position. With some irony, De La Salle closes his argument, in paragraph 5, with the words attributed to Saint Augustine, himself in debate with the Pelagians during the fifth century.

LETTER 133
To His Brother, Canon Jean-Louis de La Salle

Written by De La Salle to his brother, Canon Jean-Louis, this letter has only recently come to light, as a result of the indefatigable research of Brother Léon de Marie Aroz, who found it in the 1718 files of M. Thiénot, a solicitor of Reims. According to the terms of the Reims Agreement of 1969, the document remains the property of M. Thiénot. However, M. Thiénot generously consented to display it in the museum of the Hotel De La Salle in Reims. The files inThiénot's possession also contain, in addition to documents referring to De La Salle's immediate family, others dating back to the sixteenth century relating to the ancestors of De La Salle.

This letter was first published by Brother Léon de Marie Aroz in CL 39, under the title "Jean-Baptiste de La Salle: Une Lettre Inédite." It appears also in CL 41 I, together with evidence that Jean-Louis took the necessary steps to see that all the provisions made in this letter and all the conditions laid down by De La Salle became legally binding.

There are no paragraphs in the original letter, except in the middle of the first sentence before the words, "I hereby declare."

Letter 133: To His Brother, Canon Jean-Louis de La Salle
AM; CL 39: 26; CL 41 I: 293

Seminary of Saint Nicolas du Chardonnet, Paris
March 2, 1718

My very dear Brother,

Since you have pointed out to me in your last letter that a single letter from me will be sufficient to make known my intentions concerning the property that I still own and that is in your hands, I hereby declare that, as of this day, I transfer and cede in favor of the present and future children of my brother, Jean-Remy de La Salle, out of compassion for the wretched state to which they have been reduced, the income from the principal of 2,000 francs invested in the Clergy Fund of the Diocese of Reims. I reserve the right to myself and to those to whom I transfer this right to resume possession of the aforesaid income as I or those to whom I have transferred this right consider it advisable and pay the sum of 2,000 francs into a fund for the profit of the said children.

I also transfer and cede to them:

- two-thirds of the income payable by the Association of Locksmiths of the same city, the principal being 1,400 francs invested at four percent, the said two-thirds bringing me an income of 38 francs;

- plus half of the income from the vineyard at Thillois near Reims, the other half belonging to the said Jean-Remy de La Salle, my brother;

- together with the rights belonging to me of a house in the village of Trois Puits, near Reims, part of the estate of a certain Mathieu Menu, deceased.

As from this day the income from the above investments and securities will belong to the said children and is to be received by you, Canon De La Salle of the Church of Reims, my brother, to be distributed by you at your discretion without your being obliged to render any account to them at any time or for any reason whatever.

I am, with the greatest respect, dear brother,
Your humble and obedient servant,
DE LA SALLE

——— ✦ ———

On the reverse of this letter is written: M. De La Salle, Doctor of the Sorbonne, Canon of the Church of Reims, Reims.

Jean-Remy, the youngest brother of De La Salle, was born on July 12, 1670, just after De La Salle's nineteenth birthday. Their mother died 12 months later, on July 19, and their father died shortly thereafter on April 9, 1672. De La Salle, then three weeks before his twenty-first birthday, was named guardian of the family in his father's will. He withdrew from his studies at the Sorbonne in Paris and returned to his family home on April 23, to care for his two sisters and four brothers.

After an initial career in the army, Jean-Remy became an official in

Letter 133, to his brother, Canon Jean-Louis de La Salle

the Royal Mint in Reims, gaining the post of superintendent in 1698 at the age of 28. On May 5, 1711, he married Madeleine Bertin de Rocheret at Epernay, about 30 kilometers to the south of Reims. It is interesting to note that not one of his immediate family was present either at the signing of the marriage contract, April 29, or at the marriage ceremony six days later on May 5.

Madeleine's brother, Valentin-Philippe, recorded that "De La Salle, the Founder, came to visit Bertin de Rocheret at the time of the grape harvest of 1711," that is, some months after the marriage (CL 41 I: 258, n. 5). During the year 1711, from the end of February, De La Salle spent several months visiting the communities of the Brothers in the south of France. On August 24 he informed Drolin in Letter 29 of his intention to return to Paris, where he had been recalled to answer the charges brought against him by the father of the Abbé Clément. On his way to Paris he visited once more the Brothers of Avignon, Alès, Les Vans, and Mende. Possibly he considered that his visit to Epernay en route to the capital city was an act of courtesy to the family of Bertin de Rocheret, since he had not been able to attend the wedding.

Four children were born to Jean-Remy and Madeleine. One of them died in infancy, and the family was soon to feel the effects of more tragedy. In 1715, Jean-Remy had to retire from his post in the Royal Mint, suffering from a mental disorder. Three of his brothers, John Baptist, Jean-Louis, and Pierre, together with their brother-in-law, Jean Maillefer, the widower of their sister, Marie, drew up a deed on November 28, 1716, whereby each would provide a quarter of the cost of the maintenance of Jean-Remy and the three children. Under the terms of the marriage contract, Madeleine had retained her own private means. Jean-Remy's mental derangement worsened, and on February 15, 1717, he was deprived of all civil rights, his property was seized, and he was permanently confined to a mental institution, where he died in 1732. This tragedy was the reason for a number of letters from Jean-Louis to De La Salle and it prompted the Founder's decision, taken in 1718, to make over to Jean-Remy's children the income from the properties he owned.

It is not clear what property De La Salle retained after distributing his wealth in favor of the poor in the years 1684–1685. Acting on the advice of his spiritual director, as Brother Bernard, his earliest biographer, tells us, he kept for himself an annual income of 200 livres, "in order not to tempt Providence" (CL 4: 61). We are also told that this income was used to pay for his travels, to build up his library for his own use and that of the Brothers, and to purchase vessels and vestments for use in the celebration of the Mass. It is perhaps significant that the sum of 200 livres was the yearly stipend that De La Salle requested for the upkeep of a Brother whenever a new school was established. He had had personal experience of this need when the first schools were established at Saint Maurice and Saint Jacques in Reims. When a fifth teacher was required because of the increase in the number of students, he provided from his personal income an extra 200 livres to be added to the 800 already guaranteed by the benefactors (CL 4: 35). The retention of enough from his personal wealth to provide an annual income of 200 livres could be seen as a declaration by De La Salle that he wished to be considered on an equal footing with the Brothers, while not wishing to be a drain on their income.

At the time of writing this letter on March 2, 1718, De La Salle had already committed himself to pay one-quarter of the maintenance of his ill brother, Jean-Remy. He now made a settlement on behalf of Jean-Remy's children, thus disposing of the residue of his personal property:

✦ the 2,000 francs invested with the Clergy Fund of Reims (no further information has been given regarding this investment; it was possibly a sort of superannuation guarantee against retirement for the clergy);
✦ his share of the income from investments with the Association of Locksmiths of Reims;
✦ his share of the income from a vineyard in Thillois;
✦ his rights to the income from a house in Trois Puits.

LETTER 133(A)
From Canon Jean-Louis de La Salle to His Brother, John Baptist

This letter is probably the last letter which Jean-Louis wrote to his brother, John Baptist de La Salle. It is included here because of its close relationship with the previous Letter 133. The first two separations by paragraph are not in the original.

Letter 133(A): From Jean-Louis de La Salle to John Baptist de La Salle
AM; AMG; CL 26, D. 20; CL 41 I: 304

Reims
January 3, 1719

My very dear Brother,

Although it would appear that you are determined to forget this part of the country completely and that you have decided to cut off all communication with us for a year or even several years—so that I have only with great difficulty been able to get a reply from you in matters of great importance—I do not consider myself freed from my obligations. So I take it upon myself to write to you once more, not only to pay my respects to you at the beginning of this new year and to wish you a very happy one, insofar as there can be a happy one in this life, but mainly to remind you once more of some matters of importance to your Institute, which I have already had the honor to speak and to write to you about on several occasions.

You know that the ownership of the house in Reims is still not settled and that there are only two legal owners when there should be four. I have proposed several names to you but am still opposed to including Father Fremyn as one of the number. If your Brothers in Reims were to tell how he acts here in his capacity as their superior, you would know for yourself that it is very desirable that he have no say in what concerns the Institute. I have several times offered the name of Father Maillefer, my nephew, and there is no one whom I could name who is better disposed towards your work and more dependable in what concerns its continuance. I do not know why you hesitate to name him out of the very small number of good priests that we have today. I have proposed Father De La Salle de l'Etang, but he is now professor of theology at Rosoy. I do not see anyone else worth considering unless it be Father Legrand, at present canon at Saint Balsamie, or Father Horquette, parish priest of Saint André in the suburbs, unless you wish to choose someone from outside Reims, for example, Father Guyart of Laon.

I must not fail to remind you that you own several houses at Rethel and some properties in Reims bought in your name. It is important that you dispose of them by will, after taking legal advice, so that after your death, my brother's children, who are still minors, or those who act on their behalf, may not be able to make any claims with regard to them, on account of their father's illness, and that there may be no misunderstanding about their ownership.

At Rethel, the declaration made by Father Favart and M. Bajot concerning the Queutelot's house and the one that once belonged to Ludet states that, on your death, they will belong to those who have the management of the schools in Reims. This could give rise to some misunderstanding, as it is not clear whether it means the Superior of the Brothers or a cleric named by the archbishop as superior. It is to be hoped that this can be rectified and that Father Favart, by a new declaration explaining the previous one, can clarify the meaning in a way that is appropriate and is not liable to misinterpretation. This will be difficult, however, as Father Favart's declaration was used as a guide for that made by M. Bajot, who quotes it.

Still, I think it would be even better to have the first one explained in such a way, by a new declaration made by Father Favart, that after your death the Queutelot house will belong to the owners of the house in Reims. That will be less confusing than leaving things as they are. As for the Etienne house, I do not know what clauses are included in the title deeds, for I have never seen the contract of sale. With regard to the Charlet house, it is solely in your name, therefore is yours to dispose of. With regard to the one left by Mme. and M. Bonvarlet, you are not, strictly speaking, the owner. In Reims you have the house left to you by Father Pasté for the use of the schools. I do not know if there are any other properties. I shall make inquiries. All this might have been simplified with some discussion between us; but anyway, what I can do is remind you of it and beg you to make the necessary arrangements.

No doubt you have heard of the death of M. Maillefer, my brother-in-law, on December 7. On November 10 we lost Father Godard, our penitentiary. His loss is widely felt, as he was almost the sole support of the honorable people of this city and of the upright priests of the diocese. Our confrere, Father Jobart, died on June 27. So Our Lord is gradually taking from us the men of honor, and we see them replaced by men of quite different caliber. May the Lord look on us with mercy.

> With deepest affection and all the respect I owe you,
> I am, my very dear brother,
> Your very humble and obedient servant,
> Jean-Louis de La Salle

You have in Reims still other properties acquired in your name: the old cottage adjoining the Brothers' house, a farm at Acy, and a house in the Rue des Anges, left you by Father Pasté.

———— ✦ ————

John Baptist at 13 was godfather of Jean-Louis at his baptism on Christmas Day, 1664. When their father died in April 1672, John Baptist became the guardian of his two sisters and four brothers. The older sister, Marie, who was 18 at the time, moved out of the home in June with the youngest brother, Jean-Remy, only 23 months old, to live with their grandmother. The other sister, Rose-Marie, at 16 had already entered the convent, probably in February. Thus, in June 1672, the De La Salle household consisted of John Baptist, 21, and his three brothers, Jacques-Joseph, 14, Jean-Louis, 8, and Pierre, 6. Jacques-Joseph was the first to leave, entering the novitiate of the canons of Saint Genevieve in 1676. Jean-Louis enrolled in Saint Sulpice in 1679, and that same year Jean-Remy came back from his grandmother's to live with John Baptist.

In 1681, when De La Salle invited the teachers to live in the family home with him, Pierre and Jean-Remy were taken out of the house by their uncle to live with their sister, Marie, who had married Jean Maillefer in 1679. It was then that Jean-Louis showed his special love for John Baptist by refusing to leave him.

Brother Léon de Marie Aroz describes the close relationship between John Baptist de La Salle and Jean-Louis:

> An intimate affection united these two brothers, godfather and godson, blood brothers and also brother priests of the Lord, both students at the Sorbonne, both doctors of theology, canons of Reims, living parallel lives characterized by the same love and service of the Church, John Baptist in the ministry of the school, Jean-Louis in the ministry of the word and sacraments—the same end with different means. Learned and holy, they were inseparable until 1714, when the promulgation of the Bull *Unigenitus* provoked a schism among the clergy of France.

Those who were appealing to a general council over the head of the Pope were locked in a bitter battle with those loyal to the Pope. John Baptist kept out of the polemics except at Marseilles when he was openly attacked and forced to take part. For him Rome had spoken, the case was closed. For Jean-Louis, on the other hand, it was a matter of a sincere appeal to the General Council without, however, becoming belligerent. Yet this was enough to wound their personal friendship and end their correspondence with only two exceptions. Nevertheless, Jean-Louis remained a person trusted by his older brother and was his legal representative in Reims for the project of the schools which he had founded.

When, at the approach of his death, John Baptist needed to choose an executor of his last will, it was Jean-Louis whom he named as his heir, bequeathing to him his personal belongings willed to his nephews, the sons of John-Remy, giving him full power to dispose of them any way he saw fit in case of any controversy from whatever source. So at the hour of truth, when everything human begins to disappear in the face of death, and even doctrinal quarrels are diminished in the light of eternity, love itself reclaims its rights — John Baptist and Jean-Louis, blood brothers and brother priests of God, it must be said again, loved one another. (CL 41 I: 21–22)

In 1700 De La Salle formed a body of trustees (*société civile*) made up of himself, his brother, Jean-Louis, Canon Claude Pepin, and Father Pierre de La Val. These four as trustees were to act as coproprietors and administrators of properties bought on behalf of the Brothers in Reims, since the Society did not at that time constitute a legal entity. By 1710 De La Val and Pepin had died, and John Baptist had moved on to Paris and Rouen. Jean-Louis had been left to assume the entire responsibility for the trusteeship.

It is easy to undersand why Jean-Louis was troubled about the state of his brother's health and wished to have the number of the trustees restored to four. However, as the names suggested by Jean-Louis were those of persons who had aligned themselves with the Jansenist faction, they were not acceptable to his brother. Jean-Louis clearly draws a distinction between those whom he considered to be upright priests with their Jansenist leanings and the rest "of a different caliber."

The problems raised by Jean-Louis were solved by the terms of De La Salle's will. Jean-Louis continued to look after the interests of the Institute of the Brothers until his death in 1724. A letter written in 1723 to Canon Jean-Louis by Brother Jean, Assistant to the Superior General, in 1723, reveals the affection with which he was held by the Brothers: "In you we have found another Father to take the place of the one who has left us to go to enjoy the glory of heaven" (CL 41 I: 319, n. 3).

After his death, Jean-Louis' role of tending to the interests of the Institute was continued by his brother, Pierre.

LETTER 134
To a Brother

According to the historian Jean-Claude Garreau, who published his *Vie de Messire Jean-Baptiste de La Salle* in 1760, Letter 134 is the last letter written by De La Salle, probably in February or March 1719. It is Blain who has preserved it.

Letter 134: To a Brother
EC 110; CL 8: 170

[February or March 1719]

1 . . . Please, my very dear Brother, for the love of God, in the future you must no longer think of applying to me for anything at all.

2 You have your superiors, and it is with them you should discuss the spiritual and temporal matters that concern you.

3 From now on I wish to think only of preparing myself for death, which is soon to separate me from all in this life. . . .

———— ✦ ————

This assertion of De La Salle must be put in context with other facts of his life at this time: his effort to bolster the authority of Barthélemy on the one hand and his concluding the many details of his will on the other. He was also very involved with the life of the Institute that flowed around him at Saint Yon.

De La Salle died on Good Friday, April 7, 1719.

Postscript

In his introduction to Battersby's translation of the letters, Brother Athanase Emile, Superior General, wrote that a person who wishes to form an accurate idea of the personality of De La Salle must read his letters as they were written, chronologically from beginning to end. This documentary evidence, he said, is able to correct the bias of the biographers, who almost inevitably introduce subjective elements into their portrayal.

Another value in reading all the letters is the opportunity to witness the development of the personality of De La Salle over the years from 1682 to 1719. One sees the same idealism from beginning to end, but one also sees a maturing on the part of the Founder in his sharing these ideals with the various Brothers as both he and they confronted the vicissitudes of the project of the Christian Schools. We see also his realistic, shrewd, and even forceful management of affairs and personalities, balanced against his tender, compassionate, and patient dealings with relatives, Brothers, and others throughout these 40 years.

In the end we recognize John Baptist de La Salle for the noble person he was: not only as a saint (he was beatified in 1888 and canonized on May 24, 1900), but also as a unique, struggling, generous human being responding faithfully in the best way he could to the demands of everyday reality, which, he trusted, was God's crucible for sanctifying him and founding an Institute of Brothers to serve the Church.

Appendix A

Directories

The following five *Mémoires* are directories to guide the Brother Directors in giving their accounts to the Superior General. The *Mémoires* appear in the prescriptions of the General Chapter of 1745. They seem to be based on *Règle du Frère Directeur d'une Maison de l'Institut*, a manuscript of 1718 which Brother Barthélemy signed and sent to the Director of the Saint Denis community. In the note over his signature, Brother Barthélemy states that the document is for the Directors of the Brothers of the Society and that it was agreed upon by himself and the Directors of the Society at the General Chapter of 1717. It is significant that he does not say that it was written by De La Salle, though the Founder's influence can be considered certain.

Part of the fifth *Mémoire*, or an appendix to it, is a copy of the directory that every Brother was asked to use as a guide for his letters to the Superior. It is found as an appendix to the 1711 printing of the *Recueil*. There is evidence that it was added to the *Recueil* sometime after 1711 and before 1725. It is probable that De La Salle either composed it or had considerable influence on its composition.

The Rule of 1705 required the Brothers to write to the Superior at the beginning of each month, or if the community was too distant, to write to a Director of another community that was closer, as designated by the Superior. But there is no mention of a directory to guide such letters. It is only in the Rule of 1718 that mention is made of such a directory, at which time the letters were prescribed to be written every other month.

All of these directories were included as part of the appendix to the edition of the Letters in Circular No. 335. They are, of course, relevant to the letters that the Brothers wrote to De La Salle, but the idea of a directory for those letters seems to have developed only gradually and did not take a printed form until sometime after 1711.

First Mémoire

Matters on which the Brother Directors of the houses of the Society will give an account to the Brother Superior of the Institute at the beginning of November, January, March, May, July, and September.

On Their Conduct as Director

1   If he has conducted himself differently from what is also expected of his Brothers; if he has practiced any special prayer or mortification, or has permitted any of the Brothers to do so; if he has introduced some new practice into the community.

2   If he and the Brothers have endeavored to acquire the spirit of faith; if he expects obedience of the Brothers and if he gives them occasions to practice the virtues; if he has been careful to be recollected; if he has been vigilant to see that his Brothers are everywhere recollected and what he has done in order to do this.

3   If he has given good example to his Brothers in all things, remembering his obligation to be for them a model, following the advice given by Saint Paul through his disciple Titus for those responsible for guiding others: "In all things be yourself the example of good deeds by instruction, by purity of conduct, and by seriousness."

4   If his love for all the Brothers is impartial, especially if he has the required zeal for their progress in virtue and if he has had any trouble with any of them and in what way.

5   If he has been exact in the observance of the rules and has required the observance of the smallest details of the rules, and if he has had an esteem for this; if he has allowed any relaxation of the rules; if he has been exact to reprove even the least faults contrary to modesty, good order, and fidelity to the rules.

6   If he has given any special permission to any Brother and what it was; if he and his Brothers always retire and rise at the appointed times.

7   If he or any of the Brothers have missed any spiritual exercise, what it was and why; if he has failed to attend the recreations; how these have been conducted; if the conversation has always been about God; if they speak at this time of themselves or of their Brothers.

8   If he has taken care to be present at the beginning of all the spiritual exercises; if he has stopped everything at the first sound of the bell; if some lights have been on in the house after 9:15 P.M.; if all the keys have been given to him after night prayer and if he has checked or had someone else check the main doors of the house to see that they have been locked.

9   If he has maintained silence; if he has spoken too loudly

when it was necessary to speak; if he has asked about things out of curiosity and spoken without necessity or with familiarity to any of the Brothers.

10 If he has had the Brothers give an account of their conduct every week and if he has spoken of other things than what is in the directory.

11 If he has become friendly with externs; if he has visited them or if he has spoken with them too often; if he has taken food or drink outside the house; if these persons have come into the house or been allowed to talk with any of the Brothers; if he has asked them to do any errand and what it was.

12 If he has had any externs take meals or reside in the community; if he has had any visitors, and who they were; if he has sent any Brother to speak for him when it was not necessary that he go himself.

13 If the Brother Director or another Brother with his permission has gone out often, why and how often; if the Brother Director or another Brother has gone out alone and if every time he has gone out he has advised the Brother Sub-Director of his leaving; who the Brother is that he takes with him; if he always takes the same Brother or even if he takes the Brother Sub-Director to go out with him—something he should not do.

14 If he or another Brother has gone out of the town; where he has been, why and how often; if he or another Brother has written letters, to whom and why.

15 If he has engaged one or several Brothers to do some work and for what; if he has made some change in the house; if he has had the haircuts according to the Rule; if he has seen that the house has been kept clean; if he has had something new made for the house, such as furniture, linen, and so forth: if all this has been according to the Institute practices.

16 If he has bought something or if he has been engaged in any external matter, what it is and how many times.

17 If he or the Brother procurator has had money outside the money box with the two keys, and in what amount.

18 If he has given the Brother cook in writing the schedule for his use of time and if he has taken care to see that he has used his time properly.

(The Brother Director will omit the articles on which he has nothing to report.)

Second Mémoire

Matters on which the Brother Directors will give an account to the Brother Superior of the Institute concerning details of the last two months:

On Income and Expense of the House

1　After the Brother Director has given an account of conduct according to the preceding directory, he will present or have someone else present to the Brother Superior the income and expense of the two preceding months. After listing the receipts of these two months at the top of the report, he will add the money that was left in the house at the end of the two other preceding months, and at the bottom of the report he will record the balance of the money at the end of the month just ending, after all expenses have been paid.

2　He will then record in detail the ordinary expenses and after that the extraordinary, if there are any as, for example, for sickness, repairs, purchase of linen, and the like.

3　If anyone has given anything to the house, either some food or any other thing whatsoever; if this person has or had children in the Brothers' school.

4　If something has been loaned or borrowed, money or materials, what day, to whom, what amount; why it had to be borrowed or why it had to be loaned.

5　If something was borrowed or loaned previously; if the matter has been settled or not.

6　What is served in the dining room on meat days and fast days; on each day in Lent; how many pounds of meat have been served at each meal, each day, each week.

7　If the food has always been according to regulations, or if something extraordinary has been served; how many times and what it was.

Third Mémoire

Matters on which the Brother Directors will give an account to the Brother Superior of the Institute, the same months of November, January, March, May, July, and September:

On School Matters

1   If the Brother Director has left school for some reason, for example, to make some changes, or for some other reason; how many times and for what reason. If, when returning to the house from the school, he was always accompanied by a companion and if they have always been exact to say the rosary alternately while walking along the street.

2   If he observes and sees that others observe exactly all that is required in the *Conduite des Ecoles chrétiennes*; if he has made the examination and the changes of the students toward the end or the beginning of each month; what the number of students is in each class; if they are truant or if they generally come late to school.

3   What he has observed of note in each class; if he or some other Brother has spoken too long at the door of the school; if he has come to speak to some Brother for something other than about the students; if he has seen to it that he and the other Brothers do not speak to parents of students except during the hours of 8:30 A.M. to 2:00 P.M.

Fourth Mémoire

The personal conduct of the Brother Director (see the directory).

He Will Then Give an Account of Each Brother

1   The state of the Brother's health, if he is or has been ill and what remedy he has applied.

2   If the Brother is faithful to the rules, negligent or fervent; in what way he has observed this; if the Brother tries to be interior; if he loves prayer and interior or exterior mortification and in what way this is apparent; if he gives an exact account of his conduct and if he does this with simplicity.

3   How the Brother applies himself to prayer; what advice he has given the Brother regarding his conduct; if the Brother has been negligent and in what way; if he is making progress in perfection and how he shows this. What means he is using to help the Brother progress; what his ordinary defects are and the other defects that may not be usual; if

the Brother has endeavored to correct them; if he has done some penance that has been given him and how he has done this.

4   If the Brother has been exact in doing his work in school; if silence and order are kept there; if the students are attentive; if they are making progress in reading and writing as well as in catechism; if he inspires them to a religious spirit and if this is observed in them.

Fifth Mémoire

Matters on which each Brother will give an account to the Brother Superior of the Institute at the beginning of October, December, February, April, June, and August:

Regarding Fidelity to Rule

1   If he has rung the bell for the spiritual exercises exactly at the time prescribed; if there is a clock in the house; if care is taken to have it keep accurate time; if some of the daily spiritual exercises have been omitted or shortened; which ones and how many times.

2   If the Brothers have always taken their holiday walks together and to what place; if the advertisement of defects is held every week; if any Brother has been advised of some considerable defect and how this was taken; if this was done with charity.

3   If the Brother Director has given some serious penance during the accusation of faults; to what Brother, why, and how he received it.

4   If all the Brothers have received Holy Communion on the days prescribed, how many times; if the Brothers go to confession every week to the same confessor; if he encourages the Brothers or not.

5   If all the Brothers are fervent, recollected, silent, and who are negligent in this matter.

6   If anyone has been ill, the nature of the illness, how long, and what remedy was provided for him.

Directory according to which each Brother will give an account of his conduct to the Brother Superior of the

Institute at the beginning of the months of February,
April, June, August, October and December:*

1   How is his health; if he is or has been ill; the nature of
the illness; when and for how long.

2   If he has any spiritual troubles or temptations; what they
have been and what has been the cause; how he has coped
with them; what good or evil they have produced; how
long they have lasted; whether they have stopped or not;
if he has given or is giving occasion for these troubles and
has brought them on through his own fault.

3   What faults he has committed since the last time he
wrote; if it was with awareness or even deliberately that he
has done wrong; what have been the most usual offenses;
whether he has tried to correct himself of some; what
means he has used for this purpose.

4   If he has made progress on the way of perfection, in the
practice of virtue, or if he has become careless; in what
way has he noted this; what virtues he has tried to practice
since the last letter; if he has had any inspirations; what
they have been and whether he has been faithful to them.

5   To what does he feel inclined; if he has acted sometimes
out of whim, inclination, through bad mood, or even
passion.

6   If he has a love for mortifications, especially of the mind
and senses; how has he noticed this, or the opposite; if he
has practiced any unusual mortifications, what they have
been and if they were with permission or not.

7   How he has taken the penances that have been given to
him; whether he has performed them exactly or not; if he
has omitted any, how often; whether it was through
forgetfulness, negligence or some other reason; what the
ones were that he omitted; if they have been fulfilled,
with what motive and fervor or negligence; if this has
edified or given little edification.

---

*This directory of 31 articles appears as a printed appendix at the end of the
Recueil which has a date of 1711 on the title page. It is not clear when, after 1711,
this appendix was added, since successive printings kept the same title page with
slight alterations and retained the same date. However, one copy has been established as the oldest because it makes no reference, as the others do, to the Bull
of Approbation. From this can be established the fact that this directory was formu-
lated prior to 1725 (CL 15: vii, 122 to 130).

8   If he loves humiliations, rebuffs, and even contempt, or if
     he has difficulty accepting them and how he has shown
     this; if he, at least, has accepted them willingly and with a
     docile spirit since the last letter, and in what interior and
     exterior disposition he has received them since that time.

9   How he has received the advertisement of his defects and
     the reprimands given for them; if in different dispositions,
     how many times in one kind, how many in another;
     whether he has tried to benefit from them and in what
     way he has done this.

10   If he accuses himself of his faults each day; if of all of
     them; if with simplicity as before God; if with other
     dispositions; what these were—if good or bad; if he has
     some repugnance for this action; if it is voluntary or not;
     if he has given into this feeling, often or rarely, how
     often, approximately, since the last letter.

11   What love he has for obedience; if he is indifferent to any
     order, and disposed to obey any Director whoever, and in
     whatever he orders, without questioning, no matter how
     much repugnance or difficulty he feels about it; or if he
     feels resistive toward any Director or anything in par-
     ticular; if it is all the time or only sometimes and under
     certain circumstances.

12   If he has esteem and affection for the Brother Director or
     not and why; if he has some problem in his regard and for
     what reason; if he has always obeyed the Brother Director
     and in everything he has ordered; whether he has dis-
     obeyed; if it was often or rarely, on what occasion, how
     often one way or another and why; for what motives he
     has obeyed or lacked obedience.

13   If he has been exact to do nothing without permission; if
     he has done the least thing on his own; if he has been
     very careful about this, or if he has lost some of his care in
     this matter; if this is true always, often, rarely, and for
     what reasons.

14   If he has an esteem for the Rule of the Institute; if he
     observes the rules exactly, or has he been negligent regard-
     ing some, and which ones; whether this happened often,
     or rarely, and how often since the last letter; how he
     observes the rules, with fervor or negligence; whether this
     happens often or rarely and on what occasions; if he finds
     difficulty in keeping the rules; whether this is true for all
     of them, or only some; which ones and why.

15 If he keeps silence inside and outside the house; whether he has spoken to any Brother in particular; if this has been about good things, indifferent matters, harmful, or even bad things; whether this has been often or rarely.

16 If he has been recollected inside and outside the house; whether this has been often or rarely; whether he has remembered the holy presence of God; if this has been frequent, or even continual, or rarely; if he is mindful of his actions; if he recollects himself often or rarely, and if he has acted in a way so as to perform every action without attention to himself but to God and having God in view; or if he has acted differently, often or rarely.

17 If he has been assiduous at all his spiritual exercises; if not, at which ones he has been negligent, how many times at each and for what reason; if he has made all of them, even the exterior ones, with some interior dispositions; what they are; whether this is true always, often, or rarely; if he has made his spiritual exercises with the sole view of pleasing God and of doing his holy will, always, often, or rarely.

18 What book he has been reading for spiritual reading; if he has read much or a little each time; if he has made reflections from time to time on what he has read; with what attention he has done this; if he has benefited from this and in what way.

19 To what defect he has applied himself during particular examination; whether he has worked to correct himself of it and what means he has used for this purpose; if he has in fact corrected himself and how he has observed this.

20 To what he has applied himself during his prayer; whether he has given some time during his prayer to the presence of God; in what way; how much time and whether this has been easy for him; if he has applied himself to the acts of the first part and in what way he has applied himself to the subject of his prayer; if this has been easy for him, or if it has been difficult and why; if he has had distractions, often or rarely and why; whether they have continued for a long time; whether he has had some fervor, or aridity at prayer; whether this has been often or rarely or if this has continued for a long time; what resolutions he has made; whether he has been faithful to carry them out or not, often or rarely and why; what benefit he has received and how he has noticed this.

21 If he has always gone to confession with the other Brothers; if he has been satisfied with the confessor and why; if the confessor has been exact not to allow him to be negligent; if the confessor has encouraged him to have the spirit of his vocation both interiorly and exteriorly; if he has urged him to fidelity to the Rule; if he has had any trouble with the confessor and why he has or has not; if he benefits from his confessions and how he has noticed this.

22 If he has a love for Holy Communion and if he always receives gladly with fervor, or with lukewarmness or negligence; if he has omitted Communions at times, with permission, how often and for what reasons; what benefit he has derived from his Communions and how he has noticed this.

23 How he has assisted at Holy Mass; if every day; in the same dispositions or with varying dispositions and what they were; what attention he has had at Mass, if it is always the same or not; if he has applied himself at Mass according to the method or in some other way and, if so, what it was.

24 If he has love for his Brothers; if it is equal toward all; if his affection for them is natural or in view of God and what this view is; if he has or has had any difficulty with anyone or with several Brothers; if it has lasted for a long time or not and what the cause of it was.

25 If there is some Brother for whom he feels a particular affection and if he has spoken to any in particular.

26 If he has a love for his work and zeal for the instruction and salvation of children; how he notices this and what he does in this spirit, or if he is somewhat indifferent in this matter.

27 How he conducts himself in school; if he observes all the rules or only some and which ones he neglects; if he has wasted time often or rarely; how much each time and what it was that he was doing then; if he has always followed the lessons and been exact to correct all the mistakes; whether he has left his place; whether he has spoken in class, even if he has talked to one of the students privately without necessity; how often, how long, and why; if he has made any changes in his class, even of the grade, and if he has introduced anything new.

28 If he has taken care in school to help the students make progress in reading and writing; if they are benefiting from his efforts, or if some or many have not advanced and for what reason; if they have been promoted according to schedule; many of them, or only a few; approximately how many of each; if there are order and silence in school, and if not, what the reason is.

29 If he has taken at least as much care to have his students develop a religious spirit as he has had for progress in their lessons; if he has taken special care that they have this spirit and recollection during Holy Mass and at prayers; if he has had vigilance over them especially during these moments.

30 If he has taken care that his students attend and follow well the catechism lessons; if he has attended well to this or not; if there are many or few who are not learning and why; whether he teaches catechism according to the practices of the Institute and takes care to question the students according to their abilities.

31 How he has conducted himself in regard to his students; if he has been too rough with them, or too easy, or too familiar; if he has become impatient often or rarely toward them; toward all of them or some in particular; with what spirit and in what disposition he has corrected them; when he has done this, if he has been too quick and indiscriminate particularly toward one student or several, or acted emotionally or even in anger, and what benefit or bad effect his corrections have had.

Studies Contained in Circular No. 335

In Circular No. 335, 1952, Brother Athanase Emile, Superior General, added to the collection of De La Salle's letters two studies by Brother Félix-Paul (without naming him), each of approximately 40 pages. One is entitled "historical study," and examines in three separate chapters: (1) the authenticity of the collection, (2) the preservation of the letters through the centuries, and (3) a consideration of the letters which have been lost. Much of the material contained in these three chapters, called Part Two of the circular, has been included in the various introductions and commentaries of the letters in the present volume.

Part Three of the circular includes two other chapters on the content of the letters, one dealing with the wealth of information about the origins and early development of the Institute, and the other studying the nature of De La Salle's spiritual direction as revealed in the letters. Because these two chapters of Part Three are good examples of the scholarship of Brother Félix-Paul and because they enhance an appreciation of De La Salle's work as a Founder, a résumé of them is presented here. The numerous quotations from the letters cited by Brother Félix-Paul have been omitted to keep this appendix within appropriate limits, but where it is thought helpful, references will be given to the present volume indicating where these quotations can be found.

I. The Beginnings of the Institute

Often the letters give information about the early foundations of schools that corroborates or adds to statements of the early biographers, and in some instances the letters are the only source of information about some of the early developments of the Institute. For example, Letter 1, to the Mayor and Councillors of Château-Porcien, adds considerably to a simple remark by Blain (CL 7: 183) about the founding of the school in that town. This letter establishes the exact date of the opening of the school in 1682, the number of teachers sent to open the school, and the fact that as yet they were not called Brothers, though De La Salle does refer to his small group as "our Community." Also, some of De La Salle's expressions in this letter seem to indicate that he is at this early date beginning to have an awareness of his vocation as Founder.

The two letters to Father Deshayes (Letters 33 and 34) also supplement Blain's account (CL 8:15) of the foundation at Darnétal in 1704. The style is more businesslike than that of the much earlier letter to Château-Porcien, and it reveals that, while De La Salle was not very rigid about the stipend given for the maintenance of the Brothers, he was very firm in his commitment to keep the Brothers out of any kind of clerical activity. The letters also show his desire to have the two Brothers work together rather than in separate parishes.

Another administrative letter, written to M. Claude Rigoley (Letter 35) about the foundation of the school in Dijon in 1705, is illustrative of De La Salle's very sensitive diplomacy in dealing with the socially prominent people who were negotiating with him for the foundation of schools. At the same time the letter again shows his firmness in the policy of having two Brothers working together in a school, even in adjacent classrooms.

Letter 11 to Brother Hubert reveals how De La Salle responded to a problem that concerned the residence of the Brothers at Chartres in 1709. He employed both human and divine strategies in order to keep the Brothers in their own community rather than have them share residence with the junior seminarians, as his friend, Bishop Godet des Marais, was planning.

In Letter 53 De La Salle's administrative discretion is further manifested by the way he involved himself with his representative in the north of France, Brother Joseph, in a problem of the Troyes community. In 1710 the Brothers were asked by the new pastor to leave the residence that had been provided for them by the previous pastor. The closing of the school was threatened. De La Salle answered Brother Joseph's letter the same day he received it, telling Brother Joseph to wait for his arrival before settling, and advising him not to let anyone know he was coming, "not even Brother Albert."

Ordinarily De La Salle did not write about Institute matters in his letters to the Brothers. This reticence was, in fact, a point of Rule which he and the Brothers had established. He limited his comments to responses to matters in the letters that the Brothers had written to him. Fortunately, he made an exception to this protocol in his letters to Brother Gabriel Drolin, a good indication of the special relationship he had with this trusted Brother, and the result of which is a wealth of information about the early foundations found in the 20 letters Drolin saved. One after the other, these foundations are mentioned in the letters to Drolin: Avignon (Letter 16), Marseilles (Letter 19), Saint Roch, Paris (Letter 25), Valréas and Mende (Letter 26), Grenoble, Alès and Mâcon (Letter 27), Versailles, Boulogne, and Moulin (Letter 29).

De La Salle also writes to Drolin about some of the Brothers. He praises Brother Albert for his administrative ability in establishing the schools at Avignon, Marseilles, and Valréas. He mentions Brother Ponce, who opened the school at Mende, and notes his being in charge of the schools in the south of France. These letters to Drolin also show that Avignon was singled out to be the second capital of the Institute. De La Salle has his books approved by the pontifical censor in Avignon; here is where he has his mail sent on the way to and from Rome; here he sets up the residence for his representative in the south. These details and their precise dates are found only in De La Salle's letters to Drolin.

Of course, it is especially significant that these letters provide us with much information about the difficulties of Drolin's mission in Rome, for none of the early biographers had any access to such information.

The letters to Drolin also reveal a great deal about the personality of De La Salle, especially his reticence about his own problems. Only brief hints are given of the role of De La Chétardie (Letter 14, paragraph 17) and Clément in De La Salle's financial straits, of his distress over the defection of one of his principal Brothers (Letter 17, paragraph 12), of the unexpected death of very good Brothers (Letter 18, paragraph 3), or of his own illnesses (Letter 26, paragraph 3; Letter 32, paragraph 5).

Generally speaking, the letters of De La Salle also throw light on the Brothers who were otherwise undistinguished save for their close relationship with the Founder. For the most part they are representative of the ordinary, good-willed, but little-educated Brothers with whom De La Salle worked in founding the Institute. Blain speaks quite disparagingly of them (CL 8: 387). He makes them a foil for De La Salle's personal qualities enhanced by grace, his patient, kind, and loving commitment to those whom he felt God had sent to him for his project in the Church.

Of the 47 Brothers to whom extant letters were sent or who are mentioned in these letters, 28 are known for certain to have persevered in their vocation until death; another 12 can be considered as probably persevering (although we have no documentary proof); and only seven are known to have withdrawn from the community. This probable eighty-five percent perseverance rate is a testimony to the goodness and docility of these Brothers, and also to the strong influence De La Salle had on these ordinary men living extraordinarily heroic lives.

While De La Salle's letters do not throw much light on the secular affairs of his time, they do give some of the highlights of the ecclesiastical life of De La Salle's experience. He evidently wrote several letters dealing with questions of orthodox Catholicism, though only two have been preserved (Letters 120 and 132).

His letters to Drolin contain very precise allusions to outstanding persons in the Church: a papal legate, an ambassador for France, and other dignitaries—demonstrating that he was not uninterested in the ecclesial life of his times. He kept in touch with those who might become cardinals (Letter 17), knew in advance some nominations (Letter 18), but was wrong about these at times (Letter 21), asked his correspondent for the Vatican position on an important church question (Letter 32), spoke of some bishops as his special friends (Letter 29), and described one such person in a very frank manner (Letters 24 and 25).

De La Salle's zeal for the morality of the clergy of his day is also revealed in his letters to Drolin. There is mention of a canon of Troyes whom Drolin is advised not to trust (Letter 30), of a Breton priest returning from Rome, where the priest had stayed with Drolin for a while (Letter 24), and of a priest of the Diocese of Rouen whom De La Salle, for personal reasons, did not want restored to the exercise of his priesthood (Letter 31).

In addition to all this, the letters of De La Salle give a certain amount of information about the postal service of his day, the exchange of money between France and Italy, about the food, clothing, and gardening of the Brothers, and about some of the liturgical practices, such as the procession for Corpus Christi and the celebration of the feast of Saint Nicolas. They are simple details, but they add to an appreciation of the quality of De La Salle's involvement with the first Brothers of the Institute.

II. Spiritual Direction by De La Salle

Since much in De La Salle's letters was explicitly intended to promote the spiritual growth of the early Brothers, the letters provide accurate information about his relationship with them as a spiritual director. This correspondence supplements De La Salle's ascetical and educational books as well as Blain's writings on the spirit and virtues of the Founder. The paternal concern De La Salle had for the Brothers is revealed, showing how he adapted his advice to the unique needs of each individual Brother in the Institute.

The following observations are divided into three parts: (1) De La Salle's letters to Brother Directors, (2) his letters to the other Brothers, and (3) his letters to Brother Gabriel Drolin, which deserve separate attention because of the special relationship De La Salle had with him. An additional note about his letters of spiritual direction to persons outside the Institute is included.

A. Letters to Brother Directors

The framework for his relations with the Brother Directors was *Règle du Frère Directeur d'une Maison de l'Institut*. The earliest extant copy, in manuscript, is one sent by Brother Barthélemy to the Director of Saint Denis in 1718. Brother Barthélemy mentions in a postscript that it was drawn up by the General Chapter of 1717, so undoubtedly De La Salle had a great deal to do with its contents. No doubt it represents the practices he had worked out with the Brothers over the previous decades of their community life.

In this *Règle* mention is made of directories to guide the Director in the reports he is required to make each month to the Brother Superior. Appendix A of this present edition of the Letters gives five of these directories in the form of *Mémoires*. These were printed in the Rule after the Chapter of 1745 with some changes by Brother Timothée, Superior General, and described expressly as "composed by M. J. B. de La Salle, Founder of the Religious [*sic*] Brothers of the Christian Schools." They reflect reliance on a rather precise code, a tendency which Brother Félix-Paul contends De La Salle inherited from his father, a magistrate of a court of law.

It is probable that these directories evolved with time and that the model for them was the list of 20 articles in the *Recueil* used to guide a Brother in his weekly account to the Brother Director of his community. These 20 articles were printed in the 1711 edition of the *Recueil* but probably existed in manuscript form as early as 1700. The appendix to the 1711 edition of the *Recueil*, added sometime before 1725, is the earliest copy of a directory for a Brother's account to the Brother Superior, and borrows most of its articles from those of the weekly account of the Brother to his Director.

The Brother Director did not have to follow the directories in a servile manner. The first *Mémoire* concludes with the statement, "The Brother Director will omit the articles on which he has nothing to report." It was also clear that he could record for any given month any other topic he wanted that was not in the directory.

An examination of the letters to the Directors reveals many of the topics De La Salle valued in his spiritual direction yet frequently neglected by some of the Directors. These topics, as arranged by Brother Félix-Paul, are silence (nine occurrences), fidelity to the Rule (seven), punctuality (seven), being present with the Brothers (five). Other topics include charity, spiritual direction by the Director, uniformity in community life, the spirit of faith, obedience, good example, being sure that a Brother does not go out alone, working with the Brother in charge of purchasing, cleanliness of the house, and the scheduling of the cook's day.

The quotations cited by Brother Félix-Paul to illustrate these topics are too numerous to give in this Appendix. It would be sufficient to read the letters to the Directors, as grouped together in this volume, to appreciate his selection of these topics as illustrative of De La Salle's focus in the spiritual direction of these Directors.

In the management of his school, the Director is strongly advised against accepting pay or gifts from the students or their parents. There are also indications that De La Salle had concern for the number of students in each class, that they be taught well and treated with respect and kindness in order to encourage them to stay in school and attract other students to enroll. Part of this concern was probably the desire of De La Salle to have a school with enough students to require a community of three or more Brothers, rather than just two.

Other directives regarding the role of the Director in school include the importance of his presence there and of his speaking but briefly with persons who visit the school.

In summary, for De La Salle the Director is to be the vigilant guardian of the community's fidelity to the Rule, responsible before God for the souls of the Brothers in the same way that a Brother is responsible for his students. He himself is to be the leader for all his Brothers in this fidelity, an exemplar of all the religious virtues expected of the others. It is this characteristic that guarantees the perseverance of the Brothers and their effective work in the schools.

B. Letters to Other Brothers

There is a kind of abrupt quality to all the letters that De La Salle wrote to the Brothers. Directives follow one after the other without logical connections. Imperatives, such as "you must," "you should," "you ought to," and "take care to," most often without explanation or comment, can seem on the surface to lack paternal kindness.

It must be realized, however, that the context of this correspondence did not lend itself to a leisurely, much less a literary, style. The letters written by a Brother were monthly reports to his Superior about the Brother's observance of the Rule and about any problems which the Brother was facing. De La Salle, usually responding item by item to the Brother's letter, was forced to be brief and to the point because of his many other responsibilities, his lack of time, and the need to answer promptly. The Brothers knew, of course, exactly why he stressed certain matters; they knew too the reasons for his brevity.

It is probable that all the Brothers had the same freedom as the Directors to omit the articles in the directory of topics for their monthly letter when they had nothing to report on them. It is also possible that the Brothers sometimes reported on just a few items that were of concern to them and that De La Salle would limit his response to only one of these. For example, some of the letters preserved in Ms. 22 (Letters 88 to 94) are entirely devoted to one theme, such as prayer, self-denial or obedience, in contrast to the many topics that are dealt with in the autograph letters.

Perhaps some of these letters are only excerpts taken from one or more letters to illustrate a theme, similar to the way that Blain uses the letters in his treatment of the spirit and virtues of the Founder.

Despite the insistence on small points of the Rule, such as the immediate response to the first sound of the bell or the repetition of the same advice often in almost identical words, the letters in which De La Salle gives spiritual direction to his Brothers reveal his love and his compassion for them, his great desire to see them fervent in the service of God and of the children under their care.

Brother Félix-Paul, following the directory of the 31 articles proposed for the monthly letters, selects eight recurring themes in De La Salle's responses. These eight, in turn, can be summarized under three main headings. (1) The difficulties of health, of conscience, or of temptations experienced by the Brothers. In dealing with this honest sharing of problems of his Brothers, De La Salle shows himself to be very gentle and encouraging as well as realistic about the challenges of the spiritual life and about fidelity to God's inspirations in order to meet these challenges successfully. (2) Fidelity to the requirements of community life: obedience, fidelity to the Rule, frequent reception of the sacraments, attentive assistance at Holy Mass, silence and interior recollection, spiritual reading, particular examen, prayer, love for mortification and humiliation, and fraternal charity. (3) Fidelity to the regulations of school life, especially as detailed in the *Conduite des Ecoles chrétiennes*.

In all this advice De La Salle endeavors to apply to individual Brothers the help each one needs to achieve a balance between fidelity to spiritual exercises properly so-called and to school work in all its aspects. There is also expressed the concern to balance a Brother's commitment to the teaching of secular subjects and the teaching of religion and a balance between kindness and firmness in the discipline of the students. De La Salle warns, in particular, against slapping any of the children.

C. Letters to Brother Gabriel Drolin

The correspondence of De La Salle with Brother Gabriel Drolin is special because of the unique relationship the Founder had with this Brother, who was sent on a very important mission and left alone almost from the beginning, a Brother probably selected for this assignment because of his very particular union with De La Salle from the time of the heroic vow they made together in 1691. The 20 letters that Drolin fortunately preserved out of love for his spiritual director are also special because of the unique position he was in, without community life and so distant from De La Salle for such a long period of time, from 1702 until the death of De La Salle in 1719.

De La Salle mentions 12 times in these 20 letters his desire and plan to send a companion to be with Drolin: Letters 17 and 19 of 1705, Letters 21 to 24 of 1706, Letter 26 of 1707, Letters 27 and 28 of 1710, Letter 29 of 1711, Letter 31 of 1712, and Letter 32 of 1716. Such was the Founder's desire to normalize as far as possible the religious life of his trusted friend. To balance this unfulfilled desire, De La Salle had his usual recourse to trust in God's Providence, which he discerned in the events of his life. Perhaps as much as anywhere else in his writings, De La Salle reveals his own reliance on God's Providence in his letters to Drolin. It is in Letter 18, in particular, that he speaks so personally about his own attitude toward this quality of his life:

> As for myself, I do not like to make the first move in any endeavor, and I will not do it in Rome any more than elsewhere. I leave it to Divine Providence to make the first move and then I am satisfied. When it is clear that I am acting only under the direction of Providence, I have nothing to reproach myself with. When I make the first move, it is only I myself who am active, so I don't expect to see much good result; neither does God usually give the action his special blessing. (Paragraphs 17 and 18)

A major topic stressed in De La Salle's letters to Drolin is the importance of fidelity to the duties of Drolin's vocation as a Brother: teaching the poor without charge, wearing the garb of the Brothers, not using a Latin New Testament, and keeping up the personal contact of regular correspondence. De La Salle likewise makes delicate references to the possibility of Drolin's assuming holy orders.

In response to Drolin's own admission of failure, De La Salle frequently encourages him to avoid socializing, in order to be more attentive to prayer and the interior life. Similarly he reproves Drolin for writing "useless letters."

De La Salle was rewarded for his trust in and fidelity to Drolin over the troubled years by the responding fidelity and perseverance of his friend, even in isolation and even for years after the Founder's death. Fortunately, in the last letter De La Salle wrote to him (Letter 32), Drolin could preserve with special affection these words:

> I assure you that I have a great tenderness and affection for you and often pray to God for you. . . . I have been greatly encouraged by your last letter, and the assurance of your wholehearted affection gives me much joy. Please let me know how you are getting along. (Paragraphs 3, 7, and 8)

Perhaps this is the letter that Blain informs us Drolin always kept with him in his pocket.

D. Letters to Persons Who Are Not Brothers

There are ten letters in the collection written to members of religious communities seeking spiritual direction from De La Salle. One (Letter 105) is written to a man; Blain, who is the source of this letter, does not indicate to whom it is addressed (CL 8: 390). The others were probably written to the Daughters of the Cross, Dominicans of Paris, whom De La Salle may have been directing as early as 1703.

The style of these letters is quite different from the style of his letters to the Brothers. To the other religious De La Salle takes more care to explain his advice in logically developed paragraphs. With the Brothers he feels no need for this; he has confidence that they understand the reasons for his directions—he has guided them in the novitiate and on retreats as well as in personal encounters.

The topics of these letters include the practice of fraternal charity (Letter 105), fidelity to the Rule (Letter 106), obedience and the spirit of faith (Letter 107), trust in God (Letter 108), and the practice of silence and prayer (Letters 111 and 113). In all these matters the doctrine is undoubtedly Lasallian, though the style of presentation is more formal than his familiar style in writing to the Brothers.

The formal style is also detected in the four short excerpts from the letters to a laywoman (Letters 115 to 118), though these are almost too brief to note anything else, except that their content is focused on the spirit of faith, a topic which was of special concern to De La Salle.

Appendix C

Numbering of the Letters

Below is a comparative listing of the numbering of the letters in this volume, **LP** (*Lasallian Publications*), with **BL** (*De La Salle: Letters and Documents,* edited by W. J. Battersby, FSC), and **EC** (*Les Lettres de Saint J.-B. De La Salle: Edition Critique,* by Brother Félix-Paul, FSC).

LP	BL	EC	LP	BL	EC
1	I.1	111	31	I.39	31
2	II.4	102	32	I.41	32
3	I.2	10	32(A)	IV.Ap.2	32(a)
4	I.43	11	32(B)		32(b)
5	I.44	12	33	I.6	112
6	III.9	93	34	I.7	113
7	I.3	33	35	II.2	114
8	I.16	34	36	I.51	52
9	I.26	35	37		64
10	I.52	36	38	III.26	53
11	I.32	37	39	I.45	54
12	II.5	38	40	I.47	55
13	II.1	13	41	I.46	56
14	I.5	14	42	I.49	57
15	I.4	15	43	II.6	69
16	I.8	16	44	I.50	58
17	I.9	17	45	III.4	59
18	I.10	18	46	III.3	60
19	I.11	19	47	III.2	61
20	I.12	20	48	I.48	62
21	I.13	21	49	III.16	70
22	I.14	22	50	II.3	9
23	I.15	23	51	I.18	63
24	I.17	24	52	III.28	75
25	I.19	25	52(a)	IV.4	41(a)
26	I.21	26	52(b)	IV.4	41(b)
27	I.33	27	52(c)	IV.4	41(c)
28	I.34	28	53	I.35	40
29	I.37	29	54	I.40	41
30	I.38	30	55	I.20	42

LP	BL	EC		LP	BL	EC
56	I.23	43		96		80
57	I.24	44		97		81
58	I.25	45		98		103
59	I.27	46		99		104
60	I.22	47		100		105
61	I.28	48		101		106
62	I.29	49		102		107
63	I.30	50		103		108
64	I.31	51		104		109
64(A)		51(a)		105		119
65	III.8	92		106		121
66	III.14	71		107		124
67	III.20	72		108		122
68	III.23	88		109		123
69	III.6	91		110		125
70	III.36	101		111		126
71	III.18	73		112		127
72	I.36	1		113		128
73	III.1	66		114		129
74	III.11	67		115		130
75	III.15	68		116		131
76	III.25	74		117		132
77	III.29	76		118		133
78	III.31	77		119		39
79	III.35	78		120		118
80	III.7	82		121		115
81	III.12	83		122		116
82	III.13	84		123		117
83	III.5	85		124		2
84	III.21	86		125	I.42	3
85	III.17	87		126		4
86	III.19	89		127		5
87	III.22	90		128		6
88	III.10	94		129		7
89	III.24	95		130		8
90	III.27	96		131		120
91	III.30	97		132	IV.Ap.1	65
92	III.32	98		133		
93	III.33	99		133(A)		
94	III.34	100		134		110
95		79				

Bibliography

Cahiers Lasalliens

Volume

1   *Les citations néotestamentaires dans les Méditations pour le Temps de la Retraite.* Brother Michel Sauvage, FSC.

2 & 3   *Les voeux des Frères des Ecoles chrétiennes avant la bulle de Benôit XIII, Parts 1 & 2.* Brother Maurice-Auguste, FSC (Alphonse Hermans).

4   *Conduite admirable de la divine Providence en la personne du vénérable serviteur de Dieu Jean-Baptiste de La Salle.* Brother Bernard, FSC. (Edition of 1721, Manuscript).

6   *La vie de M. Jean-Baptiste de La Salle, prêtre, docteur en théologie, ancien chanoine de la cathédrale de Reims, et instituteur des Frères des Ecoles chrétiennes.* F. E. Maillefer. (Editions of 1723 and 1740).

7 & 8   *La vie de Monsieur Jean-Baptiste de La Salle, Instituteur des Frères des Ecoles chrétiennes.* Volumes 1 & 2. Jean-Baptiste Blain. (Reproduction of first edition, 1733).

9 & 10   *Bernard, Maillefer et Blain: Index cumulatif des Noms de lieux et des Noms de Personnes.* Brother Maurice-Auguste, FSC (Alphonse Hermans).

11   *L'Institut des Frères des Ecoles chrétiennes à la recherche de son statut canonique: des origines (1679) à la bulle de Benôit XIII (1725).* Brother Maurice-Auguste, FSC (Alphonse Hermans).

12   *Méditations pour les Dimanches et les principales Fêtes de l'année.* (Reproduction of 1730 edition).

14   *Explication de la Méthode d'Oraison.* (Reproduction of the 1739 edition).

15   *Recueil de différents petits traités à l'usage des Frères des Ecoles chrétiennes.* (Reproduction of 1711 edition).

16   *Contribution à l'étude des sources du "Recueil de différents petits traités."* Brothers Maurice-Auguste, FSC (Alphonse Hermans) and José Arturo, FSC.

17   *Instructions et Prières pour la Sainte Messe, la Confession et la Communion, avec une Instruction méthodique par demandes et réponses pour apprendre à se bien confesser.* (Reproduction of 1734 edition).

18   *Exercices de piété qui se font pendant le jour dans les Ecoles chrétiennes.* (Reproduction of 1760 edition).

19   *Les Règles de la Bienséance et de la Civilité chrétienne.* (Reproduction of 1703 edition).

20 & 21   *Les Devoirs d'un Chrétien envers Dieu.* Volumes 1 & 2. (Reproduction of 1703 edition).

22   *Du Culte extérieur et public que les chrétiens sont obligés de rendre à Dieu et des moyens de le lui rendre. Troisième partie des Devoirs d'un Chrétien envers Dieu.* (Reproduction of 1703 edition). *Cantique* (Reproduction of 1705 edition).

23   *Grand Abrégé des Devoirs du Chrétien envers Dieu. Petit Abrégé des Devoirs du Chrétien envers Dieu.* (Reproduction of 1727 edition).

24   *Conduite des Ecoles chrétiennes.* (1706 and 1720 editions).

25   *Pratique du Règlement journalier. Règles communes des Frères des Ecoles chrétiennes. Règle du Frère Directeur d'une Maison de l'Institut (d'après les manuscrits de 1705, 1713, et 1718 et l'édition de 1726).*

26 & 27   *Les actes d'état civil de la famille de saint Jean-Baptiste de La Salle.* Volumes 1 & 2. Brother Léon de Marie Aroz, FSC.

35, 36   *Les Bien-fonds des Ecoles chrétiennes et gratuites pour les*
37, 37 I   *garçons pauvres de la Ville de Reims au XVIIIᵉ siècle.* Volumes 1–4. Brother Léon de Marie Aroz, FSC.

38   *Nicolas Roland, Jean-Baptiste de La Salle et les Soeurs de l'Enfant-Jésus de Reims.* Brother Léon de Marie Aroz, FSC.

39   *Inventaire numérique détaillé des minutes notariales se rapportant à la famille de La Salle et ses proches apparentés (1593–1792).* Brother Léon de Marie Aroz, FSC.

40 I   *Jean-Baptiste de La Salle: Documents bio-bibliographiques*
40 II   *(1583–1950).* Brother Léon de Marie Aroz, FSC.

41 I   *Jean-Baptiste de La Salle: Documents bio-bibliographiques (1625–1758),* Volume I. Brother Léon de Marie Aroz, FSC.

41 II   *Jean-Baptiste de La Salle: Documents bio-bibliographiques (1661–1683)*, Volume II. Brother Léon de Marie Aroz, FSC.

42 I   *Jean-Baptiste de La Salle: Documents bio-bibliographiques (1670–1715)*, Volume I. Brother Léon de Marie Aroz, FSC.

Books

Aroz, Léon, FSC, Yves Poutet, FSC, and Jean Pungier, FSC. *Beginnings: De La Salle and His Brothers.* Edited and translated by Luke Salm, FSC. Romeoville, Illinois: Christian Brothers National Office, 1979.

Battersby, W. J., ed. *De La Salle: Letters and Documents.* London: Longmans Green, 1952.

———. *De La Salle: Saint and Spiritual Writer.* London: Longmans Green, 1950.

Brothers of the Christian Schools. *Rule and Constitutions and Book of Government.* Rome: 40th General Chapter, 1976.

Common Rules and Constitutions of the Brothers of the Christian Schools. Rome: Motherhouse, 1947.

Daniel-Rops, Henri. *The Church in the Seventeenth Century.* 2 vols. Translated by J. J. Buckingham. Garden City, New York: Doubleday Image Books, 1965.

Félix-Paul, Brother, FSC. *Les Lettres de Saint J.-B. De La Salle. Circulaires Instructives et Administratives, No. 335.* Rome: Procure Générale, 1952.

———. *Les Lettres de Saint J.-B. De La Salle: Edition Critique.* Paris: Procure Générale, 1954.

La Salle, John Baptist de. *A Collection of Short Treatises for the Use of the Brothers of the Christian Schools.* Translated into English. Paris: Procure Générale; and New York: La Salle Bureau, 1932.

———. *Meditations for the Time of Retreat.* Translated by Brother Augustine Loes, FSC. Winona, Minnesota: Saint Mary's College Press, 1975.

Lasalliana. Rome: Casa Generalizia, 1983–1984.

Lucard, Brother, FSC. *Vie du vénérable Jean-Baptiste de La Salle.* Rouen, 1874.

Rigault, Georges. *Histoire général de l'Institut des Frères des Ecoles chrétiennes.* 9 vols. Paris: Librairie Plon, 1936–1953.

The Rule of Saint Benedict. Edited and translated by Abbot Justin McCann, OSB. London: Burns and Oates, 1952.

Salmon, Dom P., OSB. "Ascèse Monastique et Exercices Spirituels dans les Constitutions (Saint Maur) de 1646." In *Mémorial du XIVe*

Centenaire de l'Abbaye de Saint-Germain des Prés. Paris: Librairie Philosophique, J. Vrin, 1959.

Sauvage, Michel, FSC, and Miguel Campos, FSC. *Announcing the Gospel to the Poor.* Translated by M. J. O'Connell. Romeoville, Illinois: Christian Brothers Conference, 1981.

Ultee, Maarten. *Abbey of Saint Germain des Prés in the Seventeenth Century.* New Haven, Connecticut: Yale University Press, 1981.

Index

A

Accusation of faults, 8, 32, 33, 46

Advertisement of defects, 8, 44, 46; appreciation of, 20, 26, 202–204

Assignments to community: indifference to, 24, 41, 132, 158, 166

Avignon: as "second capital" of Institute, 281; success of schools in, 68, 69, 71

B

Barthélemy, Brother (Superior General), 39, 244; letters to, from De La Salle, 244–249; as director of novices at Saint Yon, 141, 142, 244; deputed to visit communities concerning proposed General Chapter (1717), 120; succeeds De La Salle as Superior General, 118, 121, 122; letters of, to Gabriel Drolin, 121–125; cancels negotiations for foundation in Canada, 123; notifies Drolin of De La Salle's death, 123–125; death of, 123

Battersby, Brother W. J.: edition of De La Salle's letters (1952), 10, 11, 12

Blain, Canon Jean-Baptiste: letters of De La Salle in biography by, 3, 12

Brothers of the Christian Schools; evolution of the Institute of. *See under* La Salle, John Baptist de

C

Charity, fraternal: and bearing confreres' defects, 185, 219–220, 221; and cordial relationships, 139, 151, 185, 193

Chartres: foundations in, 45–47, 52, 54, 280; deaths of Brothers in, during epidemic, 74, 75

Château-Porcien: foundation in, 15–18, 279, 280

Church, functions in: prohibited to Brothers by De La Salle, 36, 37, 39, 40, 127, 130, 154

Class, conduct of the Brothers in: férule, use of, 147, 148, 212; impatience, 20, 36, 145, 147, 212, 216, 237; name-calling, 26; order, 42; seriousness, 36, 153, 154, 213; signal, use of, 237; silence, 146, 237; supervision of pupils, 141

Clément, Abbé: and lawsuit against De La Salle, 105, 109, 110, 118

Communion, Holy: anxiety about receiving, 145; benefits of, 210; days for receiving, according to the Rule, 47, 48; not to be omitted, 51, 141, 210

Corporal punishment of pupils: prohibition of, 27, 138, 144, 147, 155, 212

D

Darnétal: foundation in, 31, 126–130, 136, 137, 141, 142, 280

Brother Colman Molloy, FSC (1915–1986), a native of Melbourne, was for many years headmaster of the De La Salle Brothers' prestigious Saint Bede's College, Melbourne, Australia, where the library is named in his honor. He also served as Inspector of Schools and academic adviser to the student Brothers in Australia, and subsequently as Auxiliary Visitor and Visitor of the Brothers of Australia, New Zealand, and Papua New Guinea. He was a member of the 1967 General Chapter of the Institute. Later he was secretary-bursar for the Brothers of Australia and spent two years at the De La Salle Brothers' school in Kondiu, Papua New Guinea. Brother Colman died on February 24, 1986, without having had the opportunity to participate in the final editing of this manuscript.

Brother Augustine Loes, FSC, is a member of the New York District of the Brothers of the Christian Schools. He is a graduate of The Catholic University of America and holds a master's degree in classics from Fordham University. He also holds a master's degree in clinical psychology and is a New York State certified school psychologist. Brother Augustine has taught in secondary school, has served as principal or executive director of two child care institutions of the New York District, and has chaired the New York State Council of Voluntary Child Care Agencies. He was Director of De La Salle College, Washington, D.C., a major house of formation of the Brothers, and Provincial of the New York District. Currently he is Director of De La Salle Hall, the retirement home for the New York District, in Lincroft, New Jersey.